Dedication

To Truth Seekers Everywhere...

Hello...

Welcome to the Book...

Before you begin a word of caution...if you are happy to be stuck in your world of mediocrity and mundanity, asleep and numb through your anesthetised addiction to materialism, technology, consumerism, and virtual worlds...then perhaps don't read any further...

However, if you are curious and sometimes experience that feeling, that little niggle deep down within you that you just can't put your finger on, and it always leaves you feeling a little unsure like there's something just missing or there's something more...

Then please read on...

The Principles of Life/Existence

1. First Principle: You are Infinite Reality - You are Not the Body – You are Not the Mind – You are Not the - I Am.

2. Second Principle: You are trapped in a cycle of ignorance and delusion that blinkers you to the First Principle.

3. Third Principle: There are means and ways to gain knowledge and experience that will bring realisation and experience of the First Principle.

4. Fourth Principle: You will find the means and ways to gain knowledge and experience (Third Principle) that will bring realisation and experience of the First Principle in this Book...

Foreword

Throughout history, as a human species, we have experienced, documented, written, and recorded extensively about our ever-changing worlds, societies, cultures, and lifestyles. We have seen the growth and decline of empires, experienced the atrocities of War, seen countries and humanity grow from individualised states to the ever-expanding global markets of our current age, where speed of communication and technology brings material desires with a click of a button and swipe of a screen.

Yet the overarching questions that still come to us, that still niggle us:

Are we fulfilled? Are we as individuals happy? Are people happy? Can we ever find contentment and peace in this ever-changing fast paced reality of consumerism and materialism?

Is this it, is this the sum of my existence?

These questions have eluded humans and still elude many of us today. The global markets are ever pressing and pressurising us to buy and consume the products that get advertised and beamed into our lives moment by moment through our TVs, ipads, mobile phones and social media...asking us for our last penny and dime, taking our attention, zapping the life from our bodies and minds, infiltrating our personal, home, work and family lives...This sounds like a pandemic, a disease of our modern worlds, could this be the plague of the 21st Century? Is this the global addiction of our current age?

How can we possibly find contentment, happiness, and a deeper sense of who we really are, if we are constantly distracted and immersed in this material life? Well, the truth is – we can't, and that's the reality of it. You'll never find the deeper answers to life, your existence, your truth, your happiness, and contentment in materialism, it's just not possible. It's not possible because you are looking in the wrong place. It's like that old fable the 'Emperor's New Clothes' with the global markets and advertisers being the emperor desperately trying to convince you that consuming, buying, and immersing yourself in materialism is the truth, and the source of happiness. Don't listen to your own discernment or believe your own experience because that is incorrect, believe me extorts the emperor, *'look I'm not naked. I'm covered in wonderful attire, glamourous, attractive, beautiful, and adorned with speciality and joy'*…But is this really the truth, is this really what is happening? Then a small child pure and unfettered by materialism, full of truth and spirit speaks up from the crowd… *'But you are naked Sire, look he's got no clothes on, he's telling you all lies and trying to cheat you!'*…the emperor is called out on his lie, just as the advertising and marketing companies are hoodwinking you into believing that you'll find happiness, contentment and your own truth in materialism. To find your truth, to find your happiness and your contentment is to be more like the small child. Be unfettered by materialism and exist in your spirit, in your truth…and then You will see and experience a clearer picture of your reality and the worlds that You exist in. You will be able to cut through the lies, the nonsense, the glitz and glamour of the sideshows, the false empty soulless materialism and get a clearer experience of the truth, of the spirit of being human and all the goodness, joy and wholesomeness that goes with it.

We as a species are at a time of crisis. We are looking and searching for something more, but we are looking in the wrong place. We need to get back to our truth. We want to connect more profoundly. We want to create and nurture deeper bonds and wholesome relationships. You know this…just take a moment to reflect on this, give yourself the time and space to consider this…put down your mobile phone, switch of the TV and computer, turn inward and reflect on this, look into your heart…and when you do, you'll feel it, and once you feel it then you'll know it…because it's your truth, it's your inner truth. The way to contentment and happiness is found within each one of us. We all have the capacity, ability and right to this experience. It's inherent in every one of us, we just need to look in the right place…We need to find our Spirit again. Time to come home…

Matthew, S.V.

Table of Contents

Table of Figures

Reflective Tasks

How to use this Book

The book has been designed to help you unlock and access higher levels of spiritual teaching that exist within You - called your Master Plan. The book has overarching themes and specific themes that relate directly to the unlocking of your Master Plan.

The Master Plan is the genetic blueprint that exists within all of us. Each person has their own unique Master Plan that is designed for the person to achieve their spiritual growth. The themes running through this book, and reflective exercises, are designed to help you gain greater self-awareness, self-acceptance and a deeper understanding of your life and purpose. It's through the active art of listening to self and others that opens the door to your deeper learning, understanding and purpose i.e., your Master Plan.

The book not only gives you access to learning and skills but is also an expose of human existence in our current time. The knowledge is grounded in and underpins the Body/Mind/Spirit framework. It is the fundamentals of the human Body, the Mind and Spirit that we explore through relationship, and begin to understand how they are intrinsically linked to our existence.

Body/Mind/Spirit is our existence, our life and without either one of these core forms of Consciousness we do not exist in this Earth bound, corporeal existence.

As with any learning guide and map, the terrain and landscape are shown to you, but it is your responsibility, commitment and active engaging that is your learning. Once you embark on the journey with intention, and the desire to learn, in time you will access your Master Plan.

How will I know I've accessed my Master Plan?

This is such a personal question and unique to everyone, yet ubiquitous to us all...there will be certain markers - common themes - which will give you a sense of knowing, trust, and awareness of your Master Plan. The exercises in appendix 8 give a structured guide with daily practices. These practices offer awareness based in feelings, thoughts, images, and insights. When you start to gain the insights, feelings, thoughts, etc., you will be aware that you are accessing your Master Plan.

Once I've accessed my Master Plan, am I finished?

No. Accessing the Master Plan is not a process analogous to climbing a hill. We start at the bottom, and we've achieved the end goal when we reach the top. Accessing your Master Plan is an ongoing process-orientated relationship with yourself. It is not an end goal. Accessing your Master Plan is a constant relationship that needs attention, commitment, and continual care. It's where you take deep consideration and care of yourself, whilst considering others and considering how you exist in this world. There is nothing self-centred, selfish, or egotistical about accessing your Master Plan. In fact, the experiencing of these negative markers will clearly show, that you are not accessing your Master Plan and are functioning from negative egoistic energies and programmes.

How do I change these negative energies and programmes?

Within the book are certain terms, and words that create a framework to the knowledge and practice. These words are used to help give insight, understanding and meaning to how you experience yourself, others, and life. They are not definitive. However, the terms and words are an opportunity for you to make sense of yourself, others, and life. There is also a glossary at the back of the book that conveys definitions, terms, and terminology for further assistance.

One of the terms is programmes. Programmes are negative energies that block positive expression and filter the person's experience of life as negative. The negative programmes keep people and societies in Victim mode. Victim is the overarching and underpinning perception of self, others, and life in the perpetual process of 'hopelessness and helplessness'. Victim is the first lesson and perhaps the hardest lesson we as humans must face in our spiritual, physical, emotional, and psychological growth. Transcending Victim is the beginning of you experiencing your Master Plan. I will go into this in more detail throughout the book, but suffice to say, it all starts with Victim.

In respect to how you use the book, there is no single way. You could read it cover to cover, randomly dip in and out, structure the reading on certain themes, engage with the exercises, or use it as a stepping stone to other people's work, the choice is yours...

However, to begin with you might use the book in a structured and standard way as you engage with the learning, discussions, and exercises. Yet, as you begin to trust your process and access your higher spiritual teachings, greater awareness, insights, and understanding will open your learning and studying in a myriad of new and exciting ways.

A note on the reflective tasks and exercises:

The reflective tasks and exercises are designed to help you gain deeper awareness and understanding in how you think, feel, and behave toward yourself, others, and the world you live in. The reflective tasks can bring awareness to emotions, feelings, thoughts, behaviours, and relationships that make us question ourselves and others. This can feel uncomfortable, unnerving, and painful at times. When we look more deeply into ourselves, we become aware of all that we are, the good bits and the not so good bits. This is part of your learning and the stepping stones toward accessing your Master Plan. The journey of self-discovery, like any journey, can be exciting, fearful, confusing, risky, exhilarating, mundane, boring, arduous, taxing, fulfilling, and enlightening. As humans we are all these things and more, so at times we will feel, think, behave, and experience the things that we are, we must, to truly know our Self.

Due to this, it's suggested that you receive and ask for support, help and caring when you need it. This could be recognising your support networks and accessing them e.g., talking to a friend, visiting a counsellor, or engaging with meditation. You might want to go for a walk in the countryside or timetable in a Pilates class. Whatever way you choose to support yourself, please do so as and when you need to. No one is an island, and no one is supposed to be…remember to isolate and push away is Victim. To be solo and self-contained in the guise of independence with the exclusion of interdependence is Victim. We all need each other at different times and the greatest strength comes from knowing when.

Introduction

Your Master Plan is the key to positive change and to a deeper understanding of your life.

In all of us there is a plan, a blueprint to our existence. It is the blueprint to your life, your possibilities, your potentialities, your talents, your life lessons, your purpose, and your reason for being. This is called your Master Plan. Your Master plan holds the key to a life of fulfilment, achievement, and success. Fulfilment, achievement, and success are not to be solely understood and interpreted in a purely material way; although positive material things come when one has accessed and is living their Master Plan.

Your Master Plan is so much more than the material world. Your Master Plan is your blueprint to personal development and achievement in this physical life, emotional life, psychological life, and spiritual life – in effect Body/Mind/Spirit. Humans exist within this framework. The Body is our vehicle to physical embodied existence and feeling. The Mind is our platform to the emotional and psychological realm. Spirit is our connection to Source, Universe, Consciousness, God, etc., depending on how you choose to understand Spirit. This is a simple introduction to existence, as it is more detailed and complex, but this is the general overall framework and feel to Body/Mind/Spirit.

The book is structured into four sections with each section being a complete learning process. Section one is based in current secular knowledge relating to human existence and how this is understood through the framework of Body/Mind/Spirit. Section two introduces you to *the Art of Listening*, a practical and comprehensive approach to assist you daily with relationships to yourself and others, and your overall spiritual journey. Section two introduces you to sacred symbols and other methods that can help you gain access to your Master Plan and concludes by giving insight into different spiritual sources that have been shared with humanity throughout the ages. Section three looks at integrative practice and introduces different forms of therapy and therapeutic practice that are underpinned by a Body/Mind/Spirit framework. Section four concludes with the links between science, religion and spirituality and the models of pathology/illness and wellness/health. For those of you that favour and lean toward secular perspectives and the sciences then section one and section four are probably a good place to start, and those that are looking for spiritual practices and methods, these can be found in section two and three. However, it all starts with Victim so whatever direction you go I'd recommend reading section one Victim first. A glossary to help with terms and terminology can be found before the appendices, and the beginning appendixes offer a range of diagrams as visual maps of the Body/Mind/Spirit framework. Finally, in appendix 8 is a series of example study guides: including methods and exercises to help you structure your daily practice.

Section 1. - Knowledge and Understanding
Victim, Victim Mode & Victim Mentality

Ever had those days when you wake up and feel like the whole world is against you and nothing ever goes right – victim mentality.

Ever felt like you are the worst person alive and why would anyone want anything to do with me – victim.

Ever felt like it's everyone else's fault and you blame everyone and everything for not going the way you think it should – victim mode.

Is there any difference between, victim, victim mode or victim mentality, no not really, they are all the same way of saying the same thing - **'Poor Me'** ..

According to Psych Central (2023), *'A victim mentality is when a person feels like a victim across situations, even when the evidence suggests otherwise. They may feel they have no control over what happens to them.'*

The Common signs:

Behavioural signs:

- often placing blame on external factors or other people when things go wrong

- having trouble taking personal responsibility or seeing how you may have contributed to a situation

- being overly critical of yourself or others

- self-sabotage

- associating only with people who think like you

Mental (cognitive) signs:

- seeing the world as unfair or unsafe

- cognitive distortions, like catastrophizing

- harmful thinking patterns or pessimism

- ruminating over past wrongs and hurts

- thoughts of self-harm or suicide

Relationship signs:

- difficulty with intimacy and trust

- emotional unavailability

- limited empathy for others

- mistrust of authority figures

- keeping score in relationships

- trouble accepting constructive criticism

Emotional signs:

- anxiety

- depression

- feeling unseen

- guilt or shame

- low self-esteem

- resentment of others

- social isolation   (Psych Central, 2023)

Any of these signs seem or feel familiar to you? Given life and life circumstances, it's fair to say that every one of us at some point has felt, behaved, and thought like this…they are universal to us all. So, for whatever reason:

You are not taking responsibility and are not willing to actively change – You are Victim.

What can we do to change and step out of victim mode?

This depends on a few factors and why we are in victim:

1. The reason we are in victim mode is due to the programs, blocks and negative energies that exist within us. These programs, blocks and negative energies are the very cause of our victim mentality and why we exist in victim.
2. Our experiences and situations (e.g., traumas, relationships, abuses, etc.) have informed our sense of self and this informs and confirms our reality of victim.
3. There is a familiarity and delusional safety to existing in victim – e.g., if I always predict the worst then I'm prepared and ready to deal with the worst, if by some unforeseen reason it isn't the worst then I feel paradoxically better in victim.
4. I'm separate from everyone else, being close to others is risky and humans are unpredictable, this is just how life is…victim mode is confirmed.

All the above apply to victim mode and all give valid reason to why being in victim mode is a viable option. So, if this is the case, why step out of victim mode?

The reason we step out of victim is two-fold:

1. It's the very reason why we are on this planet

2. Separation/Victim is an illusion created through fear to help us spiritually grow, to understand true connectedness, and being whole - or should I say Holy.

To step out of Victim is the first lesson and step we must take when accessing our Master Plan. Victim is the illusionary state of helplessness and hopelessness. It is the very trap that holds and stops you from achieving your full potential physically, emotionally, psychologically, and spiritually. This goes far beyond positive thinking, positive self-talk, and motivation. To step out of Victim is to take full responsibility for every aspect of your existence in Body/Mind/Spirit. To step out of Victim is to take on a level of maturity that intrinsically states 'I AM'. You no longer acquiesce to your social and relational conditionings of fear that limit and block your ability to feel, think and respond in authentic ways. By stepping out of Victim, you are giving yourself permission and ability to engage with your Master Plan. You are taking full responsibility for your thoughts, feelings, and actions. You are taking full responsibility of your Body/Mind/Spirit.

A note on the Drama Triangle:

In 1961 Stephen Karpman presented the drama triangle. A diagrammatic overview of how we as humans perpetuate the drama roles and relationships in human life.

Figure 1 Drama Triangle

Persecutor   Rescuer

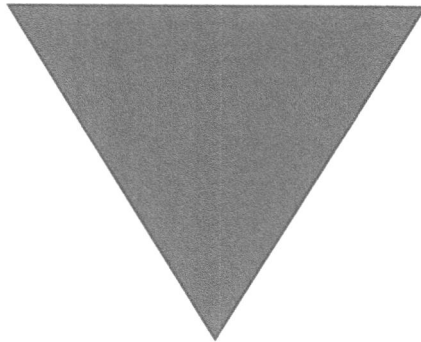

Victim

The basic premise of the drama triangle is to show and prove how we as humans are continually caught and play the roles of Victim, Persecutor and Rescuer. Within all our relationships we will oscillate and move between the three power roles, either giving or taking away our power or the other's power through the roles of Victim, Persecutor and Rescuer.

What is fascinating is that all these roles need each other to exist. The Victim needs the Persecutor, the Persecutor needs the Victim, and the Rescuer needs both the Victim and the Persecutor. Without either of these roles the drama triangle ceases to exist.

If we look at our cultural narratives, stories, media, news, social structures, hierarchies, economies, entertainment sources, cosmologies, mythologies, folklore, and fairy tales, etc…we will quickly see how the internal infrastructure of our cultures have been built around this basic drama premise of Victim, Persecutor and Rescuer. One of the first things children experience are fairy tales of the poor misfortunate child being cruelly held or punished by the wicked old stepparent or Witch e.g., Cinderella. Cinderella being the poor Victim, the wicked Stepmother being the Persecutor. However, do not despair poor Victim because you can be saved. The handsome prince, the Rescuer, will come and defeat the nasty Persecutor and 'Wisk you away' to safety, rescued from your miserable life of misfortune. What this also highlights are the perpetuation of genderism, sexism, racism, and patriarchal narratives in our cultures. I appreciate there is still a lot wrong in how we perpetuate this prejudice and discrimination. Thankfully, we are becoming more progressive and are beginning to challenge and critique this discrimination.

Yet, that simple example shows how insidious the drama triangle is from a very early age in our cultural psyche and how it underpins discrimination and prejudice in our cultures too. The news and social media are flooded with stories of Victim, Persecutor and Rescuer. Our movies, fiction, TV dramas are built on Victim, Persecutor and Rescuer. Our daily lives exist with us feeling like a

9

Victim, Persecutor and Rescuer or noticing them in others. Now I don't mean we are being beaten physically each day (although sadly some people are), or being held captive in a jail (although sadly some people are), or being cruelly bullied (although sadly some people are) - no, for some of us it isn't that extreme, it's more a mindset or feeling, a 'fed up, can't do feeling' of Victim, but however extreme or not it's still Victim. Persecutor and Rescuer are the same. You might not be physically attacking someone or holding them prisoner, but you might make a sideways comment or throw in a derogatory hurtful remark said in jest but you are still in persecutor role…the same is for rescuer, you might not come in driving your tank through the walls of the prison to save the captives but you might step in when you hear the side-ways comment and stand-up for the Victim of discrimination.

Having now recognised the roles and the dynamics of the drama triangle, they all have one thing in common – they are all in fact representatives of the all-encompassing mindset of Victim. Each aspect/role of the drama triangle is Victim with an alternate name and role, so Victim is Victim, Rescuer is Victim and Persecutor is Victim, as they are all held and are all imprisoned within the dynamics of the drama. To exist in the drama triangle and to play out the drama triangle is by essence to be in Victim, irrespective of what role you are playing…

Next is the first reflective task and exercise. This exercise is based on the drama triangle and recognising it in our lives. Now this is not a shame and guilt exercise, although these feelings might arise for you, which is common when we first start to reflect and recognise the drama triangle in our lives. We can easy attribute shame and guilt to ourselves when we recognise ourselves in these roles...Remember these roles are ubiquitous to our lives and we all play them out. Shame and guilt are the friend of Victim. Victim mentality embraces guilt and shame, they are the feelings and negative energies that Victim feeds off. We are here to engage our Master Plan, to work toward stepping out of Victim. If the feelings of guilt and shame arise, acknowledge them with respect and then send them on their way. If you get caught or hooked into the guilt and shame game you will get sent down the dark road of self-punishment, self-hurt and self-hate - negative programmes and blocks to accessing your Master Plan.

Reflective Task 1 – The Drama Triangle:

I'd like you to take a moment (between 5-10 minutes) to reflect on your life, your experiences, your relationships, family, friendships, working life, etc...to really take some time to think about the three drama roles in the drama triangle in relation to your life...Can you recognise when you have been in one of these roles? How often do you find yourself in one of these roles? What does it feel like to be in these roles? Is there a preferred role you find yourself in?

Thank you for taking the time to engage in this task...What did you experience? What were your thoughts, feelings, emotions? What roles did you find yourself in? What relationships came up for you? How was it reflecting on your own life experiences and relationships?

I hope the exercise wasn't too uncomfortable for you, although as previously stated in the 'How to use this book' section, these exercises can bring up uncomfortable feeling. If you are feeling uncomfortable and need support, please access your support networks to help you work through your experiences.

Now that we recognise Victim, why are we in Victim?

This links directly to spiritual growth and accessing your Master Plan. Victim can be understood as being imprisoned, shackled, limited, and held back. For us to achieve ultimate freedom and to move beyond the Earth-bound realm, we first need to be in Victim. Victim is our starting point, our point of departure and the end game here on Earth. If we look at this as a simple game analogy, Victim is the first level which we need to complete before we can move on to the next stage.

Does this mean that every human on Earth is in Victim?

It means that there will be a substantial percentage of the human population in Victim, and a very small percentage of humans that have stepped out of Victim. Those that have stepped out of Victim will know they have and will have a deeper fundamental knowing and awareness of Body/Mind/Spirit. They will be free from self-judgement, self-punishment, and self-hate. They will be compassionate, empathic, and authentic to self and others. They will be open to their experience and will not discriminate through social conditioning and social constructs. They will be spiritually, psychologically, and emotionally mature. They will be attuned to their Master Plans and living them out in-line with the greater Divine Plan. Examples of humans that have stepped out of Victim in our history are Shakyamuni Buddha. Jesus of Nazareth, Mary Magdalene, Dogen Zenji, Shinran Shonin, Francis of Assisi, Jalāl ad-Dīn Muḥammad Rūmī, Juliana of Norwich, Sai Baba of Shirdi, Ramana Maharshi and the Dalai Lamas. These are examples of humans that have progressed spiritually through their learning and development from many, many thousands of past lives here on

13

Earth. They have achieved true spiritual awakening and have completed the Earth-bound game.

Seven Spiritual Principles that underpin our Existence:

There are seven spiritual principles that underpin our existence and life in this Universe. These seven principles are our foundation for growth, development, and healing. These seven spiritual principles are also the bedrock and foundation of SRT - Spiritual Response therapy – which I will discuss further in section three. Kathryn Hamilton-Cook (2006) presented these seven principles of healing, and they are given to SRT trainees as part of their training to become SRT practitioners. If we also explore and research spirituality and certain religions, you will also come across these principles embedded within their belief systems and cosmologies.

Spiritual Principles

1. We are spiritual beings expressing through a physical body. Separation from SPIRIT is an illusion.

2. As spiritual beings, we have access to higher spiritual guidance in the form of High Self. High Self works with the Soul to research and clear programs.

3. The Soul is ultimately in charge of its own healing. Nothing happens that is not planned for or allowed by

the Soul. As divine beings creating our own reality, we cannot be victims.

4. It's not what happens to you, but the energy you attach to it. This is the Law of Mind Action: What you think and attach an energy to, you create.

5. As spiritual beings, we've lived thousands of lives, many on other planets, and in other dimensions and galaxies. The accumulated energy from these other lives can and does affect the current life. If we hold energy on something, we must deal with it.

6. Only love has the highest outcome. Fear is a misperception that we can be separate from SPIRIT and SPIRIT is the highest expression of love.

7. Everything is in Divine Order.

Now when you first read these principles you may start to think, ok, here we go, it's getting all esoteric, mystical, hanging out with angels and believing in things we can't evidence! That would be a fair appraisal for some of you…others might be thinking, ok, I'll have an open mind and see where he's going with this and others might be saying at last, he's telling me what I've always known – there is a system/cosmology that exists, which gives clarity and meaning to life.

My job isn't trying to convince you or to persuade you to believe in angels, archangels, cosmic and galactic committees, high powers,

God, Universe, and Spirit…my job is to present this system and process of healing for you to think about, consider, possibly try, and engage with. You can make up your own mind, decisions, and choices around what you wish to believe in or not.

Humans are a fascinating species, we are quick to condemn, ridicule and eradicate anything which we feel goes beyond our 'ordinary way of life'. Our history is riddled with persecution, war and violence, and even current life (just watch the news) where we are confronted by things that we believe will usurp or unhinge the status quo. If it doesn't fit within the groups everyday vernacular, ideology, and belief system we are quick to feel defensive and to defend ourselves against whatever this scary, different, strange, weird, or threatening thing might be. Yes, you've guessed it FEAR has been allowed to enter the room…and we are fixed in Victim.

Huntington (2023) states:

> Fear is a universal human experience… fear is the experience we have when we feel threatened. Whether the threat is an upcoming performance review at work, the steep slope of a mountain you've chosen to ski down, or the sound of footsteps behind you at night, fear is a full-body, stressful experience of anticipating something bad might happen.

Fear, therefore, is a process that not only stops us from engaging in aspects of life and being able to 'do life'; it is also experienced as a full mind/body reaction, and it is due to this full mind/body reaction that prevents us from doing and fulfilling our full potentials.

Common Symptoms of Fear:

- Rapid heartbeat

- Sweating

- Trembling

- Shortness of breath

- Wobbly legs

- Dizzy or lightheaded

- Feeling of choking

- Indigestion

- Chest pain

- Getting chills

- Flushed face

- Dry mouth

In addition, to these physical symptoms, people often report feeling overwhelmed, out of control, nervous, or numb, when they are afraid (Huntington, 2023). Given the universality of FEAR in human experience it would be fair to say that everyone of us at some time in our life has experienced these symptoms and feelings. It would also be fair to say that not one of us when we experienced this dark FEAR enjoyed it, or it made us feel good.

In respect to human development FEAR is the factor that keeps us isolated and separated from the source of our existence and universal connectedness to all. FEAR is the misperception that we are separate from SPIRIT, and SPIRIT is the highest expression of Conscious existence LOVE.

That might be all well and good, but what about the evidence? Where is the evidence base to all this?

Reflective Task 2 - Victim:

I'd like you to take a moment (between 5-10 minutes) to reflect on your life, your experiences, your relationships, family, friendships, working life, etc...to really take some time to think about and feel those experiences (please practice self-care around this task as some of you reading this may have had trauma, abuse, deep hurt, etc., so please be kind to yourselves and edit what is safe to reflect on)...think about those people you love, think about those people that love you, think about the good you have experienced as well as the not so good...allow yourself to feel the range of your experiences in life, allow yourself to evidence your own existence – your experiential processes.

Thank you for taking the time to engage in this task... What did you experience? What were your thoughts, feelings, emotions? Who did you think about? What relationships came up for you? How was it reflecting on your own life experiences and relationships?

Whatever you experienced, and I'm not even going to hazard a guess, is your evidence base. It is your way of validating and confirming your thoughts, feelings, emotions, behaviours, and processes in your life. Again, it is not my job to convince you or to persuade you to believe in anything. I'm here to offer a framework that can help you heal, develop, and grow, and an opportunity for you to try this out and make up your own mind. From the reflective task you will have experienced and reflected on situations, relationships, and dynamics that made you feel good (I hope) and those that produced the opposite. If you struggled to find any positive experiences or relationships, then I am truly sorry and hope in time, and with the right healing, you can come to experience the good in the world as well. For those of you that were able to experience the good as well as the bad, I hope it has shown you the range of human experience and that the good is underpinned by connectedness, kindness, care, and love. The very things that enhance our wellbeing and are the opposite to pain, fear, isolation, and separation; the very things that block/prevent the enhancement of your wellbeing.

Taking Charge of Your Own Existence

Now that we know that Fear causes Victim, it's time to shine the light on what we can do to step out of this mode...

If we refresh ourselves on principle three of the seven spiritual principles that underpin our existence:

> **The Soul is ultimately in charge of its own healing. Nothing happens that is not planned for or allowed by the Soul. As divine beings creating our own reality, we cannot be Victims.**

This is a key statement and a key step when we decide and apply the courage to step out of Victim. There are three fundamental premises to this statement and these three premises give justification to step out of victim.

1. You oversee your own healing - therefore you can do this and ultimately this is your responsibility.

2. Everything you experience in this life, has already been planned for and is happening and will happen because You have agreed to it – therefore you are already responsible for it...

3. As a Spiritual Human Being we create our own perceived reality – therefore you are already creating your existence and therefore

you can also change it – leading to the ultimate realisation that You are not a Victim. Victim is a delusional state that you've created using FEAR...

Yes, I know what you are going to say, well if everything has already been planned for and agreed, how can we change it? The answer is this – the change process/learning experience has already been agreed to and planned for; therefore, the change is part of your already pre-planned agreement and process of learning. It's the same as learning anything in life, you decide what you want to learn, you study and engage with the knowledge, then you apply the knowledge/skill and integrate into your existing life. How many of you learnt to drive a car, learnt to read, learnt to walk, etc. It's the same process. You had to learn how to do it, and the very first step to learning was You agreeing and planning to learn.

So, we can see how fundamental spiritual principle three is, because what it tells us is that we agreed and planned for this. So how can we blame anyone or anything else – we can't because to do so would be to undermine and block the very thing we came here to learn – and the thing we came here to learn was to step out of Victim and to take responsibility for our development and to access our Master Plan, which includes the remaining spiritual principles:

4. It's not what happens to you, but the energy you attach to it. This is the Law of Mind Action: What you think and attach an energy to, you create.

5. As spiritual beings, we've lived thousands of lives, many on other planets, and in other dimensions and galaxies. The accumulated energy from these other lives can and does affect the current life. If we hold energy on something, we must deal with it.

6. Only love has the highest outcome. Fear is a misperception that we can be separate from SPIRIT and SPIRIT is the highest expression of love.

7. Everything is in Divine Order.

So, if everything has been planned for (principle 3) and everything is in Divine Order (Principle 7), where does the idea of 'free will' come into play? That would be Principle four:

4. It's not what happens to you, but the energy you attach to it. This is the Law of Mind Action: What you think and attach an energy to, you create.

Principle four is the perceived process of 'Free Will'. I say perceived as it is the process of 'doing' and 'apply'. We perceive action taking place and perceive action in our self and others through the 'applying of' and the 'doing of'. For example, when I first began learning to walk, I observed others walking, which created a visual map/picture for me. When you are learning to walk you don't need to create images in your mind - you watch others around you that are 'doing walking' and you apply the image you've just gained from watching. You see the process of walking and how it's done, so you then take the image, attach the energy, and then start to create walking. With time and practice you eventually become competent at it, and it becomes integrated into your body – this is the Law of Mind Action (principle 4). This is the Law that gives us our perceived process of 'Free Will'. We are the creators using the Law of Mind Action to create; therefore, we believe we have 'Free Will' to create, and overall, through this process it is true – we do have 'Free Will'.

This is also the process that helps us spiritually develop and create the fulfilling life we dream of by accessing our Master Plan…interesting I said dream, what are we doing when we dream? We are creating images, ideas, pictures, identities, landscapes, etc. of the possibilities and potentials of what we want to be or the change we want to see in ourselves. The Law of Mind Action first starts with an idea, concept, image or thought. We first create or see the image we want before we begin to attach the energy and bring it into being. Ask any successful businessperson, personality, or anyone that's created anything, and the first thing they did was conceptualise the very thing they wanted. This must happen before we can apply the necessary energy to create it and bring it into existence. Want to be rich and famous? Apply the Law of Mind Action. Want to have fulfilling relationships? Apply the Law of Mind Action. Want to find contentment and feel sorted in this world? Apply the Law of Mind Action. It's a simple and as easy as that…or is it?

This is where it gets a bit trickier, principle five:

5. As spiritual beings, we've lived thousands of lives, many on other planets, and in other dimensions and galaxies. The accumulated energy from these other lives can and does affect the current life. If we hold energy on something, we must deal with it.

Past lives and accumulated processes of the Law of Mind Action over many lifetime's causes accumulated energy that we hold onto and bring into our current life. This accumulated energy has an influence and impact on how we experience ourselves and life around us. If this energy is not cleared it will continue to affect us and the choices, we make in life. Ultimately this accumulated energy is what puts us in Victim and if it's not cleared will hold us in Victim. On a wider spiritual level these accumulated energies affect our overall spiritual existence. In our current life they affect how we perceive, think, feel, and behave about our self and others. The more negative accumulated energies you hold, the perceived harder, more painful, and difficult your experiences will be and will generally feel. Now, this is not about falling either further into Victim, e.g., I've experienced myriad forms of trauma, abuse, hurt, suffering, etc., so therefore I must have been an awful person and done awful things in past lives. No, that's a blame game and victim mentality – it's the 'poor me' again – No we don't want to fall into that old trap. It's about recognising and going back to the very first principle:

1. We are spiritual beings expressing through a physical body. Separation from SPIRIT is an illusion.

You are a spiritual being having a human experience on this wonderful planet and your illusionary state of separation is your way to spiritual growth, development, and enhanced wellbeing. So, you might have done many horrendous things in previous lifetimes and done horrible things in this lifetime that you regret but what we are looking for is not to blame or condone. We are looking for change and growth. Now I don't want to get into a deep discussion regarding ethics and morals. Ultimately, as we grow spiritually and self-develop, we step out of Victim and begin to take responsibility for our actions, choices, and life. This is what we are aiming for…principle five states that we have lived, many, many thousands of lifetimes, and past lives – are you telling me you've been a Saint and a morally upstanding person in everyone? I don't think so because if you had you wouldn't be here now working through all this and having this human experience. Every single one of us at different points in our past lives have lived the full range of light and dark. The light and dark need each other, you can't have one without the other, look at the imagine of the Eastern philosophical symbol of Yin and Yang fig.2:

Figure 2 Yin & Yang Symbol

In the light is the dark and in the dark, you'll always find the light. Lighter consciousness, darker consciousness...Lighter matter, darker matter. Lighter material, darker material, and the range of this. As we get darker material, we get denser material and as we get lighter material, we get less dense material. It's evident in our natural world as well as our spiritual world. So, we are not looking to blame and condone. We are looking for change and growth. We are looking to access our Master Plans.

Connecting to Spirit and the Spiritual Realm

For some of you, the thought of being spiritual and connecting to spirituality may already be a given. You may already have an established way of connecting to Spirit and the spiritual realm that works effectively and you are happy with. If this is the case, you can either skip this section or happily read on to explore further…

Connecting to Spirit and the spiritual realm – what do we mean by this?

For centuries human existence, culture, and societies have always had some kind of spiritual connection, framework, or ideology that underpins them. This can be housed in organised spiritual groups, religions, cults, and personal belief systems. Every country, culture and society will have some form of recognised spiritual/religious organisation that serves the people and offers spiritual solace e.g., Islam, Christianity, Hinduism, Buddhism, Judaism, etc… (PBS, 2023). Within our societies these religious, spiritual, and philosophical belief systems are taught to us and our children in schools, home, church, temples and groups by teachers, parents, spiritual leaders, Imams, Elders, Rabbis, Priests, Ministers, and followers/believers. I suspect many of you have come in contact at some point in your life, be it through one of these contexts e.g., school, with some form of spiritual/religious teacher. My children go to a state school in the UK, and the state school is Church of

England, so my children will have been taught Christian teachings and doctrine.

Now for the sake of ease and uniformity, I am using spiritual and religious interchangeably at this stage. I appreciate there is a very grave distinction between both for some, especially given the history and levels of persecution, violence and war that has and still is going on in the name of certain religions. To quickly touch on the differences between religion and spirituality, Cline (2020) states:

> Religion describes the social, the public, and the organized means by which people relate to the sacred and the divine, while spirituality describes such relations when they occur in private and personally.

This is a surface level look at the differences, and I'd suggest that you do further research into these very different but at times similar forms of engaging with the sacred or divine (Cline, 2020; Pargament, Exline, & Jones, 2013).

I will use the example of Robert Detzler the founder of Spiritual Response Therapy (SRT) to illustrate this further. Robert Detzler was practicing as a Minister for an organised religion when he started to work and establish the SRT systems. He approached his Church for support and integration of the system with his congregation. The Church did not allow this integration and finally gave Robert an ultimatum – either stop practicing SRT and stay being a Minister or leave and stop working as a Minister. Luckily for us Robert chose the latter, but what it highlights is that some religious groups can be fundamental and exclusive with their practice and belief systems, causing negative outcome for their followers/believers.

Going back to our original question - connecting to Spirit and the spiritual realm, what do we mean by this? We can see that due to the different forms of spirituality and religion, it is not as straight forward as simply picking up the phone and dialling up the spiritual helpline...or is it.

If we accept that religion according to consensus is an organised belief system that consists of mainly five beliefs:

1. there is a supreme deity,

2. this deity should be worshipped,

3. the most important part of religious practice is the cultivation of virtue,

4. one should seek repentance for wrong-doing, and

5. one is rewarded or punished in this life and the next.

and these beliefs are administered through a hierarchical system of leaders, teachers, elders, priests, ministers, etc. (Cline, 2020; Pargament, Exline, & Jones, 2013; Schilbrack, 2022). Therefore, the belief system, knowledge and power of that religion is firmly held in the hands of a group of people that are allowed to administer it; therefore, the people in positions of power within that hierarchy. If we take the Catholic religion as an example, we can see a very clear hierarchical system of human power starting with the Pope at the top, then Cardinal, Archbishop, Bishop, Priest and then finishing with the Deacon. The Catholic religion is controlled and administered through the people that undertake these roles and who interact and share the teachings and beliefs of the Catholic Church with the laity its followers. The laity or laypeople do not have any control in the administration of the knowledge, practice, or power of the religion – they must follow, believe, practice, and not change any element they have been taught or that has been shared with them. The religion has a very clear established set of beliefs, ways of 'doing/practicing' the rules that underpin it, that the human hierarchy controls and polices. If you question, change, or step out of line, the organised religion will give you an opportunity to repent or step back inline, and if this is not an option, then you'll be asked to leave that religious group. As per the example of Robert Detzler being asked to leave his religious Church group as he was no longer in line with their doctrine/belief system and practice, according to the Church leaders/administrators.

So, if we are following a religious belief system that has a human hierarchical system of power controlling the religion, it may not be as simple as picking up the phone and dialling up the spiritual helpline. The religious hierarchy has the control and monopoly of connecting to the higher levels of spiritual consciousness. Yes, we can pray to the supreme deity (God), if it falls in line with our allowed religious practice, but the answer and waiting time might be a long one due to the complex and convoluted administrative system that controls it...not dissimilar to a state administrative system here on Earth. I'm sure we've all been on hold at different

30

points in time and passed around administrative systems when we are looking to get in contact with state and government services. I know I have, and I know how frustrating and time consuming it can be – it can be a long, long, long wait time.

A note on spiritual leaders, charismatic leaders, and gurus:

Ultimately, my understanding of being spiritual and spirituality is grounded in certain values, qualities, and beliefs about what it means to be spiritual and how we engage and connect to the spiritual. If we accept, or at least are open to the possibility, that spirituality is connecting and developing a relationship with higher levels of consciousness that exist to support and guide in our daily existence, then we have a good starting point.

When we decide to engage with the spiritual there are certain pointers, emotions and experiences that can help us recognise that we have connected to something greater than ourselves, and that this higher level of consciousness heightens us positively.

Miller (2020) links to self-transcendent emotions as markers to connecting to the spiritual:

- Compassion

- Awe

- Gratitude

- Appreciation

- Inspiration

- Admiration

- Elevation

- Love

Those of you that have experienced connecting to, and connect to, the spiritual will no doubt have experienced these, and if you continue to connect will have noticed these heightened levels become grounded into your daily existence. In turn they make yourself and life feel better and more positive.

What Miller (2020) goes on to say, from a positive psychology perspective grounded in spirituality, is that these self-transcendent emotions help us focus on others as well as our self, which in turn fosters more meaningful and purpose-filled relationships generally. So, we can evaluate, and we know from our own experience, that when we embody, feel, and communicate from these self-transcendent emotions, better relationships are fostered with our self, others, and the environments we live in.

Another aspect Miller (2020) highlights is that:

> Many positive psychology interventions are grounded in ancient religious and spiritual teachings, which are not typically included in treatment for psychopathology. There are empirically validated interventions for the following four virtues: hope,

gratitude, forgiveness, and self-compassion (Rye, Wade, Fleri, & Kidwell, 2013).

Miller here is bridging the gap between science (scientific rigour) and spirituality, something I will come onto later in section four when discussing how science and spirituality can work together, instead of being presented as diametrically opposed.

How does this fit with spiritual leaders, charismatic leaders, and gurus?

It's very simple and something that we can evaluate either in the moment or on reflection when we meet and interact with someone that presents in this role. These self-transcendental emotions Miller (2020) highlights can also be markers to spirituality and how well it's being fostered and presented by spiritual leaders, charismatic leaders, and gurus You can also go through a series of steps, I've noted 5 below, which give an easy method to evaluation.

5 Steps to evaluating the authenticity of spiritual leaders:

1. You must always remember and come back to the fact that this person is another human being, just like you! They are not God, an angel, higher spirit, God's right-hand person, etc…they are just like you! A spiritual being living a human existence.

2. How does what they are saying and preaching affect you? Do you feel safe? Do

you feel a sense of openness? Do you feel positivity?

3. Are their teachings inclusive or exclusive? Therefore, are they openly accepting of all, or do they have conditions e.g., asking for money from you?

4. Do they expect you to follow them and follow their teachings only?

5. Do they expect you to evangelise and preach their teachings?

If on reflection and evaluation of these five steps, you come up against any doubt, fear, negativity, or confusion, then I'd say be cautious of the spiritual leaders, charismatic leaders, and gurus. What we tend to find is that the person's ego is running at a high percentage, and they are looking to gain and profit from your passive engagement and subjection to them. They want followers that will idealise them, put them on that pedestal and subject themselves to them by handing over their power, money, decision making and autonomy. In effect you are enslaving yourself to them, their teachings/beliefs and allowing yourself to exist within their limited and confined reality. An example of this is pyramid schemes, motivational speakers, cult leaders and radicalisation. You are no longer living in your own reality; you are living in theirs - You are once again in Victim.

What we are looking for from spirituality, and the people that teach, share, and promote spirituality, are the embodying, sharing, and experiencing of positive qualities, beliefs and values that exist. We are looking for relationships, connection and engagement grounded in ethics, I turn to my psychotherapy ethical framework (BACP, 2020) to assist here:

1. Being trustworthy: honouring the trust placed in the practitioner.
2. Autonomy: respect for the client's right to be self-governing.
3. Beneficence: a commitment to promoting the client's wellbeing.
4. Non-maleficence: a commitment to avoiding harm to the client.
5. Justice: the fair and impartial treatment of all clients and the provision of adequate services.
6. Self-respect: fostering the practitioner's self-knowledge, integrity, and care for self.

The six ethical principles can give a good starting point to help us evaluate and foster these ethics within ourselves and recognising them in others. What we want from our spirituality, teachers, guides, and helpers are the embodiment and commitment to uphold and relate from these ethical positions that promote wellbeing, openness, integrity, and compassion.

If spiritual leaders, charismatic leaders, and gurus do not embody, foster, or promote from these ethical positions then perhaps it's time to re-evaluate.

Connecting to Spirit and the Spiritual Realm – revisited

Do we need anyone else to connect to the spiritual realm? No.

Is this something I can learn to do and feel confident with? Yes, any one of us can learn to connect to the spiritual realm, be confident with how we do this, and trust this connection.

Ways to connect spiritually can be found in section two and three. However, engaging and being spiritual is a personal process. There are lots of ways to engage with the spiritual, some people find this when they go out in nature, climb a mountain, walk in a forest or swim in the sea. Some people find it through meditation, painting, music, and the arts; others might find it in science, social sciences, and the natural sciences. There is no right or wrong way to be spiritual, it's about finding the way that works for you! The key is being open to spirituality, inviting it in and allowing it into your life…

So, you can now see that it is straight forward and simple, just pick up your spiritual phone and dial up the spiritual helpline… You don't need any spiritual leaders, charismatic leaders, or gurus. You don't need any convoluted, complex administrative religion or hierarchical system of power.

All you need is **openness**, **invitation** and **allowing** of spirituality into your life.

Connecting to the Body

The body is a wonderful and marvellous instrument. It has many capabilities, functions, and aptitudes, in essence it's a gift…without the human body we wouldn't be able to do, function, process and engage in our daily lives; you wouldn't be able to read this book or make decisions. You wouldn't be able to drive your car, take your children to school or meet your friends for coffee. You wouldn't be able to get out of bed in the morning or get into bed at night. You wouldn't be able to laugh with your partner, get angry with your partner or make love with your partner. The body is our way of navigating the social world and a hub of pain and pleasure. The body is essential to life.

Bryson (2020) gives us a comprehensive look at the human body and its wonder, and interestingly calls his book a 'guide for occupants'.

The human body is the machine, instrument, and avatar to embodied existence. It gives us the possibility, potential and opportunity to engage with others, our self, the natural world, and life, but most of all it's yours. The body is your personal vehicle and from a very early age you begin to learn and spend most of your life learning how to use it and figuring out what it can do. It really is a marvel.

So, why then do people take it for granted?

Sadly, our human existence has layer upon layer of negativity that impacts human life and most definitely impacts the human body…our history and current life are riddled with war, violence, hate, hurt and punishment (just watch the global news). In countries around the world atrocities, violence, trauma, and suffering are happening daily. Wars are happening, there's violence on the streets, in homes, in schools and in workplaces. Abuse, domestic violence, torture and people trafficking are happening. Self-harm, self-punishment, addiction, and suicide are happening. All this is happening on an emotional, psychological, and physical level, which means it's happening to our bodies. We are a traumatised species that keeps on repeating and playing out our trauma, time and time and time again… (Mate, 2023; Van Der Kolk, 2015; Van Der Kolk, McFarlane & Weisaeth, 2007).

I guess it's hard not to take one's body for granted when we are dealing with all this trauma and suffering. We are constantly distracted, and our attention is elsewhere. Plus, we've had our body since our birth, so it's always been there. We are constantly using it and it's constantly doing stuff that most of the time we don't even consider or think about e.g., breathing, pumping blood and processing information. So, it makes perfect sense why we would take it for granted…

But what happens when something starts to go wrong?

The body is many things but most of all it's the Master of Communication. Not only is the body a master of verbal, sound, language communication it is the master of non-verbal communication, including sign language, eye contact, facial expressions, gestures, posture, use of objects and body language. In fact, Hull (2016) suggest that 70% of human communication is non-verbal leaving only 30% verbal, which demonstrates the power of non-verbal communication and how it impacts our human communication pathways and relationships.

One aspect of the non-verbal communication the body is intrinsically linking with and does on an ongoing basis is communicating to the self. Your body is in constant communication with you and that ongoing communication is either 'in and/or out' of your awareness all the time. The most obvious level the body communicates is through our feeling and sensory processes e.g., taste, touch, smell, sight, and hearing. Our senses are the touchstone to our relationships with others and the external world. It's through our senses that we can experience and orientate ourselves through our day-to-day living. The senses help us make sense of people, objects, and the world. The body is a master communicator.

It is this master communicator that brings our attention and awareness to our body and self when something goes wrong. When the body starts to go wrong, we usually stop taking it for granted. This is seen with the 'wakeup call' or 'alarm bells ringing', when the individual realises that their choices, actions, and behaviours e.g., cigarette smoking, are hurting and destroying their body and sense of self. This can be experienced through pain, illness, and suffering. So, the individual acts and decides to change their habits, choices, and behaviours. They quit smoking and take responsibility for their own health and wellbeing. They stop hurting their body.

Sadly, for some people, even the pain, illness and suffering don't have the desired impact the body is communicating. This level of body communication can still be ignored, distorted, or denied, finally leading to the death of the body. We see this often with substance abuse addictions, where the individual knows that the substance e.g., alcohol, is killing and destroying the body; yet sadly the individual continues to harm and destroy the body finally leading to death. As tragic as this is, and it is tragic, it also highlights the level of control and overriding the individual's sense of self/ego has over the body. The body can be screaming out to the self/ego, through pain, suffering, discomfort, illness, and confusion; yet the self/ego can still find ways to ignore, distort and deny these levels of sensory communication. This perhaps is needed on some level, especially if we revisit trauma in our history and societies, as the body does need to function. If the human self/ego didn't have the capacity to distort and deny some levels of human experience then the body would be in constant shutdown, non-functioning, and catatonic. It would be in a constant state of overwhelm. This extreme level of shutdown is evident when choices, lifestyle, and relationships are not conducive to positive living and wellbeing. This is when your blocks, negative programmes and negative energies are impacting your life to such a degree that you are struggling to live positively and make positive choices. You are so entrenched in Victim that you are harming self and therefore harming your body. Extreme cases are when the individual decides to 'take their own life', sadly, they can't see another way out. The only option is suicide, so they decide to kill the body.

Suicide is a tragic answer to suffering, pain and torment in our cultures. It highlights the absolute disconnect and sense of separation from the body and one's existence. The body is therefore a vital element to our existence not only from birth but also to death. It allows us to be born into corporeal existence and it also allows us to exit corporeal existence. It's our vehicle for life but also our vehicle for death. Without the body we do not exist corporeally, we need it to navigate human experience on Earth. So, we can see how vital the human body is to our existence and therefore an essential element in body/mind/spirit integration.

How do I connect to the body?

Connecting to the body suggests that there is initially a disconnect, a misnomer that I will explore later. However, there are reasons why we don't always allow feelings and sensory processes to register with us e.g., trauma, abuse, violence, etc. So, we disconnect from our sense of the body to manage and not feel, in essence we allow a numbing or desensitising to happen so any feelings that we might experience in the body are dulled or switched off to awareness. This tends to be the case with emotion and forms of hurt, pain and suffering e.g., violence, abuse, trauma, etc...therefore the mind/body connect is strong and this demonstrates how they are linked. As in our previous examples with self-harm e.g., substance abuse with alcohol, the mind overrides the body's communication systems of pain, illness, discomfort, and suffering, to allow the individual to keep using the harmful substance (alcohol) and in effect damage and toxify the body. Alcohol is a powerful substance as it not only depresses the body's ability to feel through sensory processes, but it also alters our mind state creating an alternate state of reality and perception of self, others, and environment. This can be the case for many forms of mind-altering substance e.g., pharmaceutical drugs, painkillers, anti-depressants, and anti-psychotics. For further information on this I'd suggest reading Peter Breggin's views and research on psychiatry and medication drugs.

The human's ability to change and affect our sensory systems body/mind is clearly inherent in our cultures (how many of you drink alcohol and take pharmaceutical drugs?). Humans have been using mind/body altering substances since we can remember, and our history and cultures are drenched with them. I'm not going to go into the reasons why we as humans do this because there are many books, literature, podcasts and information cites out there that can do this – suffice to say the usual forms of pain-killing, distraction, escapism, numbing and avoidance of our daily relationships, jobs, etc,…we use these substances to take us away from our 'normal realities', whatever our reasons are..

Reflective Task 3 – The Body:

I'd like you to take a moment (between 5-10 minutes) to reflect on your body and bring awareness and attention to your body...to really take some time to focus in on your body and experience your body. Bring your attention to your feet to begin with and then move up through your legs, hips, abdomen, chest, down your arms and then back up through your neck and then into your head...

Thank you for taking the time to engage in this task...What did you experience? How did this feel? Were you able to feel your body and body parts? Did you feel a sense of connect or was there disconnect?

The idea of disconnect is a misnomer. We are never disconnected from our body as long as we are alive. The only time there is a real disconnect is when we leave the body, and the body dies. However, we use the term disconnect as it gives us an understanding of the different levels we experience when our senses are either heightened or dulled in respect to the body. For example, in the previous reflective task you were asked to bring attention and awareness to certain aspects of your body e.g., feet. In our daily goings about we don't generally bring awareness to certain body parts unless we encounter an experience that causes this...so we wouldn't bring attention to our feet normally unless they start to ache from prolonged use, or we drop an object on them. When this happens then our attention and awareness is drawn to the body part (feet), as the body part and the body in general, is communicating to us that something has happened, is happening, and our attention is needed to do something about it. In our previous examples with tired feet or dropping an object on them, the resolution or action needed is - we need to rest, recuperate, and heal them.

What this shows is that we are never disconnected from our body, only that our sense of perception and feeling work in accordance with awareness. It is the illness, hurt, pain and discomfort, the body is communicating, so we bring our awareness to the body for understanding and healing.

Connecting to the body: revisited

Are we ever disconnected from the body? No, only in death.

The disconnect or lack of awareness is the process of the body or aspects of the body in a limited and/or an out of awareness way. The body is a master communicator that is designed to help you navigate your reality and the shared worlds you live in. Without the body we do not exist in corporeal form and are not able to 'do' and 'be' in the world. Your body is your highly stylised and personal vehicle and as Bryson (2020) states we are occupants. Therefore, as occupants it's seems only sensible, ethical, and reasonable for us to take care and nurture this wonderful gift we have. If you want it to run more efficiently, effectively and have longevity then you must look after the body. **Be aware of what you put in it, how you use it and most of all nurture the Body.**

Connecting to Mind

The mind and concept of mind is a fascinating and well explored aspect of being human. Depending on what discipline be it biology, psychology, developmental psychology, psychotherapy, sociology, philosophy, neurobiology, interpersonal neurobiology, education, neuropsychology, and any other 'ology' you can think of there will be some theory, concept, or application of what the Mind is…

Developmental psychology tells us that Mind or Theory of Mind is the ability of the individual to attribute mental states to ourselves and others e.g., emotions, beliefs, desires, knowledge, etc. This helps the developing child to learn and predict social interactions, behaviours, and communications, so they can navigate their social worlds more competently. Recent developments within our developing sciences e.g., Interpersonal Neurobiology, and the proponents of this like Dan Siegal, have introduced us to mind, as a self-organising relational processing system that is individual to each human as well as sharing a consensus relational reality that we communicate through. We have an internal processing system that regulates the flow and ebb of information and energy through our bodies and relationships. Kenneth Gergen, from the world of philosophy and relational psychology, would go one step further and say that Mind isn't bounded within the individual, Mind is a purely relational process and embodied through our actions and interactions in all aspects of our relationships. Mind is born and dies in relationship; we are not a separate bounded information and energy processing system but an aspect of a greater relational processing system that we exist in. This links and fits within the spiritual concept and process of being One with everything. This is essentially the same as spiritual principle one:

1. We are spiritual beings expressing through a physical body. Separation from SPIRIT is an illusion.

We are not a separated individual being but an aspect of a greater central energy force Spirit that exists and is the oneness of everything. Everything is Spirit and Spirit is everything. Mind therefore is a central processing system of Spirit and as spiritual beings expressing through physical form we access and exist through Mind and therefore Spirit.

Whichever way you choose to understand Mind and make sense of Mind, ultimately, it's an experience and process that you as an individual are involved in. There is a process of consciousness or being aware of utilising and engaging with information/energy and how that exists within your sense of reality. How you make sense of Mind will also be a good indicator and highlight your sense of connection or disconnection with your body and Spirit. The greater the sense of separation, boundedness, and isolation from self, others and social context will be indicative of this throughout your life. If you believe your Mind to be a separate entity and disconnected from life, then you will experience yourself and life as that. If you believe your Mind to be an aspect of a greater social world and a processing system of that world, then you will feel closer and more connected to self, others, and the social world.

Reflective Task 4 – The Mind:

I'd like you to take a moment (between 5-10 minutes) to reflect on Mind, and bring awareness and attention to Mind...to really take some time to focus in on Mind and experience Mind...

Thank you for taking the time to engage in this task...What did you experience? Could you make sense of Mind? Were you able to feel or grasp Mind? Could you connect to Mind? Was there connection to relationships, the social world? Or was Mind isolated, bounded, and separate?

Pease don't worry if you couldn't make sense of Mind or connect with Mind. This reflective task can be difficult and almost impossible from an experiential process. Mind unlike the body is not a tangible and corporeal object, it isn't something we can grab hold of physically like a hand or even a brain. Although, some people will associate the Mind with the brain and even residing or existing in the head or brain. Again, there's no right or wrong concept of Mind, only what it means to you and how you make sense of it. My job here isn't to get into an academic discussion to prove or disprove a theory, concept, or practice. Only to present ideas and practices that will be beneficial to you and the people you relate to.

How then do I connect to Mind?

You don't need to connect to Mind, you already are...

Connection to Mind or awareness of Mind is to do with utilisation of Mind, how we go about using Mind in our day-to-day lives. As with the Body we are connected to the Body until we die and it's a process of awareness of body and body communication. Mind is similar in that we are always connected to Mind and even quite possibly after death (although, this is for another discussion later). Mind is also a platform for communication and utility as is the body, however, the difference is that Mind is not corporeal, is not physical and therefore not organic. Mind is the ultimate processor, the design hub, the world of symbols and signs - it's our download station and our non-organic central processing system. Mind is the place where objects, shapes, images, pictures, movies, language, text are created. It's the potentiality of creation - where everything created by humans was once conceived, be it cars, furniture, clothing, houses, gardens, computers, theories, language, mathematical equations, and chemical formulas. Mind is the place where every great discovery was first made in science, social sciences, and the arts. However, I pose the question - were they discovered or were they downloaded from the ever-expanding Mind/Universe where the potentiality of everything already exists? Is the individual human so great, so clever, such a genius to create this brilliance or does the greater source of Spirit already contain the possibility of everything? Perhaps the brilliance and genius are that the individual has reached a point in their development, to be ready to download this information and to share it for the development and growth of humanity?

Remember if we go back to spiritual principle seven:

7. Everything is in Divine Order.

There is a divine plan to our existence, life, the Universe, and everything else. Just like healing, only the individual can heal when they are ready. The time must be right. There is an order, a divine plan that is happening that goes beyond our physical existence that we as spiritual beings are a part of. Source/Spirit is the central hub of Oneness, everything is part of Spirit. Spirit is expanding, so therefore so are we. Just like systems theory there is a balance and the whole is greater than the sum of its parts just like the Body. The Body is a system of many thousands of parts that run and work to uphold the greater system of body efficiently, effectively, and harmoniously. There must be balance for the system to work, therefore there is a plan. Our lives and existence are analogous to this – instead of it being a physical corporeal system i.e., the body – it's a spiritual, divine existence that incorporates everything, and for that system to work there must be a plan. Just as the hand is a part of the body, each of us is part of Spirit working efficiently, effectively, and harmoniously as part of the whole. We are part of the divine plan just as the hand is part of the body plan.

What is fascinating and links into micro and macro and is reflected in every aspect of our lives is the existence of systems. The system maybe organic e.g., the body; non-organic e.g., virtual, conceptual, practical, logical, digital, you name it there will be a system. Where did this system first originate? The very source of existence Spirit. In certain religions, spiritual beliefs, and philosophy there is a premise – **As Above So Below.** In effect as divine/spirit as physical/corporeal - Heaven upon Earth. If we explore this further, it is saying that what exists in the divine is being reflected in the corporeal; albeit on a lower spiritual vibrational level but it's still existing on Earth. So, when certain spiritual leaders and masters have posed – to know oneself is to know God – they once again are presenting the reflection that the human was made in God's image. The closer we can get to understanding how we work and what the system of the human is, the closer we get to the divine. The human system is analogous to the system of the divine; again, albeit on a lower level of consciousness but still reflected and analogous. Spiritual principle number one - We are Spiritual beings having a human experience.

Connecting to Mind: revisited

How do I keep the Mind clean?

Just like the Body, the Mind is similar – if you put toxins in the Body, you will damage it and it will start to go wrong. The Mind is the same – if you engage with negativity, harmful language, harmful images, harmful relationships and harmful thinking and processing then you will damage your Mind processing system and it will work against you…Buddhist philosophy and Western Cognitive therapies e.g., CBT, discuss the importance of language, thinking and feeling in relation to the Mind. A healthy Mind is fuelled and fed with nurturing, caring and kind thinking and processing toward self and others and the world in general. Be careful what you allow yourself to engage with e.g., pornography, violence, aggression, hate, negative news, etc., all these leave a toxic trail in the Mind. Just like the Body if you overload with toxins e.g., junk food, you will start to feel sick, ill, anxious, and depressed, and with the Mind this will be reflected in your mental health, and it will even start to impact your Body as well.

So, as with the Body we need to be aware and conscious of what we engage with, put in the Mind and how we process. We are looking for enhanced wellbeing, positivity, and growth, and having the discernment to know what will nurture this.

Be aware of what you put in it, how you use it and most of all nurture Mind.

Connecting to Body/Mind

Now that we have established that connection to Body and Mind is a given whilst we are alive, connecting to Body/Mind should also be a given? The answer is a definite yes. However, what we are looking at here is not necessarily connection to Body/Mind but more integration or a system of complex ongoing communications between the Body and Mind and how this is regulated and achieved. From an Interpersonal Neurobiological, Neuroscience and psychotherapeutic viewpoint the interface or processing system is the brain organ (Cozolino, 2017; Schore, 2012; Siegal, 2012, 2016). The brain sits within the skull of the body at the top of the spine and links to the body's central nervous system, and from this position is interconnected with every aspect of the body through the peripheral nervous system. Hormonal systems, impulses, communications, blood flow, immune system and all the neural energy and information flows through and are regulated to some degree by the brain organ. It's our processing hub and our connection to and link between Body and Mind. Just as the High Self is the connecting operator between Self and Spirit from a spiritual perspective, the brain is the connecting operator (a simple analogy) between Body and Mind. Obviously, the Body and Brain are a complex system made up of thousands upon thousands of connections, impulses, cells, organs, etc...but this gives a simple way of understanding the relationship between Brain, Body, and Mind. The Mind needs the brain and without the brain the Body doesn't have a processing system to access the Mind. They are integral to the human being and assist us in being able to 'do and 'be' in the physical world, in the Mind world and in the spiritual world, whilst we are alive in this world.

A note on neuroplasticity:

Neuroplasticity is the term that denotes the ability to change our neural pathways and therefore the circuits of the brain. When we engage and learn with language, observation, social interaction, and relationships the body and brain create neural pathways to assist us with repeated thinking, feeling, and acting. We want short cuts so we can 'do' without applied thinking and application of knowledge. A classic example of this is learning to drive a car. At first you are all fingers and thumbs, reminding yourself to shift gear, brake, look at the road, watch for pedestrians, etc., but in time and practice this skill set becomes embodied and embedded within you – your brain and body remember. In time, you just drive the car, you don't have to think about it or remind yourself what to do, you just 'do' it…and it's the neural pathways created in the brain and the body's actions that help you do this. Without those neural pathways you would be a continual learner and never become competent at driving. Overtime and the more times you 'do' the activity the greater the neural pathways get embodied. Think about a virtuoso violinist or pianist or master craft-person, they can get to the level and standard they do due to those neural pathways. Of course, there's more than just neural pathways to becoming a virtuoso but without them they wouldn't even get passed the first hurdle. They are an intrinsic aspect of human development and learning.

However, the Body and Mind can get exposed to and can encounter harmful experiences e.g., abuse, trauma, violence, hate, etc., which leave a harmful trail and impact the individual in negative ways. So, just as the person can learn and develop from positive experiences to enhance their sense of wellbeing. the person if exposed to negative experiences will learn and develop survival and coping strategies to keep themselves safe, protected, and alive. If the person is exposed to a lot of repeated negativities their neural pathways will develop in self-protective, defensive, and less prosocial ways. For example, if the child is repeatedly abused, they will develop coping strategies that keep them alive and physically, psychologically, and emotionally safe. When they move into adulthood and the abuse stops, they will bring those coping strategies with them as the neural pathways and processes have been embedded and embodied. The adult may find they are struggling to have 'normal' relationship due to the abuse and trauma they suffered in their childhood.

One way to help the individual is therapy. Therapy, therapeutic relationships, interventions, and support can help the adult to work through their past trauma and abuse to find a sense of healing. A part of the healing process would be the creation of new neural pathways to override the old survival/protective/defensive pathways. Through the therapeutic relationship the individual would relearn to trust self and others creating more positive neural pathways of increased self-worth, self-value, self-compassion, and trust of others. In effect, they would create new ways to live and release the old ways of survival/defence and eventually heal. This change of neural pathways for the individual through positive relationship and attention is the process of neuroplasticity. Again, this is a positive example, but it can go either way. Neuroplasticity is the potential for neural pathways to change.

A note on the Pineal Gland:

Figure 3 Pineal Gland

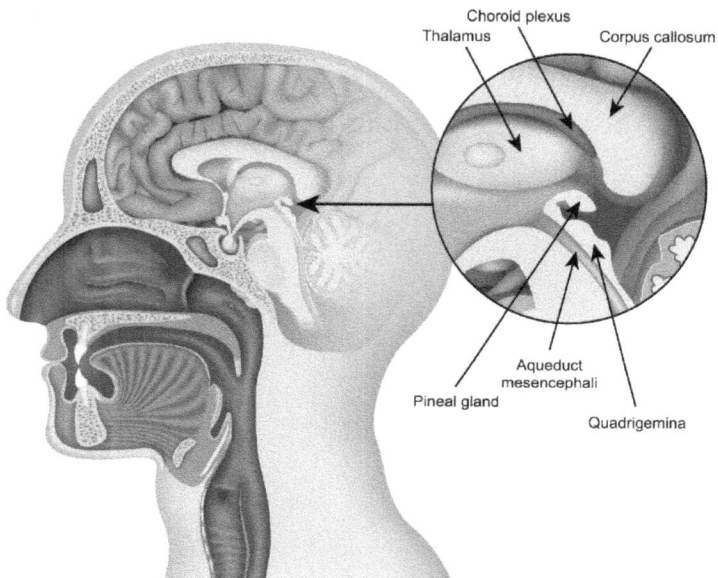

Your pineal gland, also called the pineal body or epiphysis cerebri, is a tiny gland in your brain that's located beneath the back part of the corpus callosum. It's a part of your endocrine system and secretes the hormone melatonin. Your pineal gland's main job is to help control the circadian cycle of sleep and wakefulness by secreting melatonin.

Cleveland Clinic (2022)

From a medical perspective, the pineal gland is one of the least understood glands of the human body. It's mostly understood as a regulating gland to help us maintain good sleep patterns, and possibly balance aspects hormonal levels and support good cardio-vascular health, but these are not understood or researched sufficiently to make any definite claims.

A 2022 paper by Arendt and Aulinas looked at the 'Physiology of the Pineal Gland and Melatonin' making links and examining the biological function of the pineal gland and how it regulates the production of the hormone melatonin and the therapeutic uses of this. They state in their abstract that the pineal gland *'is to receive information about the state of the light-dark cycle from the environment and convey this information'*, this is an interesting point and one that has been researched further by academics, practitioners and researchers making the link between neuroscience, neurobiology and how this links to forms of spiritual awareness through the pineal gland releasing dimethyltryptamine (DMT) which opens a greater sense of awareness and connectedness to all forms of life, the Universe and is sometimes called the door way to God…In yoga it's known as the third eye or Anja chakra.

I'm not going to say too much about the pineal gland. Other than suggesting researching this amazing pinecone shaped gland further and see where your researching takes you…

Principle One of Life/Existence states:

1.   First Principle: You are Infinite Reality - You are Not the Body – You are Not the Mind – You are Not the - I Am.

Light comes into Being, comes into the Body/Mind to create a finite reality (relative time and space) that we as humans perceive and engage with…This Light of Consciousness projects/superimposes onto the memories, identities and relationships that create our life (the movie of our Minds)…that reflection in its purest form is the I AM…if this is so what then is the pineal gland?

Connecting to Body/Mind: revisited

The body and brain are not separate. The brain exists in the body and therefore is part of the body. So, when the body is discussed and presented, the brain is automatically included. When we think of the body or discuss the body general, we don't exclude any of the parts of the body. It would be a strange presentation of the body to exclude body parts discriminately…so why then separate the brain? I appreciate that the brain plays a fundamental role within the body's functioning, but I don't think we need to give it centre stage. For me, the Body is enough and inclusive of all the necessary organs, parts, cells, hormones, fluids, etc. The brain doesn't function on its own and is a part of a highly stylised, complex, and marvellous system that is the Body. The Body is far greater than the sum of its parts. From personal experience, and communications with others, the Body holds a collective wisdom that far exceeds individual cells, body parts and organs.

Body/Mind is an ongoing system based in relationships. The Body and Mind relationship is interdependent, existing of flows of information, processing and regulating. There is an integral connection between Body/Mind that co-regulates the human experience in relationships. In effect, the person needs both to function effectively in this corporeal existence. We are by no means passive in this relationship, the spiritual being (You) is the occupant of the body and the user of Mind. We have the potential to utilise these two – Body/Mind – to fully achieve a fulfilling existence. They are our amazing tools, the greatest gift imaginable and without them we cannot 'do' or 'be'.

Connecting to Body/Mind/Spirit

Now that we've discussed connecting to Body and Mind and the degrees of this. The next step is linking to Spirit. As previously discussed, connecting to Spirit can be as straight forward as simply picking up the phone and dialling up the spiritual helpline. All we need is **openness, invitation** and **allowing**. When we cultivate this openness, invitation and allowing, we develop a relationship.

In the Beginning is the Relationship

Kenneth Gergen

Relationships are the fundamental ground of human existence. If you consider every aspect of life, from the earth we walk on, to the air we breathe, to the people we engage with, to the dreams we dream – everything is in relationship. We cannot exist without being in relationship. The Body and Mind, our environments, our transactions, our languages, our thoughts, our feelings, our hurt, our pain, our desire, our pleasure, our love is all in relation to something else. We feel pain, yes, but where do we feel pain? We feel love, yes, but love for whom or what? Nothing exists alone and in isolation. We may think we are alone, or isolated, but we never are. If we are shut away or imprisoned from others, we are still in relation to the things we are shut away from and imprisoned from. Everything has a reference and relation to something else. You exist because everything that is You is in relationship with all those things that make you, You...

So, just as spiritual principle one states: Separation from SPIRIT is an illusion. Aloneness, isolation and disconnect is an illusion. How can we ever truly be alone when we are always in relationship. Even when we die, we are not alone. How can we be alone in death when we have a Body to leave? How can we be alone in death when there is Spirit? Whatever your personal beliefs on death, the Soul, and afterlife - when you die, you die in relationship.

It might be all well and good for me to exclaim the certainty of relationships in human existence. That relationships are a given, the fundamental ground of existence, and the very source of our being. Yet not all relationships produce a good outcome for those involved.

Not all relationships leave you feeling enriched, connected, and loved. Some relationships leave you feeling quite the opposite. If relationships are the ground for positive human existence, they are for certain the ground for negative, painful, and frightening human existence too.

When relationships go wrong:

I appreciate on a theoretical level that aloneness, isolation, and separation may be an illusion. Yet, given the complexities of human life, the experience of aloneness and isolation albeit an illusion, can feel very real for some people. When one has experienced abuse, violence, hate and trauma, the sense of isolation and disconnect from self and others is a real experience. An experience that all too often is overwhelming, confusing, and full of pain.

The Earth-Bound Process

In Buddhist philosophy, according to the realisation of the great spiritual teacher Shakyamuni Buddha, there are four truths to human existence:

1. **Dukkha - Pain and suffering is ubiquitous to us all in our lifetime**:

   Everyone will experience pain in their life be it birth, sickness, grief, anxiety, not getting what they want, end of pleasurable experiences and old age.

2. **Pain and suffering have a cause and origin – Samudaya:**

   It's the experience and drive for pleasure and desire that keep us held into the feedback loop of suffering (Dukkha).

3. **Nirodha – the ceasing of pain and suffering is achievable and possible to gain:**

   By stepping out of the feedback loop of pleasure and pain and understanding our relationship to it - suffering will cease.

4. **There is a way to stop suffering and pain – the following of the eight-fold path:**

   By following and practicing the eight-fold path will cease your relationship to suffering.

It is the human's relationship to self, others, and life in general where we experience the first two truths expounded by Shakyamuni Buddha. Through our relationships to ourselves, to other people, and the environments we live in, will be the fertile ground for pain and suffering. How many of us suffered the pain of learning to walk? How many of us have felt guilt and shame from what we have said or done? How many of us have felt the pain of sore muscles, a headache, stress, and anxiety? How many of us have felt the pain of loss and grief in all its forms, from experiencing pride to losing a job to the heartbreak of the death of a loved one?

Pain and suffering in human existence are inescapable. We try to deny, distort, and avoid it, mitigate it, risk assess it as best as we can, but we never really escape it. How can we escape it when the very factor, our desire for pleasure, happiness, contentment, joy is always impermanent, fleeting and comes to an end. We can never live in an eternal feeling of pleasure or happiness on Earth. The Earth is bounded and exists in cycles of finite processes and structures. We see this in the seasons, through birth and death, with the rising and setting of the sun, the continual moving of the tides and their relationship to the moon. Earth and all its life forms are in a continual process of birth and death, beginnings, and endings, so to think we can feel happy forever and to desire to feel happy forever is a nonsensical delusion that goes against the very nature of the Earth-bound existence.

Therefore, everything in life, including You, is in relationship and relationships are the origin of emotions and feelings. It's unavoidable that you will experience pleasure and pain throughout your life. The Earth-bound existence has been designed that way. The Earth-bound realm has been designed perfectly and constitutes the ideal place for spiritual growth, which is one of the Earth's main functions. Mother-Earth is here to assists humans in their evolution as a species and to help us spiritually develop and evolve. She is integral to human development and advancement as a species in Body/Mind/Spirit. Without Mother-Earth we cannot evolve and take our species to the next spiritual and evolutionary level. And we do this by understanding our relationship to self, others, and our environment, by accessing our Master Plan and stepping out of Victim.

The Sufferings of Humans:

Human suffering and pain can take many forms. There's physical pain, the stubbing of a toe, falling over and grazing a knee to more severe forms like disease, organ failure and cancer. There's emotional and psychological pain experienced through abuse, discrimination, bullying, grief, and loss. There's the combination of the combined effect of suffering and pain when physical, emotional, and psychological pain are experienced together. Pain and suffering are unavoidable throughout our lives.

Reflective Task 5 - Suffering:

I'd like you to take a moment (between 5-10 minutes) to reflect on your life, your experiences, your relationships, family, friendships, working life, etc…to really take some time to think about pain and suffering and your experiences of it, of yourself and in others…Can you recognise when it happened? How it happened? Who was involved? What were the causes of it? Was it anyone's fault? How did it make you feel? Thinking back to the drama triangle, what roles did you play in this?

Thank you for taking the time to engage in this task...What did you experience? What were your thoughts, feelings, emotions? What roles did you find yourself in? What relationships came up for you? How was it reflecting on your own life experiences and relationships?

I hope the exercise wasn't too uncomfortable for you, although as previously stated in the 'How to use this book' section, these exercises can bring up uncomfortable feelings for us. If you are feeling uncomfortable and need support, please access your support networks to help you work through your experiences.

Attachment:

In the 1950s, Psychiatrist and Psychoanalyst, John Bowlby established a theory of human development called attachment theory. Taking his theory and insights from ethology and Lorenz's (1935) study of imprinting, whereby young ducklings had an innate drive to attach to the first object (Mother duck) for survival. Bowlby hypothesised that through evolutionary processes the human baby and mother had developed, like Lorenz's Imprinting, an innate biological bond to attach for safety, nurturing and growth. The mother and infant had an inherent need to stay close to each other for the beneficial co-regulation and development of the growing child. Bowlby's theory of attachment is essentially a theory of spatial parameters between the child and parent. From the processes of attachment, it was found that if the child feels secure and safe with the primary carer (usually, but not always the mother) then a secure attachment is established, leading the child to develop greater self-confidence within its environment. If there is an insecure attachment with the primary carer (the child feels unsafe and unsure) then the child potentially develops fear, anxiety, and a lack of self-confidence within its environment. Psychopathology or the degree of mental suffering is dependent on the severity of the insecure attachment e.g., if there's abuse, neglect and/or trauma. The greater the insecure attachment the greater potential for the adult to develop psychological problems i.e., depression, anxiety, stress/fear responses to more severe presentations leading to mental health diagnosis like Bi-Polar, General Anxiety Disorder (GAD), Emotional Unstable Personality Disorder (EUPD) and Narcissistic traits.

I've worked in education, healthcare, therapeutic services, drug and alcohol services, the Criminal Justice System, and social-work settings, alongside professionals from all disciplines including Psychiatrists, Psychologists, GPs, Social-workers, Nurses, Teachers, Police Officers, and Service Users. In all my time over the last twenty plus years, I've never met a person who had a secure attachment with their parents. I appreciate my work does bias towards people who have had problems in their childhoods; however, it still highlights the prevalence of insecurely attached people in our world.

Dr Allan Schore has written extensively on attachment theory and the connections to neuroscience bringing awareness to the dangers and pervasiveness of insecure attachment in Western culture. These dangers are being witnessed in our ever-advancing technological cultures more and more. People are becoming dependent and addicted to all manner of substances, activities, and technologies. If you are interested in looking further into these issues, I'd suggest reading Dr Allan Schore's work and research.

Addictions & Capitalism:

In the 21st Century there is a pandemic, and I'm not referring to the recent Covid 19 pandemic. I'm referring to the global pandemic of addiction. As a child of the 1970s and 1980s I grew up in the post-highs of the anti-violence, anti-establishment counter cultures, where free love, drugs and challenging the establishment (the 'Man') was very much still flowing through collective Western psyche. This like any movement has a timeframe, which subsided and led into the Capitalist, money driven, materialism of the 1980s and we are to this day still very much in the throes of a Capitalist mindset.

Cambridge University press (2023) define Capitalism as:

An economic and political system in which property, business and industry are controlled by private owners rather than by the state, with the purpose of making a profit.

Capitalism is the free market, it's the place where anyone with an idea, strong business acumen and a driven mindset for production, sales and marketing can make a profit and collect financial gain. It's the playground of the rich and famous and has shaped Western culture and the collective Western psyche for the last 30+ years. If you want to be rich and make loads of money, the Western world and Capitalism are your foundation. However, what was once thought as a solely Western enterprise has now become a world-wide global enterprise with a large majority of the countries and nations around the world adopting and existing within the mindset and political frameworks of Capitalistic culture.

All well and good you might ask, but what has Capitalism got to do with addictions?

Capitalism is all about selling products and making the seller rich. It's a continual cycle of production, advertising, sales, and marketing. The free market is always in need of a new product and needs products to be sold and bought. The free market of Capitalism exists, grows, and feeds on consumerism.

> Consumerism refers to the consumer ideology of Western society, which revolves around a social and economic structure in which customers are encouraged to buy anything, regardless of whether they need it. Such consumer desires are more often driven by

lifestyle obsession rather than a requirement, giving them a sense of happiness and fulfilment through material possession. Wall Street mojo Team (2023)

Consumerism, the collective disease of the 21st century, not only wants you to buy for necessity, but it wants you to buy irrespective of necessity. It wants you to buy for the feeling of pleasure, gratification, for the dopamine high and feel-good vibe. Consumerism is the 21st century drug of choice. Forget alcohol, forget cannabis, forget psychedelics (LSD, Mushrooms), forget stimulants (Cocaine, Crack), forget painkillers (Heroin, Valium, and Morphine), forget your over-the-counter prescription drugs, these don't compare to the instant, online buzz and high of surfing the internet dopamine high of buying and receiving that product almost within a few hours – now that's addiction!

Let's also not forget the bedfellow of our other globalised drug of choice - refined, it's in almost everything we eat and consume – Sugar!

Consumerism and Sugar make the perfect team. They feed into each other to produce and hook the individual into the highs and buzz of consuming and buying. What better way to get your fix and high from your sugar rush drink, sweet, chocolate bar, pastry, or fast food, whilst flicking through your phone, laptop, ipad or computer, they go together like cigarettes and alcohol once did (although they are old school and out-dated now). Yes, the drugs of choice for our 21st century are sugar and consuming. These are our global pandemics – these are our insidious global addictions!

Thank you for taking the time to engage in this task...What did you
experience? What were your thoughts, feelings, emotions? What did
you discover? Were you surprised with what you found? Has this
given you any thoughts for change?

We may be incredible with our technological advances, there is no
question of that; however, as I've previously highlighted, they do
harbour and foster a darker shadow-side too. The ongoing and
constant engagement with technology and the e-worlds e.g.,
computers, gaming, iphones, ipads, etc., accompanied with the
ongoing consumption of refined sugars constitutes a major concern
for the evolution of our species. Not only are we becoming mass
addicted, but we are also slowly losing touch and connection with
our natural world. The real-time spaces that we as humans need to
connect with each other are diminishing. More and more people are
becoming fixed to their mobile phones, their technology, and virtual

worlds, to the exclusion of real human to human interaction with the natural world. Children as young as two are being soothed and pacified by their parent's mobile phone through apps and games, missing out on the natural connection and secure attachment they need to develop into emotionally and psychologically healthy adults. Young people and young adults are becoming more and more based within the isolation of their own homes and bedrooms, only communicating and engaging with their friends through social media apps and gaming. Adults are more inclined to meet over the phone app or virtual meeting room e.g., Teams, Zoom, than be bothered or motivated to meet in a park, or venture to each other's homes or a social meeting venue. Technology for all its ease and convenience is slowly detaching us from our natural worlds and opportunity to engage with each other in public spaces. Ironically it has opened the global market, we can chat and see each other and communicate in conferences, meetings, and social gatherings from all over the world, yet for all its ease, it is isolating and containing us within virtual worlds away from the very spaces that nurture and support our physical and mental wellbeing. It's slowly sucking the life out of us. We are giving over our life force to it and its slowly killing us – the same way that smoking cigarettes leads to heart disease and cancer – it's only a matter of time with our virtual worlds too.

Dr Gabor Mate brings our awareness through his writings, interviews, and conferences, to the toxicities and dangers of our modern cultures and societies. I'd recommend taking the time to engage with his work and to listen to his wisdom. He brings awareness and highlights the issues, problems and dangers of addictions and the toxicities of our ever-growing globalised planet. And like so many of us in the fields of wellbeing he also offers 'pathways to wholeness', integrity, and healing...

So why I am highlighting and bringing awareness to these addictions and problems within our global societies? Am I just a harbinger of doom?

If we are to resolve, change and move forward progressively, to heal our collective and individual sufferings, pain, and traumas, then we need to understand what is happening to us and why it's happening. If we as a species are to step out of Victim, then we need to understand why we are in it in the first place and what is keeping us trapped and fixed within this cycle of continual 'pleasure/pain'. Why do we continually do this? Welcome the universal drive, urge, motivator, and generator of pleasure/pain - human desire.

Desire:

Buddha's eightfold path shows a way out of suffering – it offers a method that can bring the end/cessation to the trap of the pleasure/pain cycle – samsara.

But what drives the suffering in the first place, why do humans suffer?

Humans suffer due to the powerful urges that exist within the body and the mind. These urges come in many shapes and forms from the feeling of being liked, from the feeling of achieving, from the feeling of success, from the feeling of gaining something (e.g., an object of desire, a new outfit, a new job, a new computer, a new phone, a new friend, etc.), to the human orgasm…and from the ubiquitous relief of pain, and the relief from whatever we perceive to be holding us back and/or is blocking our way to pleasure, or as we incorrectly perceive it Happiness…

Human desire in its causal root form is the human drive to find Happiness…humans want to be Happy. Ask anyone what they want ultimately and when you strip away the object of desire and the name and form that the human is projecting their desire onto - you will always find hidden underneath it the need to be happy. The human's pursuit for pleasure is the human's desire for eternal happiness. Most human's if you offered them the choice of being eternally happy would take it – wouldn't You?

So how do we find eternal happiness in this finite Earth-bound world?

Well, the simple answer is you don't if you continue to place your desire on finite objects of the world. If you continue to place your desire on material objects e.g., money, consumerism, technology, etc., and/or conceptual objects e.g., fame, knowledge, success, likeability, image, etc. – you will never find true happiness. True happiness cannot be found or gained by grabbing and craving external objects of desire…it can't be found in objects due to the finality of the objects and the finality that you experience once you've 'got what You wanted'. Once you've 'got what You wanted' and experienced the pleasure of it, the happiness of it, the pleasure

73

hit subsides, and you're left with the low feeling of loss...so what do you do then? Well, you move onto the next object hoping to achieve the pleasure feeling again (this will make me happy!), and so on and on it goes a never-ending cycle of highs and lows, of pleasure and pain driven by the human desire for eternal happiness...and our current age of Capitalism and Consumerism knows this very well...

Capitalist consumeristic culture and societies are the perfect fertile ground for the continual cycle of 'pleasure/pain'. The perfect fertile ground that 'hoodwinks' us in to thinking that they can satisfy our continual desire for eternal happiness. It is through our addictions/desire to buying and consuming in and outside our virtual worlds, with the accompaniment of Sugar constantly fuelling the high/buzz, that keeps us well and truly anchored in the 'pleasure/pain cycle'. Yet, once the high of the sugar and sale has gone, we are left with the low, the emptiness, the void of feeling miserable, the pain...so we start it all over again. We plugin into our virtual world, drink down our sugar drink, or take a bite out of our convenience sugar filled food, and start the whole cycle again, and again and again, stuck in the 'carousel of consuming'. A slave to the consumeristic system – stuck in the continual world of Victim, stuck in our suffering – stuck in Dukkha.

The great Shakyamuni Buddha realised the four truths of human existence: Dukkha (Our suffering), Samudaya (the origin of our suffering), Nirodha (the possibility of the ceasing of our suffering), and the Eightfold Path (A way to achieve the ceasing of our suffering). He gave us a remarkably simple yet wonderful framework to assist us in our spiritual, physical, emotional, and psychological growth. By recognising and understanding what we do, why we do it, what causes us to do it and then the possibilities of change; we have a very real way of understanding the processes, thoughts, feelings, and behaviours that make us who we are as individuals and as a collective.

Consciousness

What is life? What are humans? What are objects? What are animals? Where do we all fit in this Universe? How do we make sense of all this? What's it all about?

Humans have been asking these questions since time immemorial. The pursuit for knowledge, understanding and meaning has been a part of our existence since the beginning... science, religion, philosophy, psychology, and the myriad of disciplines have been searching for the answers and understanding - asking the same questions repeatedly – what's this life all about?

Depending on the discipline and school of thought, you'll receive some kind of understanding, some kind of insight, some kind of knowledge, but do you ever really get the full picture? Do you ever get the complete answer, or are there always doubts, uncertainties, fears, anxieties? It kind of fits or because we need an answer and are so desperate for an answer, we make it fit. Like a tight pair of shoes or an oversized jacket, we like the way it looks, we like the colours, the design, the overall feel but it just seems to miss the mark, it just doesn't fit completely...

Now I'm going to go out on a limb here and say what could be considered as a very bold statement. I'm going to say that all these schools of thought, all these disciplines and all these teachings are correct. Every single religion, philosophy, and every single 'ology' and teaching to some greater or lesser degree are correct...let Indra's net explain...

Indra's Net:

They are all correct due to the fundamental interconnectedness of every single aspect of reality. Everything in our Cosmic reality is essentially infinite in nature and holds the blueprint to All reality within it, just like each cell of the human body holds the genetic blueprint to the whole organism. We are All One and One is All. The metaphor of Indra's net used in Vedic and Buddhist teachings offers us the understanding and knowledge that All life is One; therefore we are not separate independent beings isolated within a separate essential form of existence or self...we are essentially All the same Being (verb not noun) having a muti-dimensional existence at different points of reality, which when perceived through the delusion, illusion and ignorance of ego identity (You, Me, We, etc) is experienced as separate individualism and psychopathologised through a form of mental psychosis/illness. You think you are an individual person because You identify with

76

the body and mind (finite reality) believing that You are a separate being having an individual independent existence. This causes You suffering, mental and physical illness/distress grounded in Fear of Death, because you identify with the body and mind (egoism) and believe you will eventually Die…

This is the fundamental error of human existence and the cause of All human suffering here on Earth. Vedic and Buddhist philosophy, study and practice help to enlighten and liberate the human being from this fundamental human delusion/error thus ending the cause of human suffering…

The philosophy of Hua-yen Buddhism taken from the Avatamsaka Sutra (Flower Garland Sutra):

> *Far away in the heavenly abode of the great god Indra, there is a wonderful net that has been hung by some cunning artificer in such a manner that it stretches out infinitely in all directions. In accordance with the extravagant tastes of deities, the artificer has hung a single glittering jewel in each 'eye' of the net, and since the net itself is infinite in all dimensions, the jewels are infinite in number. There hang the jewels, glittering like stars of the first magnitude, a wonderful sight to behold. If we now arbitrarily select one of these jewels for inspection and look closely at it, we will discover that in its polished surface there are reflected all the other jewels in the net, infinite in number. Not only that, but each of the jewels reflected in this one jewel*

is also reflecting all the other jewels, so that there is an infinite reflecting process occurring.

Cook (1977, p.2)

Brahman is responsible for the interconnectedness of things and has become the living and the non-living; the visible and the invisible; the creatures which are two-footed and those that are four-footed. He became the subtle body and then the gross body by means of a subtle instrument known as the subtle body. This very Being became the vital consciousness of all. This is known as the Madhu-Vidya, the sense of the 'honey' of all beings, the knowledge of the inter-dependence of things and the vital connection of everything, under every condition, at every time, everywhere.

Bṛhadāraṇyaka Upanishad

Indra's net helps us to realise that everything in perceived and lived reality that is known and not-known, is understood and not-understood, is correct and not-correct, in awareness and out of awareness is therefore paradoxically correct and is One subjective Consciousness...Indra's net is a cosmology and it tells us that every part of the Whole (therefore each jewel in the net) contains the Whole and is therefore the Whole at different points of the Whole reflecting the Whole back to the Whole in a never ending and beginning mirror of reflections upon reflections upon reflections infinitely... like a hologram i.e., One Consciousness subjectively existing in a reflective process infinitely...

78

How can they all possibly be correct?

When we take Indra's net as our example and go back to the original discussion regarding human belief systems and schools of thought we find that every single culture has a cosmology, an origin story of the species, group, and collective that tells of how the Universe was created and how we as a species, and organic and non-organic life has a place in the Universe. We see this in Christianity, Hinduism, Islam, Judaism, Buddhism, Taoism. We see this in physics, social sciences, and philosophy. We see this in every culture around our globe, from the collectives that live in India, Africa, China, Indonesia, Korea, America, and Europe. Depending on what collective group you are considering, they will have some antecedents to a cosmology or belief system that underpins the culture of that group, even if they are aware of it or not...you might not even be aware there is a cosmology to your belief system or that the belief system you follow has an antecedent cosmology. However, if you go searching and studying and look deeper into the origins of that belief system, you will find a cosmology. For some belief systems this is more obvious than others, for example, Hinduism and Buddhism have explicit cosmologies that are openly taught to their followers through texts/teachings, as does Judaism and Christianity through biblical teachings. Other schools of thought are not so obvious and can be seen as mythology, folklore or fairy tale by contemporary science and organised schools of thought. These mythologies could include Norse cosmology (Germanic origin), World Tree cosmology (Mesoamerican culture), Greek mythology (Homeric) and Druidism (Europe).

What is the difference between cosmology, mythology, folklore, and fairy tale? In relation to an underpinning or over-pinning origin story, structure, or belief system, I'd go so far as to say not a lot. If the story has an origin source, an explanation to structure in the Universe and how conscious and non-conscious beings and existence are positioned in the Universe then there's not a lot of difference, other than how certain groups hold sway, importance, value, and power over their origin story within the global marketplace. Christianity in the West and even some aspects of the non-Western worlds, has held a strong hold for a long time. This is evident in the USA and Europe, but we are beginning to see this fade, as other belief systems are being considered and adopted e.g., Buddhism, Taoism, and Islam.

Some societies and groups have become so disillusioned and lost from their antecedent ancestral origin stories that they are open to adopting more modern sources of myth and story e.g., Tolkien's Lord of the Rings, Stan Lee's Marvel, and George Lucas's Star Wars. Are these real? Well, they are real enough for the people that wish to follow them, and it gives them an opportunity to engage with something that exists beyond them. These stories open a door to something greater than our ordinary lives. They are an invitation to move beyond our ego-self and to consider something other than what we think we know. They open our Minds to the possibility of Spirit, to being spiritual and understanding our species as embedded in something far greater (e.g., Indra's Net – One Consciousness) …but are these the same as science, philosophy, and religion?

I stated earlier that every single religion, every single philosophy, every single 'ology', every single teaching to some greater or lesser degree is correct. A bold statement indeed. Now, I'm also going to include all mythology, folklore and fairy-tale as correct too. Yet, what of fiction, story, and tales? Yes, you've guessed it all stories too, including Lord of the Rings, Marvel, and Star Wars.

Why and how can they all be correct?

They are all correct because they are all Spirit/One Consciousness and therefore contain the essence of the Whole (Indra's net), and Spirit as previously stated is the source of All. Every idea, every thought, every concept, every creation, every story, every tale, every cosmology, every religion, every philosophy, every science, every belief system, every language, every formula, every equation, everything you can possibly think of or engage with in this life and beyond is Spirit. There is nothing that exists in this Universe, multi-Universe, Galaxy, Solar system, Star system, Earth system, all physical forms of matter, irrespective of what vibrational frequency they are existing on is Spirit. Everything physical, organic, non-organic, fluid, elemental, gaseous from the smallest atoms to the largest Galaxy is Spirit. Every non-material existence be it Mind, thought, concept, idea, word, language, and imaging are Spirit. What distinguishes these creations are the vibrational levels at which they exist. As previous stated in a simple distance analogy, the closer we get to Source/Spirit the higher the vibrational energy level or frequency and the further we are away from the Source/Spirit the lower the vibrational energy/frequency. And what do all these frequencies/vibrational energies have in common? Yes, you are correct they are all Spirit, which also means they are Consciousness too. Why? Because Spirit is One Consciousness and One Consciousness is Spirit.

> *We are not necessarily pointing to consciousness as awareness of self, others, life, etc...although that is an aspect of Consciousness...No, we are referring to the ultimate ground of existence, the fabric of life. That which is manifested into a perceived reality through the Cosmic Universal substances that constitute finite reality – That which is Known and That which is Unknown – That which is in Awareness and That which is out of Awareness – That which Is...no more and no less.*

Consciousness with a big 'C' is the ground of everything that emanates from Spirit the creator/source of All (i.e., Indra's Net).

If Consciousness is then the manifested and unmanifested of All, what is the point to cosmology?

Plus, surely some cosmologies are more correct than others?

The point to a cosmology really depends on the use for the individual or group. The question to ask oneself is - why do I need a cosmology?

Thank you for taking to time to engage with this reflective task. I'm curious to know what you made of this task...I'm wondering where it took you mentally...what images, pictures, ideas, or thoughts came up for you? Were you taken to the realms of Goblins, Elves, to Middle Earth, or were you taken through the skies or galaxies in Star Wars? Or did you connect deeper into something further back in your history, in your culture? Did you see symbols, hear sounds? Were you confronted by images or beings that you only dream about or see in the imagination? Did you feel the presence of something else, of something you couldn't quite put your finger on? Or maybe you experienced nothing, a void, an emptiness?

Whatever you experienced or didn't experience, again is your experiential process, and a point of access to something else that exists outward or that exists inward or both...the key is not to question or judge your experience or yourself...the key is in the allowing, the invitation, the curiousness of experience, to being open to whatever comes or goes – to acceptance.

So, why do we need a cosmology?

A cosmology or mythology can offer a variety of uses or opportunities to the individual or group. If you are going down the science route it offers explanations, reasons and understanding to the physical universe e.g., physics and astronomy. If you are going down the religious or belief system route it offers understanding to origins, structure and evolution based on the belief systems or religion's perspective and traditions e.g., Hinduism. If you are going down the fiction route it offers a contextual backdrop, structure and/or underpinning explanations, philosophies and reasons to the story or stories being presented e.g., Tolkien's Lord of the Rings.

Cosmologies and mythologies from a spiritual perspective, like religious or belief systems, can give us a structured framework to our spiritual communications, connections, and actions. They can give us a system with names and reference points to differing levels of consciousness, which is not dissimilar to other naming systems we use in life. We see this in biology, where different species, organisms and life are divided into seven major groups, (1) kingdom, (2) phylum or division, (3) class, (4) order, (5) family, (6) genus, and (7) species. Basically, it's a classification system to help us make sense and create an order. For an example of a cosmology go to the spiritual cosmology example in section two.

Safety - perceived or real?

Human beings like to name and order their life. By doing so we have a way to make sense of and to organise what otherwise could appear to be unpredictable, uncertain, and insecure. Humans need to feel secure in their lives and overall safe. The classification, naming and ordering of life not only gives us an order and classification system, it also can give us that illusionary feeling that we are in control. By having a sense of control and predictability to our lives, we feel in control and safe. We can predict another's behaviour by learnt body cues and non-verbal language embedded through our culture. We can predict verbal language through our day-to-day social rules and structure of language e.g., If I say, 'Hi' there is a predicted expectation that the other person will respond with, 'Hi' too through social rules of engagement. We can predict the weather through our satellite systems and belief in our weather presenters. We can predict what another driver will do on a traffic interchange due to shared social rules of driving. We know if we stop at a red traffic light others will do this too, the light then goes to amber and then when green we can go – it's safe to go! We as a species have designed and constructed our groups, societies, cultures, and environments in such a way as to create and predict safety. We are a risk assessing species, it's in every system we've imagined, designed, and created, be it in the 'real-world' or virtual world. Of course, life isn't as predictable as we would like it to be...but that doesn't stop us from wanting to control it.

Reflective Task 8 - Safety:

I'd like you to take a moment (between 5-10 minutes) to reflect on your day-to-day lives and take a moment to identify and recognise all the different ways we keep safe… think about the objects and design of your homes…think about how you organise your life…think about the wider public areas you inhabit real and virtual, e.g., the pedestrian systems, traffic systems, virtual highways and webpages…what things are in place and what do you put in place to make your lives safer and easier to navigate?

Thank you for taking to time to engage with this reflective task. I hope this task has given you further insight into how we as a species are constantly and consistently working to keep us all feeling safer.

So, the structuring of life and the creating of order is a necessary way for humans to feel safe and make sense of life. The cosmology/mythology not only gives a framework and order but it's through that order and framework where we as a species create safety.

What really drives that sense of safety and predictability in the 21st Century, is the need to know, understand and feel like we have a place, purpose, and reason for existence. Therefore, the spiritual cosmology/mythology gives an answer, structure, and process to one's existence.

If we revisit our seven Spiritual Principles:

1. We are spiritual beings expressing through a physical body. Separation from SPIRIT is an illusion.

2. As spiritual beings, we have access to higher spiritual guidance in the form of High Self. High Self works with the Soul to research and clear programs.

3. The Soul is ultimately in charge of its own healing. Nothing happens that is not planned for or allowed by the Soul. As divine beings creating our own reality, we cannot be victims.

4. It's not what happens to you, but the energy you attach to it. This is the Law of Mind Action: What you think and attach an energy to, you create.

5. As spiritual beings, we've lived thousands of lives, many on other planets, and in other dimensions and galaxies. The accumulated energy from these other lives can and does affect the current life. If we hold energy on something, we must deal with it.

6. Only love has the highest outcome. Fear is a misperception that we can be separate from SPIRIT and SPIRIT is the highest expression of love.

7. Everything is in Divine Order – i.e., Indra's Net.

We not only have an overview and reason to existence. We also have a process of understanding development, enhancement, and growth. The seven spiritual principles give a framework, purpose, and reason to our existence. Ultimately, we are spiritual beings having a human experience that has been happening throughout many thousands of lifetimes, to assist our spiritual growth through developing vibrational consciousness, to ultimately return to source achieving Oneness and Becoming through an ever expanding and growing Universe.

You might be thinking, really that easy, that simple, why haven't other people been saying this through space and time? Well, the simple answer is they have. Our stories, our histories, our religions, our cultures, our cosmologies/mythologies have all been saying this since time immemorial in one way or another. This isn't new knowledge. This isn't a revelation that has been hidden from the masses. This has been available to us all at any-time, throughout all time, in all lifetimes, in every culture. This is the reason and purpose to your existence. Your ancestors knew this, the Earth knows this, the Stars know this, the Planets know this, the animals know this, the plants know this, the rocks know this, the elements of earth, fire, water, and air know this…how because they are

Spirit/Consciousness and that is the divine plan. It's embedded in our blueprint, in our Master Plan. Just like it's embedded in the Master Plan of everything. You are Spirit/Consciousness your purpose has always been there through all your lifetimes and most definitely in this lifetime. It's no secret…You are a Jewel of Indra's Net…

The great Humanistic psychologist and therapist Carl Rogers, once spoke of the organism (the body) being cluttered up and covered with ideas, conditional ways of living, social expectations, and social constructs of groups through one's mind/self that limit and block the individual from experiencing their life in a more authentic and congruent way. Almost like your Body/Mind is being covered in murky mud making it hard for you to experience a sense of You. Through therapy and the offering of empathy, acceptance and genuine relational engagement, the client/person would be able to identify these limits, these blocks, these expectations, these conditions from themselves, others, and society. Once identified and understood the client/person would then be able to change, have greater choice and start to feel and experience a greater authentic way of being – being true to themselves, others, and life. The client/person in effect is recognising the murky mud, where it's come from, how it got there and then having the choice to clean it off. Just like washing the dirt away…and once the dirt is washed away…You begin to experience the cosmology of You…Your Master Plan starts to appear and your ability to connect and engage with it is made available.

Why haven't I been able to see and know my purpose, my Master Plan?

It's been covered in murky mud. Once the dirt has been washed away, you will begin to see and experience yourself and life more clearly. What was once hidden from you by the murky mud, will now be revealed and the beauty is… it has been there all along. You don't need to go searching outside of yourself. Everything you need to know is already in You, is You!

The great spiritual masters and teachers have been saying this for centuries – know thy self.

Know thy self and you know your purpose, and reasons for being here…what you need to learn, what you need to develop, what you need for spiritual growth. You therefore know your Master Plan.

How do I know thy self?

To know oneself is the Master Plan, your Master Plan, your plan of self-discovery and understanding. Our Earth-bound existence is to grow and develop spiritually. Sounds wonderful and easy but how are we supposed to do this when we are living hand to mouth on the streets? How are we supposed to do this in a war-torn environment? How we are we supposed to do this when we're addicted to substances? How are we supposed to do this when we are trying to organise a family? How are we supposed to do this when my boss wants that deadline and presentation yesterday? How are we supposed to do this when there just isn't enough time in the day to do everything life is asking of me?

The Art of listening:

In every culture, there are certain people that stand out and make a difference. You might have heard of these people through school, from parents, in the news, in books or from the people that share and celebrate their endeavours. These are the people that we admire, that inspire us, that we respect and that make us want to be a better person. These could be people of spirituality and religion e.g., Mahatma Ghandi, Sai Baba of Shirdi, Joan of Arc. They could be people of science e.g., Albert Einstein, Marie Curie. They could be people of politics e.g., Nelson Mandela, Dalai Lama, Mary Church Terrell. People of entertainment and music e.g., Handel, Beethoven, the Beatles, Elvis, Aretha Franklin. They could be people of the arts e.g., Caravaggio, Michelangelo, Jackson Pollock, Laura Wheeler Waring. These people are the ones that are living out their purpose – their Master Plan.

What differentiates you from them? Nothing.

They are spiritual beings having a human experience for spiritual development just the same as you. The only difference is the uniqueness of the individual Master Plan. Those people that are perceived to make a difference are supposed to. It's part of the divine plan - spiritual principle seven. They have chosen as part of their spiritual development to live out a life on the wider world stage that gives them the opportunity to share and develop for themselves and for everyone else. It may seem a glamorous, powerful, and wonderful life to appear on the world stage to influence and connect with many thousands of people, but everything has a cost. You may sit at home with your family or friends and long for this life...I'm not saying don't wish for it but is it part of your Master Plan? Is it where you want to be or just an illusionary side-show, a distraction from an opportunity to learn a deeper lesson?

Inside of each of us is our Master Plan – our purpose, our life lessons, our journey, our talents, our wisdom, our darkness, or shadow side and our light or evolutionary side. Inside each of us is everything we need to develop and to enhance our self spiritually, physically, emotionally, and psychologically. It's there within our core of being, our blueprint, our DNA, and low and behold we have access to it...

How do I access it?

All those people you admire and inspire you all have one thing in common...the art of listening. They have all developed the attuned ability to listen deeply to their core being, their wisdom, their knowledge, their abilities, their potentialities, their high-self – they have all been able to access and listen to their Master Plan. So, if they can do it so can you...

If there's a Divine Plan, why should I bother with listening and my Master Plan?

The hardest lesson and one of the first lessons we must learn, to engage our Master Plan is stepping out of Victim. If you 'give up', 'resign yourself', make excuses and acquiesce to 'checking out', then you remain in Victim. Victim is your hopelessness and helplessness card. By remaining in Victim, you close yourself off to growth. You close your self-off to your Master Plan.

We as a species are constantly evolving and changing due to the ever expanding and evolving Universe. Spirit/Consciousness is ever expanding and growing. Human beings are moving away from dualism and the playground of opposites. We are moving away from a fear animal-based survival instinct, which sits very deep within our programming to a more collective, empathic, other-attuned process-orientated species. Don't get me wrong, I'm more than aware of the fear-based atrocities, violence, hate, abuse, and trauma that exists every day but ultimately, we are changing, and eventually in time and with healing the human species will evolve and become free of Fear.

Carl Rogers (1959) spoke of a human being becoming 'Fully-functioning':

1. Being more self-aware, open to experience, and non-defensive

2. Having true self-acceptance and true acceptance of others

3. Living an unconditional life with an inherent trust of self and others

93

4. Perceiving the ability to make decisions and the choice as residing within oneself

5. Experiencing life as interpersonal, interrelated, and harmonious.

What Rogers was presenting back in 1959, is a human more evolved and potentially able to transcend Fear. The human is so accepting of experience, self and other, is so open to experience, self and other, so integrally attuned to experience, self and other that Fear is a non-entity.

With fear transcended and the human being fully-functioning - Victim is gone, violence is gone, hate is gone, abuse is gone, trauma is gone - with fear transcended there is no reason to defend oneself. We've transcended our fight, flight or freeze animal survival mechanism. It's no longer needed as we've evolved beyond it. Our cultures, environments, groups, and societies are based in a foundation of acceptance, care, honour, respect, empathy, and Love.

Ever wondered why certain spiritual teachers e.g., Shakyamuni Buddha, Jesus of Nazareth, Jalāl ad-Dīn Muḥammad Rūmī, Juliana of Norwich, Sai Baba of Shirdi, Ramana Maharshi have been able to do the things they have and shared the teachings they have...because they've been fully-functioning and living out their Master Plan. So now is the time more than ever, to engage with yourself and connect to your Master Plan through the art of listening, for the good of yourself and for the good of All.

Section 2. – The Art of Listening

Deep within our cultures are certain markers, certain symbols, signs, sounds and shapes that when actively engaged with can unlock and open the door to spiritual awakening. There is nothing unusual or secret about these symbols, or even particularly special about them, other than what they can facilitate given the correct focus of energy. You will know some of these symbols and have probably engaged with some of them already. These symbols when given the correct attention, respect and focus will start your journey to accessing your Master Plan. These are the keys that will assist you and can potentially open your awareness to self, others, and life. These are the keys to your Master Plan.

Sacred Geometry

What is similar and unique to all these symbols are the geometric shapes and structures. Sacred geometry is the study and engagement of geometric mathematical shapes that have certain rules and laws. These shapes when understood and actively engaged with help us connect to the infinite universal structure of life. For example, the Flower of Life, the Gayatri Yantra, the Buddhist Dharma Wheel, the Pentagram, Star of David, etc., are all forms of sacred geometry.

It is through sacred geometry that the very structure of life is formed, from the smallest atom to the largest Galaxy. Sacred geometry from a mathematical perspective is the rules by which the structure of life is created and governed. In effect, we can see these shapes: the triangle, square, circle, spiral in all forms of life, including humans. Your Master Plan is sacred geometry, as is your life course, journey, growth, and spiritual development. To know thy Self is to know true connectedness to All and Oneness to Spirit/Consciousness. Out of Spirit comes levels of existence and forms of creation e.g., the Human Body, thought and sound, all life-forms and therefore sacred geometry.

Below in no order are examples of sacred symbols and sounds (mantra: a short spoken, chanted, or sung phrase) that you can use to engage with, meditate on, speak (to yourself or say out loud), print out, draw, memorise, wear as pendants, some people even get tattooed, the list is endless. There is no right or wrong way to engage with these symbols if your intention is positive and nurturing to self, others, and the environment.

Now positive intention is an important note to remember and actively ritualise when you are engaging with these symbols. These symbols have been used and shared for many centuries through differing cultures and societies. They are powerful energy forms and have the potential to change how you not only experience yourself and others but life itself. When you engage with your Master Plan you are actively intending to step out of Victim. These symbols when given the correct focus and attention can assist you in stepping out of Victim, and the intention before engaging with the symbol of your choice is to say: **I intend to step out of Victim and engage my Master Plan.**

It's a simple as saying that statement to yourself or out loud before you engage with one of these symbols. It doesn't matter what symbol you choose; the choice is yours…As a suggestion maybe look at all the different symbols at first, and then depending on the one you are drawn to, use that symbol to begin with. You might already have forms of practice that you do e.g., meditation, walking in the countryside, that you could incorporate the symbol into. For example morning meditation is great to introduce the symbol into, for you to contemplate, visualise, look at the symbol on a printed out piece of paper, or you might go for a daily walk contemplating the symbol or saying it to yourself a few times along the walk; or you might want to hold the image or sound in your Mind throughout the day, again the choice is yours. The power and key to the symbol is you discovering and finding the right way that works and resonates with you – this is part of the learning and self-development. It's about discovering your way through your own practice and having fun. Remember your Master Plan is unique to you – so the accessing is also unique to You too. No one can tell you how to access and engage with the life that is You. You must learn, discover, and understand how you tick, find the keys to help you do this and then keep practicing and staying open to the unfolding of your life's journey – Your Master Plan.

Sacred Symbols and Sounds

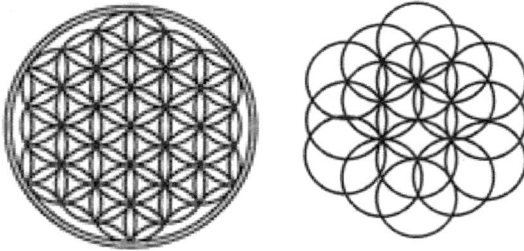

Universal Flower of Life/Seed of Life – Creation patterns to existence – Indra's net

The Universal Flower of Life - The most important and sacred pattern in the universe. This is the source of all that exists. It is found in everything ranging from the human body to the largest Galaxies, e.g., DNA, molecular structures, minerals, tissues, and plants. This symbol represents the emerging form and patterns of life as they arise from Spirit. All that there is originates from source and it's these patterns that underpin existence. This symbol is found in and is synonymous with all cultures and we experience many variations of it in e.g., mathematics, music, religion, philosophy, and medicine.

Gayatri Mantra

The Gayatri mantra has 24 syllables with phonetic pronunciation in brackets:

Om bhuh, bhuvah, swaha (*Aumm Bhoor Bhoo-va Su-va-ha*)

Tat savitur varenyam (*Tat Sa-vee-toor Var-ayn-yam*)

Bhargo devasya dhimahi (*Bar-go Day-vas-ya Dhee-ma-hee*)

Dhiyo yo nah prachodayat (*Dhee-yo Yo Nah Pra-cho-da-yaat*)

Divine knowledge & Illumination - This symbol and mantra when spoken represents the illumination and awakening of Spirit and the wisdom of life. The generalised meaning to the words and sounds of the Gayatri Mantra consist of engaging with Spirit whose divine light illuminates and shines forth to all realms of the physical, mental, and spiritual. Therefore, let us be one with this divine light for our own illumination/awakening.

The Sri Yantra – From the Hindu traditions, this symbol links to the divine and the creative forces of life. A symbol of transformation and manifestation, it has a powerful potential to bring balance, coherence and harmony leading to spiritual awakening and growth.

The Shin Buddhist Nembutsu – Namo Amida Butsu

When one recites and speaks the nembutsu '**Namo Amida Butsu**' in Shin-Buddhism, they are taking the first step and vow toward refuge and alignment with Amida Buddha. To do so is to take support, love and nurturing from the Infinite Buddha of life and light. Reciting, chanting, singing, or speaking of '**Namo Amida Butsu**' is to bring peace, joy, wisdom, and wholeness to assist one's journey and path toward spiritual awakening and growth.

Eyes of Buddha – The symbolism of the eyes, looking into the Soul, is accompanied by the divine feminine energy of life. The Third Eye in the centre represents spiritual awakening with the unity symbol below it representing Oneness. Compassion, respect and honour of Self and others is engendered through the engagement of this symbol.

Dharma Wheel – The Eight-fold path

In Buddhist tradition the eight-fold path is represented by the Dharma wheel. The eight-fold path consists of right view, right intention, right speech, right action, right livelihood, right effort, right mindfulness, and right concentration. This symbol assists in the cultivation of the eight-fold path.

Om (Aum) – The Sacred Sound of Creation - This sound is the primordial sound of life and creation. Spirit/Consciousness in all realms of existence from the past, present and future all blend into this one all-inclusive sound. When chanted or concentrated on, Om or Aum frees the individual to remember and engage with the natural state of infinite energy of Creation, and one's connection to it.

Om Mani Padme Hum mantra – pronunciation: Ohm – Mah – Nee – Pahd – May - Hum

This extended inclusive mantra and phrase is a purifier and process to spiritual awakening for anyone who decides to incorporate this into their daily life and practice.

Om – generosity and the sound of all creation

MA – ethical life dissolving jealousy

Ni – patience purifying desire

Pad – diligence dissolving our judgements and prejudices

Me – renunciation of greed and negative vices

Hum – wisdom purifying aggression and hate

The Dalai Lama states, Om Mani Padme Hum has the power to:

"Transform your impure body, speech and mind into the pure body, speech and mind of a Buddha."

For Tibetan Buddhists, the connection and deep holding of this phrase within one's life, and daily practice, is the gateway to attaining spiritual awakening.

Om Shanti, Shanti, Shanti – mantra

The literal meaning of Om Shanti, Shanti, Shanti is Om Peace, Peace, Peace found in Hindu, Buddhist, and Yogic practice. It is used to bring purity to mind, body and soul leading toward a sense of calm, joy, and bliss, fostering spiritual attainment, growth, and self-realisation. The pronunciation of Om Shanti, Shanti, Shanti is a process of full embodied resonance. Hold the 'a' in Shanti for two beats with it being sounded like the 'a' sounded in father. The 't' being pronounced by pressing the tongue against your teeth, which is not the same as in the 't' in English language.

Soham (pronounce Sohum) or Hamso

Soham is the primordial breath and sound of existence, which is life itself i.e., the pulse and flow at the heart of all creation. From the Sanskrit – Sah 'He' or 'That' followed by aham 'I am' – Soham 'I am He' or 'I am That'. 'He' or 'That' corresponds to the non-dualism of existence, that which is beyond time and space, depending on your religion or spirituality this could be God, Allah, Universe, All that There is, Brahman, etc. Through the mental repetition of this mantra and synchronising it with your breath, *So* inhaling and *Hum* exhaling, one is connecting and invoking the Divine presence within and cultivating a stronger awareness and unveiling of our Divine existence.

Earth Medicine Wheel – Sacred Hoop of infinite knowledge

This symbol is synonymous with tribal communities representing harmony and the boundary existence of the Earth. It consists of four quadrants that signify four within the Earth realm, e.g., four seasons, four elements, etc., and the flow and ebb of harmonious life. Mediating on this symbol can engender spiritual energy, harmony and love of self and others.

Pentagram – Found in Celtic, Pagan, mystical traditions, and religions as well. The five-pointed star bounded within a circle represents all aspects of life. Spirit is found at the top of the star with the other four points representing all the elements of the Earth: earth, fire, air, and water. Togetherness, harmony, integration, and wholeness are all epitomised here.

Hexagram or Star of David – Union of Opposites

This symbol is present in varied belief systems and religions across the globe ranging from Judaism (Star of David) to Kabalistic practices to Wiccan and Pagan traditions to Magic in the Occult. Its fundamental premise is the union of opposites and their deep connection e.g., God and Human, male and female, Heaven and Earth, Fire and Water, with the centre representing the heart of power.

Lotus - From the Mud emerges transfiguration into the Divine

In Eastern philosophies the image of the lotus (water lily) rising from the depths of the murky muddy waters signifies transformation, growth, spiritual awakening, and the power of potentiality. The power of resurrection, change and transformation is used to help us remember the 'flux of life', the constant change of everything and the continual impermanence of All.

Luna Goddess - An ancient symbol of birth, the giver of life, and bearer of creation. She is the holder of knowledge and wisdom and all that is creative here on Earth. With a deep connection to water and the tides, she extends her power through the ebb and flow of life representing the sacred gateway to the feminine and the divine.

The Spiral – One of the oldest symbols known to human existence. Originating from the void and representing the patterns of existence, growth, and evolution. The spiral can go up or down depending on the focus and intention of existence. We see this ancient sign in all patterns of life from the minerals in the ground to organic life, humans, animals, plants, the weather, and the natural world. Synonymous with fertility, womb, and birth it assists us in connecting to the divine source and embracing the multi-facets of the continual changes of life.

Yin & Yang – the Eastern Taoist symbol of light and dark, the flowing interplay of the divine forces of the Universe. Like the Hexagram, we are seeking the unity of opposites – male and female, dark and light. We see the primordial forces of life itself through the continual flow of the receptive, cold, passive, feminine energy of Yin flowing into the male, potent, dark, heat energy of Yang and back again. Spiritual growth and balance are attained through the unity of the opposites - from ignorance (the dark) we step into illumination/knowledge (the Light).

9

Number 9 – is the Magic number - Completion

The number nine is a fascinating symbol. In numerology we see transformation and transition toward completion but don't misunderstand this to mean the end. Completion is of a cycle and the beginning of another. In Tarot we have the Hermit, the introspector and searcher of spiritual growth and development. In mythology and religion nine represents structures, frameworks, and good luck, all leading to development and completion of life stages. The number nine is a very special symbol and a powerful image to contemplate and reflect on. It can be incorporated into any aspect of your life from counting your breaths in a breathing exercise to structuring your environment. 9 is the magic number!

Vibrational Energy

Everything in life, including You, has a vibrational energy, a frequency that it vibrates at and exists at. For example, in the Earth-bound realm humans, animals, plants, rocks, water, etc., all have their own vibrational energy, a frequency at which that form of Consciousness/Spirit vibrates. Depending on your species, form, shape, etc., e.g., animal, plant, mineral, human, etc., will determine the vibrating energy. However, we are all vibrational energy existing at levels and this is also dependent on our level of spiritual growth and development. Again, spiritual principle one:

1. We are spiritual beings expressing through a physical body. Separation from SPIRIT is an illusion.

As spiritual beings we are existing at a vibrational physical body level when we exist in the Earth-bound incarnational realm. The human body has a vibrational level that allows it to exist in the corporeal world due to the vibrational energy level of Consciousness/Spirit. If we go back to my original distance analogy regarding spiritual principle one and separation from Spirit is an illusion; the further we get from Spirit the denser or lower the vibrational energy form, the closer we get to Spirit the higher or lighter the vibrational energy form. So, depending on where you are existing within the structure and levels of Consciousness/Spirit, will determine what existence you are having and in what form that existence is being presented.

If we look at the example of a spiritual cosmology of the levels of Consciousness Fig 4., we can see a structured overview and framework to the different levels of vibrational Consciousness/Spirit in our existence.

Spiritual Cosmology Example:

Levels of Consciousness

Incarnation Level

Below Incarnation Level

Figure 4 Spiritual Cosmology Example

Levels of Consciousness	*Incarnational Level – Earth Realm
The One – Monad	Human
The Trinity:	Human Bodies:
1.Prime Mover - Omnipotent	1.Causal Body
2.Creational Energy – Omniprovident	2.Astral Body
3.Name & Form - Omniscience	3.Physical Body
High Levels of Consciousness: Celestial Choirs of Divine Presentations	Animals, Birds, Sea creatures, Plants, Bacteria, Microbes, Rocks, Soil & Nutritive elements, etc., inclusive of all organic life & inclusive of all non-organic life
Godhead	
Virtues	
Elohim	
Archangels	
Angels	
Human – *Incarnational Level – Earth Realm	
Denser Forms of Matter/Energy - *Below Incarnational Level – Under World	*Below Incarnation Level
	Hellius Inferno
	Vices
	Fallen Angels
	Satanics
	Demonics
	Hell Beasts

111

Fig.4 above shows a structure to Conscious existence. In the left-hand column, it shows the highest level of Consciousness/Spirit and then all the descending vibrational levels of consciousness until they become the denser reaches of matter and Consciousness below incarnation level. Incarnation level is our Human Consciousness and Earth realm, the corporeal existence that is you reading these words and living an Earth-bound life. If you look at the right-hand column, you can also see the human-bodies that make up the human being here on Earth and the other forms of Consciousness, e.g., animals, plants, etc. We can also see life forms/expressions of Spirit/Consciousness below the Earth realm incarnational level that exist within denser forms of matter e.g., Fallen Angels, Demonics, etc. This cosmology is by no way a definitive prescriptive cosmology, it is an example only, a possibility to represent vibrational energy by name and form...and those of you familiar with Christian symbolism and Yoga philosophy will recognise links to this. What I'm presenting is by no means or related to the ideology of Christianity that gets taught in schools, etc. No, what is presented is an example of a structured form of Spirituality based around some elements of Christian symbolism/mythology and Yoga. This is not a controlled or convoluted hierarchal religious system governed by humans. This is also not about the battle between good and evil, although certain mythology and cosmologies have been created that way. This is about levels of Consciousness that help us understand the various levels of existence from Spirit to the denser forms of Matter. We can, as humans do, place value judgements and morality onto this framework if we wish to use it that way for our spiritual growth but that aside it can be seen more as a map of name and form. We see this also in other spiritual and religious cosmologies and systems but they are represented with different naming and symbolic forms, for example, the Hindu system/cosmology has their own naming of deities and structural forms, Judaism has their particular system, Yoga has their own, as does Buddhism, Islam, etc, etc...all these different religions and spiritualities have their own unique system but when we dive deeper into each system, we begin to see the comparisons and overarching principles and forms that are representing the same core themes and structures. Remember we are working with symbolic representations of energy manifestation, a naming system that gives shape and form to vibrational energy, this is not to be understood in the literal sense but as a symbolic representation of levels of energy that constitute and vibrate at different frequencies, speeds, and patterns. If we were coming at this from a quantum physics perspective, we would be looking at the 'physical characteristics' e.g., wave forms, particles, atoms, etc. This example of a spiritual cosmology is coming at it from a religio/spiritual perspective based in ancient Christian symbolism and aspects of Yoga philosophy.

What has this got to do with the Art of Listening and sacred symbols and sounds?

The art of listening is a way of tuning into the vibrational energies of existence, dependent on how that form of Consciousness is presenting, be they human, animal, plant, or mineral. However, it goes far beyond just listening and tuning into organic life. It's also about tuning into non-organic life, conceptual life, symbolic life, sound, thought, image, fluid, solid and air. The art of listening is developing the skill and attunement to life itself and the different forms of vibrational energy. When we tune into other forms of existence, be they another human, animal, plant, thought, word, sound, symbol, book, story, musical composition, song, or crystal, whatever it may be - we have an opportunity, a real opportunity to experience different forms of life and to connect with the Other. We move into a perceived connectedness of Oneness, of integration, our illusion of separation is lifted, and we experience Togetherness. The Divine in Me connects to the Divine in You.

Accessing My Master Plan

In Appendix 8 you are given structured guides to practice that can assist you in accessing your Master Plan and stepping out of Victim. Accessing your Master Plan is a very personal and unique process. No two people will access their Master Plan and step out of Victim in the same way. Some people will find that they are more actively engaged in physical practice incorporating exercise, walking, Yoga, Pilates, etc. Some people will be less active and incorporate more meditation, stationary breathing exercises or contemplation on symbols and mantras. Others might incorporate a mixture of both doing yoga twice or once a week and then doing visualising exercises or meditation using symbols or sounds on other days. The key is finding and discovering what works best for you. This is the fundamental premise to the entire process, it's through trying different ways and exploring what works that gives you the confidence, self-worth, and autonomy to know yourself, and it's only when you truly know yourself that you step out of Victim. This is not blind faith whereby you hand over your thinking, feeling, and behaving to an established 'off the Shelf' ideology, religion, or belief system. No, this is a process of self-discovery, self-understanding, self-knowledge, and relational living which underpins how you think, feel, behave, and exist. The Earth is our playground, our matrix, our maze, our landscape, our journey into self and others. The Earth is our gift of physical existence, the place where you can use your embodied form to experience life in all its fascinating and exciting ways, which lead ultimately to the reason you are here: to spiritually grow and develop by accessing your Master Plans and stepping out of Victim and completing the Earth-bound game.

The Game analogy

Modern advances in technology over the last eighty years have given us wonderful and exciting ways to exist and communicate. Radio, Telecommunication, Television, Computers, Mobile-phones, Internet, E-technology, have completely revolutionised and changed how we live. The ability to access information, communicate and engage with each other and to share information is almost instant and infinite. Children as young as four will have access to some form of device e.g., a parent's mobile-phone, where they can play games, access music and open apps that deliver educational mind stimulating sources and escapist forms of entertainment to soothe or distract the infant i.e., a techno-dummy/pacifier. Now, I'm not going to go into the potential issues and problems that this can cause as I've discussed this in section one; if you haven't got to that part yet, I'd suggest reading the dangers of the technological advances in our cultures and how these are impacting our development as humans.

However, what technology has given us, is the ability to immerse ourselves into a virtual reality of game playing. Side-stepping the negative issues, what gaming has given us is the potential metaphorical platform to understand the quest, adventure, exploration, and problem-solving, by over-coming obstacles and challenges resulting in growth and character development. We also see this in table-top games, role-playing games, adventure/quest books, movies, plays and live-action role-play. The game analogy is the ground to understand the highs and lows of adventure, exploration, and questing to achieve a set goal. By engaging with one's landscape, relationships, work, employment and examining of one's situation we have focus, purpose, and possibility. This is not new, if we investigate our cultural histories, stories, narratives, literature, folklore, and tales, we are inundated with the Hero quest. The Hero's quest is a journey of self-discovery. We see the Hero quest as far back as the 6th century in the tale of Beowulf, in the 8th century we have Homer's Odyssey all the way up to current times with Tolkien's Lord of the Rings, Lucas' Star Wars and even JK

Rowling's Harry Potter. The quest of self-discovery, to overcome adversity and win is inherent in all our cultures. So, the game analogy works very well in our techno-modern times, especially in the consumeristic cultures that present the concept of 'manifesting', 'levelling up' and following an 'influencer'.

But where's the place for spirituality, for embodied connection and the natural worlds?

The natural worlds are the wellsprings of vitality, nurturing and harmony, and the places for harshness, extremes, and adversity. They offer us real landscapes that present the range of corporeal existence from the harshest colds of Siberia to the moderate woodlands of the UK to the nurturing sunny beaches of California. What the natural worlds offer are real opportunities and myriad forms of organic life that we as embodied humans can engage with and experience. The Earth is our corporeal playground, our game landscape that we as humans can move through, engage with, explore, examine, use and live-in/on. The Earth is our life support system that helps keep our Body, our Mind, and our Spirit alive. So, if we continue with our game/quest analogy, the Earth is our place to play this out. You cannot access your Master Plan and step out of Victim in a virtual world, it's just not possible because the virtual worlds in essence are doing the very thing you are trying not to do – they keep you in Victim.

How do the virtual worlds keep me in Victim?

Virtual worlds by essence are based in consumerism that's how they are designed and that's how they function. Virtual worlds are constantly in a process of selling, advertising, and marketing products. If you are in service to a consumeristic mindset, mentality, and mode of existing you will never step out of Victim. The consumeristic mindset, mentality, and mode of existing wants you to be subservient to it, it must be that way so you will buy into it and consume the products in the market. The organisations, institutes, governments, and people that administer it need you to keep feeding it, without you the markets will collapse and cease to exist. You the consumer are the vital ingredient that upholds and supports this consumeristic culture and system, without you they are nothing. So, you are in Victim mode in relation to it, even the multi-billion-dollar CEOs and companies that exist in the top 1-5% are Victims to it, they need the system; they think they control the system and the markets, but they are slaves to the system. Yes, they may have all the top material trappings and lifestyle with their multi-million-dollar life, but they are still Victims/Slaves to a system that controls them, and feeds off them.

How can we exist without our virtual worlds and market?

In the globalised markets and cultures, it would seem impossible or even impractical to exist outside of these virtual worlds, they are so intrinsically embedded within our lives now that we couldn't even imagine living without them. So don't worry, I'm not asking you to live without them. What I'm asking you to consider is your relationship to them and how they influence, impact, and govern you...

Reflective Task 9 – Virtual Worlds/Internet:

I'd like you to take a moment (between 5-10 minutes) to reflect on your day-to-day lives and to consider your relationship to the virtual worlds you live in and global consumeristic markets that you engage with... think about the websites you visit daily...think about how you engage with social media...think about the products you buy, the advertising you see, the people and products that 'influence you'...think about the constant messages, words, images and sounds that stream through every aspect of your life...are you in control of any of this?

Thank you for taking the time to engage with this reflective task. I hope this task has given you further insight into how You as an individual relates to the virtual worlds and markets. Sometimes we just need a moment to reflect and take stock of our thoughts, feelings, and behaviours in relation to an aspect of our life, especially one that can feel all consuming.

So, to truly step out of Victim you need to understand your relationship to these virtual worlds and how much of a slave you are to them. It's not about living without them, although that would be an ideal solution; it's more about how you allow yourself to be blindly governed by them.

Do we need the natural world to step out of Victim and access our Master Plan?

Yes, you do. We have a beautiful, wonderful, and exciting natural world that has everything we need to assist us in accessing our Master Plan and stepping out of Victim. We are organic embodied humans, the natural world (Earth) is organic and embodies all forms of corporeal life. We need the Earth; we may think we don't due to consumeristic lifestyles, but we really do need her. She is our home and embodies everything we need to step out of Victim. So, your job is to go out there, engage with it, and experience it...

Eco-Living, Existing and Listening

The Earth is a fascinating and wonderful form of existence. She is the home to a wealth of varied ecosystems that exist throughout the planet forming our Biosphere/Ecosphere. Our ecosystems are the spaces where life exists and co-habits through harmonious and supporting relationships. Humans, animals, plants, and other organisms depend on each other and work together to form co-existing relationships in their environments, consisting of land, water and air spaces that allow the perpetual cycle of life to continue.

The biosphere is sometimes thought of as one large ecosystem—a complex community of living and non-living things functioning as a single unit. More often, however, the biosphere is described as having many ecosystems.

National Geographic (2023)

Therefore, the Earth holds the keys to aiding you in accessing your Master Plan, and as we are embodied and organic in Body, we need the Earth and its many forms of life to help us step out of Victim.

The natural world and our wellbeing are interconnected, there's no getting away from this basic principle. The natural world has the ability and potential to nurture our Body/Mind/Spirit. It's through our relationship with the natural world that we feel calm, settled, and centred. The natural world allows relationships and spaces that foster positive energy exchange, nurturing and growth. A positive mindset, energised feelings, and a sense of connectedness can all be engendered through the natural world. By relating and engaging with the plants, animals, organisms, and landscapes, we have the possibility to receive positive energies that can assist us in transcending and moving beyond our closed fixed urban lifestyles. Over the last twenty years research has shown and is still showing that engaging with the natural world boosts positive wellbeing. It helps us destress, fosters positive mental health, assists with overall resilience, and helps us develop positive coping skills (Brown, 2021,

Jordan & Hinds, 2016, Tariki Trust, 2023). To engage with the natural world is the potentiality of being enhanced through the development of Body/Mind/Spirit - therefore accessing your Master Plan and stepping out of Victim.

How do I engage with the natural world?

There are many ways to engage with the natural world, in fact you probably already are but don't necessarily recognise it. How many of you have a garden, indoor plants, a fish tank, pets, parks you visit or exercise in? How many of you engage with outdoor activities like running, sailing, kayaking, climbing, surfing, swimming, walking, and hiking? How many of you meet your family and friends outside in parks, on beaches, by rivers, at lakes or in the countryside? I can guarantee that a significant percentage of you will be engaging with at least one of these, if not several of them on a daily, weekly, and monthly basis. So, for some of you already, you are engaging with your natural world and the many forms it takes…If you don't feel you are engaging with your natural world then it's as easy as buying an indoor plant or taking a walk-in a nearby park or the countryside. You don't need to go climbing mount Everest or sailing down the Congo or crossing the Gobi Desert. It's as simple as watching the birds from your window or stroking your cat on your lap or taking your dog for a walk. It's as simple as taking a blanket on a summer's day, lying down on the grass, and watching the clouds float by.

But surely, it's not that simple, is it?

It is and it isn't. In life there are degrees to what we do and experience, and engaging with the natural world is the same. It comes down to two basic principles: 1. our intention and 2. our attention. By actively intending to engage and actively attending to the focus of our intention will determine our level of engagement and our level of awareness. It's not necessarily what you do but it's how you do it and this is the fundamental difference between being a spectator and always having distance or becoming a participator and being actively involved in the game. When you engage with the natural world, we are looking for you to participate through your intention to engage and then your active attention to what you are doing. So, if you are taking the dog for a walk, it's not just blindly and thoughtlessly ambling along lost in a void of non-engagement, no, it's about actively participating and being aware of your surroundings, your thoughts, your feelings and noticing what is going on around you – your intention to engage and the attention you apply to it. It's about chatting to your dog or noticing the wind on your face, or that jogger turning a corner, or the warm sun on your back. It's about noticing and being aware of yourself and others around you. It's about being alive, noticing and attending to all the levels of relationships you are having as you take your dog for a walk – don't be switched OFF – be switched ON to all that there is around you. When we start to become aware and attend to all our relationships, and continue to do so throughout our life, then we are truly starting to practice the true art of listening. We are beginning to attune to the different vibrational energies that exist within us, within others and between us, we are allowing ourselves to engage into a process and experience of Togetherness.

Cultivating the Art of Listening

Now that we know what the art of listening is, it's time to understand and learn ways to cultivate and develop this discipline. I call it a discipline due to the nature of it being an art form that is continually crafted and embedded over time. We all have the potential and ability to practice and cultivate this art, again it's through one's intention and then attention to this art form that we as practitioners can really begin to understand and hone this skill.

The art of listening is simply being able to attune yourself to the vibrational frequencies of self and others in such a way as to bring understanding and connection. If we can attune to ourselves and others, then we have a gateway and a bridge to each other and the world around us. By mastering the art of listening we can remove the illusion of separation and realise our connectedness to All that there is – Oneness – Spirit, i.e., spiritual principle one: We are spiritual beings expressing through a physical body - Separation from SPIRIT is an illusion.

One of the first factors that we must realise, is that the art of listening is not solely a hearing process linked to the auditory system. This is not an exercise in being able to hear higher frequencies and sounds. This is an art form that requires your complete system, your whole Body/Mind. When we develop the art of listening, we are using and attuning all our senses, all our bodily processes, the very being that is You is focused to such a degree that your whole Body and Mind are attuning to yourself and your surroundings. Yes, your auditory system is being used as part of this system but it's not a solo activity. To think and use only the hearing to listen, is to limit, block and undermine your whole being of existence. The art of listening requires the whole of You and nothing less.

How do I cultivate this whole Body/Mind art?

There are many ways, exercises, and practices that you can use, even an experienced practitioner can still go back to basics to remind themselves of the fundamentals and grounding principles. In fact, the best practitioners have the fundamentals embedded deeply within their Body/Mind system through diligent, mindful, and skilful practice overtime. A virtuoso or expert pianist, violinist, sportsperson, craftsperson, artist, scientist, etc., are all at the position they are and existing at that level due to their committed and mindful way of practice and development. The art of listening is no different. To be a master of this art takes time, commitment, and skilful practice, the same as any other. The only difference with the art of listening is that this art is ubiquitous to us all. We all have the universal ability and potential to develop this. It's designed in our blueprint just like wings are designed for flight for the Hawk and Falcon and gills are designed for fish to breath underwater. So, we can all develop the art of listening, we need it for our personal development here on Earth, to step out of Victim and to access our

Master Plan. So, the potential for the art of listening is already built in.

Empathy

One of the first ways we can cultivate this skilful art is through the understanding and practice of empathy toward ourselves and to others. Empathy is quite simply the ability to understand an experience, thought, feeling and behaviour of our own or another. We see empathy developed and used in professional helping roles, for example by therapists, counsellors, psychotherapists, psychologists, teachers, doctors, nurses, etc., to assist the practitioner in understanding the concerns of the person they are working with to help them devise and implement an effective therapeutic intervention or pathway. I give a clear example of this in section three when looking at the role of a psychotherapist and integrating practice in the case study of Tara.

How do we develop and practice empathy?

The best way to develop empathy and start to practice this is first listening to your Body and/or other people. Meditation and Mindfulness are also an effective way for developing empathy and practicing empathy, by taking time to sit or walk with the intention to develop empathy and with the attention toward our feelings, thoughts, and bodily processes. We need to be curious explorers toward ourselves, asking such questions as: What are my thoughts telling me about this experience? Why am I feeling that emotion? Why is my body tense or shoulders raised, or neck aching or chest tight? What do these feelings tell me about me at this current moment? Why do I feel that way when my partner says that? Why do I lack patience with my work colleague? How come I have so much time for my children yet lack it for my parents?

These are just a few examples of the way we can explore our thoughts, feelings, and behaviours with ourselves and others, which in turn helps us develop a deeper understanding of ourselves and our life, therefore developing empathy.

Taking time and exploring our self can be challenging in and of itself – sometimes it's not always comfortable to feel and experience thoughts, feelings and behaviours associated with our relationship to ourselves and other people. So, taking this to the next step can be even harder for some people, when we must metaphorically 'walk in someone else's shoes' or allow ourselves to experience the other's world from their perspective without being biased or blinkered by our own. This at times can feel almost impossible. To do this requires practice and personal development. The first step in being able to do this is being able to understand our values and beliefs that underpin how we experience and perceive life. For example, if you have a strong belief and value that others should be treated equally and without judgement – you no doubt will find it difficult to understand and empathise with someone that doesn't believe or practice this – in fact this person might even provoke a judgmental or negative reaction in You. If for example you are an animal rights activist – you will find it difficult to empathise with a cattle farmer or scientist that uses animals for experimentation – again, I imagine it will cause a strong judgemental reaction within you and vice versa. Another example could be that a person has a strong belief and faith in a religious theology and/or religious text e.g., the bible, so they would find 'it difficult to' empathise perhaps with an atheist or agnostic that not only doesn't believe their faith but actively denies or doubts it.

So, we can see from these examples that the ability to empathise with another is not just about understanding the other – it's being 'able' to understand the other. Which is foundationally based in being able to suspend judgement not only of the other but also of ourselves. To be able to suspend judgement of the other we must first undergo a deeper exploration of ourselves to know what our own values and beliefs are and how these influence our opinions, feelings, and behaviours. So, to begin with you must start the journey toward yourself – now this doesn't mean self-righteously being opinionated, arrogant or dismissive, no, quite the opposite. The intention is to understand the judgements, values, and beliefs that you hold, why you hold them and why they are there in the first place. When you find the answers to these questions you will have a clearer picture and understanding of the person that you are and why you are the way you are, why you think the way you think and why you feel the way you feel – i.e., you are becoming more self-aware.

Why does being more self-aware help the development of empathy?

Time and time again, spiritual teachers, spiritual masters, great thinkers, philosophers, arahants, Buddhas, prophets and holy people espouse the need and fundamental ethic of compassion. From the teachings of Shakyamuni Buddha to Jesus of Nazareth, to Jalāl ad-Dīn Muḥammad Rūmī, to Juliana of Norwich, to Sai Baba of Shirdi to, to Ramana Maharshi, to Swami Sivananda, to the Dalia Lama, they all have and still advocate the need for human beings to be more compassionate to each other on a fundamental level… Why do they do this? They espouse this for many reasons – the first is somewhat obvious – if we are more compassionate to ourselves and others then our existence will be more pleasant and enjoyable. However, it goes further and deeper than this surface level understanding. What these spiritual teachers knew and know and had experienced through their spiritual development and awakenings was that we are all fundamentally Spirit – we are all One and that our separation from each other and Spirit is an illusion – spiritual principle one. They realised that we are fundamentally connected, so to judge another or hurt another was in effect to judge and hurt ourselves, and not only hurt ourselves it was ultimately blocking and limiting our own ability toward spiritual growth and awakening – the very thing we are here on Earth to achieve. If we as individuals and as a collective are to experience spiritual growth and awakening then we must first stop judging others, which in effect stops us judging ourselves. If we are to step off the 'merry-go-round' ride of the pleasure/pain cycle, Shakyamuni Buddha's second truth to human existence the origin of suffering, then we must first master the ability of empathy through the holding of true compassion for ourselves and the other.

129

The ability to foster empathy and compassion toward self and other in a continued process throughout one's life moving us ever closer toward stepping out of Victim and taking full responsibility for ourselves. This developing self-awareness assists us and gives us lived experiences of the benefits of developing empathy/compassion and the offering of it to ourselves and others. It's through your experiences and practices of empathy/compassion to self and other that you really start to see, feel, and experience the positive benefits of trusting, loving, understanding, caring and compassionate relationship. It's through these relationships being fostered through empathy/compassion that you begin to experience your life more positively. Clearer and more honest communications begin to happen. Greater respect, understanding and care begins to be experienced and a greater sense of community, togetherness, and fellowship starts to appear between groups. We as a species begin to trust each other, understand each other, and begin to care for each other. We want to care for each other as our processes of fear and separation begin to diminish leading to greater honesty, care, and love.

Spiritual Teachings

True spiritual teaching is a constructive process and
a process of fulfilment

Swami Jyotirmayananda

Our cultures, education systems, institutes, societies, and homes will currently be affiliated to some form of religion. Our public places, schools, and home life, if we wish to believe it, accept it, or even acknowledge it has at some point been the place where religious systems have had an influence. Were you Christened as a baby? Have you been to a funeral? Did you go to a school that has a religious affiliation? Have you been to a wedding held at a church? Have you watched a TV show that has had one of these in its story or plot? Have you gone sightseeing in a different city, landmark or country and visited the cathedral, temple, church, or holy place? In fact, I'd say it's hard not to have had some sort of connection to religion…have you ever watched a state funeral of a monarch e.g., Queen Elizabeth II, or a President, head of state or state leader? If you have then you would have seen this being held and conducted through that country's state religion e.g., Italy (Catholicism), UK (Church of England), So, for most of you out there, you would have experienced a form of religious teaching.

Religious teaching or education is instructing an individual or group about the belief and practices of a certain religion. For example, in a Roman Catholic school, there will be a strong emphasis on teaching the school children about the beliefs and practices of Catholicism with a concerted effort to indoctrinate the children into followers of Catholicism. This will be the same for any school affiliated to a religion. I gave the example earlier about my children going to a state school in the UK affiliated to the Church of England. The UK schools have an agenda to educate, instruct and indoctrinate the children into followers and believers of the Church of England. I use the word indoctrinate here, not as a sinister form of brainwashing, but as a process of indoctrination through a fundamental, biased, and focused instruction. The religion has an agenda to amass followers, so schools are the perfect fertile ground to influence and teach developing young people. This is the same for any form of value or belief that is passed down through a group system be it the family (parental values and beliefs) or a public institute e.g., a school. We indoctrinate, have been indoctrinated and continue to indoctrinate through a process of ignorance. Very rarely do parents question the values and beliefs they pass onto their children because those values and beliefs were passed onto them by their parents and so on and so forth down the generations. We only really start to question those family 'values or beliefs' when they begin to clash with an experience or relationship that causes us to question or that challenges those beliefs. A stark example of this was experienced in the civil rights movements in 1950s and 1960s America, where generation upon generation of young white people in America had been indoctrinated by their families and institutions into racist values and beliefs against Black people. Due to the non-violent civil rights movement young white people started to question legalized racial segregation, discrimination, and disenfranchisement of Black people. Black Americans began to speak out and stand up for their civil rights challenging white legalized racial segregation, discrimination, and disenfranchisement, publicising the inherent racism within white America. This made the whole country question its inherent racist beliefs and values and the institutional systems and structures that upheld this, finally leading to the civil rights act of 1964 (although white culture in the USA and UK still has a long way to go even in our current times regarding the insidious racism that exists within white culture). So, we can see how generation upon generation passes down values and beliefs ignorantly to their children without question until something, someone or some experience challenges those values and beliefs, and we see this repeatedly with religion. Woe the child that questions or challenges the parent's religious beliefs or values – they are usually met with irritation, frustration, anger, or sadness, whatever the form of emotion that is expressed, the usual intention is for the parent to close-down the questioning or challenge with an outcome for the child to know that their questioning or challenge was inherently wrong and incorrect.

> *In the future, my child, this should not happen again –* **creating a conditional dynamic of worth within the child** *– if you want my parental love and acceptance then you do not question me or my belief, in fact you take it on as your own and then all will be well again…*

133

So, we see the power of indoctrination and how easily and ignorantly its used to pass-on embedded forms of beliefs and values that are held by individuals and groups. The whole idea of evangelism within the Christian Church is to pass-on, preach and share the Christian beliefs and values of God with the inherent agenda to convert people to the Christian faith. It's not even hidden or disguised through this act. There is a focused, concentrated and committed effort to pass-on, preach and share the 'good news' to people, so they may find the word of God and be brought to salvation…and this could be said generally for a lot of religions that have a structured belief system and value structure that is run through a hierarchical administrative system. It's in the administrative systems best interest to amass followers and convert people to the religion. The more followers you have the stronger and more powerful the religion becomes; if you have any doubt, take a moment to investigate the history of religion, especially the more global powerful religions of our world e.g., Christianity and its many forms e.g., Catholicism, etc. Take a moment to see and observe the countless levels of violence, war and human atrocities that have and still are being performed in the name of religion, and that is on a grand scale, but also let's not forget the localised judgement, exclusion, bullying and discrimination on a daily level that exists too. When we follow a belief system to the letter with prejudice, fundamentalism, and exclusion, we walk the road of narrow-mindedness, cruelty, violence (non-truth) and ignorance, and it is this ignorance that causes defensive thinking, speaking, and acting, which always leads to suffering and pain.

What is the difference then between religious teachings and spiritual teachings?

Have you ever heard the suggestion or term to get into 'the spirit' of something? If we look at the surface level meaning of this, we see a suggestion or motivation to enter whatever you are doing with 'enthusiasm and general good mood', throw away your cares and have fun, which on a general level seems good advice. Why get bogged down with the stresses and worries of life, let them go and enjoy yourself…However, if we look a little deeper and reflect more skilfully, perhaps there is another meaning, a meaning that exists just below the surface that holds a deeper significance. To be 'in the spirit' of something also suggests that the 'spirit' could also mean in the 'essence of'…the 'essence of' something is that of a deeper quality, that thing which is not obvious to first sight, that which is out of awareness, below the surface, hidden and not yet discovered. Another way of looking at this could mean 'to be in the spirit of' is that which is not literal. To be in the 'spirit' of something is to not take that thing on face-value or literal terms, there is a deeper meaning here that needs to be discovered and experienced, so the experiencer can get the full and whole value of the deeper quality of that which is being experienced. So, in basic terms do not take the literal meaning of something, do not follow the letter or literal words of the phrase because if you do you are missing the true message and meaning.

Now I'm not applying this to basic laws or structures of living, we do not want people getting to a red light on a traffic intersection and then deciding and taking a moment to reflect on the deeper meaning of the colour red and the sequence of lights, no, that would be ridiculous and probably dangerous leading to traffic jams and potential traffic accidents, no some rules do need to be followed to the letter for basic communal safety and order. What I'm asking you to consider are teachings, beliefs and values that underpin and exist through ideology. Ideology being a set of ideas, beliefs and philosophies that are held by individuals and groups e.g., religious beliefs, political beliefs, economic beliefs, etc. We are moving beyond the basic rules and structures of basic living e.g., rules of traffic, and reflecting on the ideas, beliefs and values that govern our opinion, motivations, thinking and acting. Those beliefs and values that we hold dear or that challenge us, those values and beliefs that cause and are connected to judgements, feelings, and emotions. The things that enlighten us, depress us and those things that enrage us and everything in between. We are moving into the realms of morality, ethics, and evaluation of us as a species and the things we think, say, and do to ourselves and to each other locally and globally. You are now being asked to get into 'the spirit of' something...

Spiritual teaching is simple getting to the meaning below the literal meaning. The great spiritual teachers and masters had and have a wonderful, gifted, and profound ability to share the teachings to any number of people from different races, classes, backgrounds, and cultures. The spiritual messages they shared did have literal meanings but more often there was a greater deeper message that was also being shared. The teachings of Shakyamuni Buddha, the teachings of Jesus of Nazareth (Christ), the teachings and poems of

Jalāl ad-Dīn Muḥammad Rūmī, of Dogen Zenji, of Shinran Shonin, the teachings of Juliana of Norwich, of Sai Baba of Shirdi, of Ramana Maharshi, of Swami Sivananda, to the Dalia Lama, all these great spiritual teachers were and are able to share their teachings to anyone that wishes to learn and understand them. A true spiritual teacher and master can communicate and share with anyone, from any walk of life, which is the gift of the spiritual teacher and master.

Bringing this back to religion we see and understand that:

> *Religion is not to be taken literally, to do so is to become cruel, bigoted, narrow-minded, rigid, and destructive. Religion is to be taken figuratively – in the Spirit of religion. Take religion as your starting point toward inner-searching, self-discovery, self-realisation, and spiritual awakening...do not follow blindly – follow intelligently, with discussion, with exploration, with a skilful curiosity that examines, analyses, and critically evaluates the teaching...search for the essence of the meaning, search for that which sits below...*

A true spiritual teacher does not try to convince, influence, or prescribe their teaching to you. They do not use fear, domination, ridicule, or violence to bring understanding to you – to do so goes against the very nature of their enlightenment, awakening and spiritual attainment. A true spiritual teacher offers compassion, understanding, kindness, love, and respect – they offer the teachings not of their own but of the greater wisdom, knowledge and divine cosmic love of a higher power that is the source of all that there is, of Spirit, of Consciousness, of life itself. It is solely up to you and you alone if you wish to listen, understand, and study the teachings. They are there for you just as they are there for any human being. A true spiritual teacher does not discriminate, exclude, or deny anyone the teachings. The teachings are there for us all – it just depends on our ability to understand them, hear them, experience them, feel them, and comprehend them. Have you ever had one of those moments when you feel your body tingle, or shivers go down your spine, or you get 'goose bumps' not in a frightened fearful way but in a good wholesome positive way. You experience a feeling deep within you that reverberates your whole body. This is a good sign and a deeper sense and knowing that what is happening within you, in response to that experience is impacting you in a deeply profound and positive way - so therefore take heed, acknowledge, observe, and learn from this…a true spiritual teacher can attune to your vibrational energy (the art of listening) and connect to You.

But I'm not religious, I'm secular, how will they benefit me?

You don't need to be religious or follow a religious group to benefit from religious teachings. There are so many reasons to engage with the deeper spiritual teachings of religion:

- they are profoundly nurturing, they offer deeper wisdom to life generally,
- they give us an ethical way to exist in the world that can benefit us all,

- they are wonderful stories, parables, fables, and poems in their own right
- they offer us an opportunity to go beyond our ordinary daily lives but most of all they offer us an opportunity for spiritual growth.

If you can allow yourself to hear, experience and understand these messages and communications, by getting out of the way of yourself. If you can begin to suspend your judgement and cultivate empathy – this will not only assist you in cultivating the art of listening – in turn it will help you move ever closer to achieving spiritual growth and awakening.

Forms of Spiritual Teaching

In this next section I'm going to introduce you to several forms of spiritual teaching that exist within our cultures. These come from different schools of religion, spiritual collections, philosophical teachings, and religious texts – some may be familiar, and others may be new to you. You may already have preconceived feelings, thoughts and opinions about certain texts, parables, fables, poems and teachings – all I ask is for you to try and suspend your judgement and perhaps enter with a fresh and open mind - remember these teachings have been acquired by particular religious organisations for the administrative, evangelical and marketing promotions of the religion; if you harbour any affiliation to these groups either good or bad, please remember that the original spiritual teacher, speaker and communicator of these teachings had no affiliation to any non-profit charitable organisation...

Shakyamuni Buddha

The son of a King and prince to a noble land, Siddhartha (wish fulfilled) Gotama was born in 623BC on the outskirts of Nepal. A spiritual ascetic and teacher to the king on seeing the new born child, instantly praised the baby as the Enlightened One and Buddha to be...his father the king desperate for his son to become the next great ruler and king, tried to nurture and shape his son for this role, offering him the best the world could offer, education, fine foods, riches, beautiful clothing, dancing, music, warriorship and marriage but all to no avail. One day while walking in the park Siddhartha came across the first of four sights that would change him forever. The first sight was of an old decrepit man, the second a diseased person, the third a corpse and the fourth a dignified hermit. The first three of these sightings proved to him instantly of the true nature of life and the process of suffering eventually leading to death. The fourth signified the means to overcome the suffering through a focused practice leading to a sense of peace and fulfilment. The young Siddhartha having now experienced these sights renounced his royal life and left the palace for his journey to become Buddha. Over the next few years Siddhartha met with many ascetics and learned scholars in search of enlightenment, until finally after being so weak and skeletal due to lack of food and nourishment he sat under the Bodhi tree, whereby he faced his final challenges, overcoming primordial fears, animal instincts and base existence to achieve full enlightenment 'awakening'.

This is a very brief overview and introduction to Shakyamuni Buddha – if this sparks your interest, I'd suggest doing further research and looking more deeply into the history and texts of Buddha's life and journey toward enlightenment. There are many enjoyable books, websites and organisations that promote and support Buddhism and the life of Buddha.

So, what did Shakyamuni Buddha teach us?

The Buddha taught us that human existence is based on four truths, which are known as the four noble truths due to their reality, infallibility, and permanence.

The Four Noble Truths:

1. **Dukkha - Pain and suffering is ubiquitous to us all in our lifetime**:

    Everyone will experience pain in their life be it birth, sickness, grief, anxiety, not getting what they want, end of pleasurable experiences and old age.

2. **Pain and suffering have a cause and origin – Samudaya:**

It's the experience and drive for pleasure and desire that keep us held into the feedback loop of suffering (Dukkha).

3. **Nirodha – the ceasing of pain and suffering is achievable and possible to gain:**

   By stepping out of the feedback loop of pleasure/pain and understanding our relationship to it - suffering will cease.

4. **There is a way to stop suffering and pain – the following of the eightfold path:**

   By following and practicing the eight-fold path, your relationship to suffering will cease.

The four noble truths are the alpha and omega, the beginning and the end of Buddha's teachings and underpin everything that was communicated to others throughout his life. In Buddhism there is a basic belief of Samsara – the continuous cycle of life, death, and rebirth – which is governed by karma the law of action and reaction (what goes around comes around). The Buddha taught that the cause of Samsara is suffering (noble truth one) and the reason we continue on in Samsara and do not get off the 'merry go round' of suffering is due to noble truth two – our desire and experience for pleasure which then leads to pain - this is what keeps us held in the feedback loop and the continual cycle of life, death and rebirth. It's our constant cravings and the impermanence of pleasure that always leads to dissatisfaction, irritability, and suffering. Karma, as the

Buddha taught, is our intention expressed through our actions, nothing more and nothing less. It's our intended actions that produce either positive outcomes or negative outcomes dependent on the natural law of karma. For example, if we offer intended positive outcomes e.g., compassion, through our thinking, speaking, and acting then compassion will come to us. The same is true for intended negative outcomes. If we offer intended negative outcomes e.g., ridicule, we will get back ridicule.

The Buddha said: *If you speak or act with a pure mind then happiness follows you like a shadow that never leaves. If you speak or act with a corrupt mind, then misery follows you like a wheel of an ox car follows the second leg.*

So, we can see that the Buddha also espoused an ethical way of living and being, which is underpinned by the natural law of karma. If you want a good life, you need to live a good life because the law of karma, the law of cause and effect, the law of moral causality wills it so.

How do we live a good life?

Buddha taught us that suffering, and the cause of suffering can cease (noble truth three) and the way to cease this suffering and step off the 'merry go round' of pleasure/pain (Samsara) is through the undertaking of noble truth four - the eightfold path.

The Eightfold Path:

1. Right view/understanding
2. Right thinking/intention
3. Right Speech
4. Right Action
5. Right Livelihood
6. Right Effort
7. Right Mindfulness
8. Right Concentration

Right view/understanding is linked and underpinned by two overarching principles in Buddhism the four noble truths and the law of karma. Right view/understanding is to know and comprehend these principles and to apply them to one's life. To benefit fully from life is to live in an ethical way through minimising harm to self and others, through the awareness of our thoughts, speech, and actions.

Right thinking/intention: from unclouded vision or understanding (right view) we are led to right thinking/intention, which is the focused and committed attention to clear thinking. It is our thoughts that either defile or purify us, so it is our responsibility to foster positive thinking to aid our wellbeing.

Right speech comes from right thinking/intention and leads us to speaking with clarity, care, and consideration. We move away from frivolous talk, slander, unkind words, and falsehood. We do our best to communicate clearly, truthfully and with non-violence.

Right action is our intention to refrain from harmful action towards others. We do not kill, steal, and cease from sexual misconduct in all its forms. We foster positive boundaries, actively support life, and develop positive relationships.

Right livelihood is the practice of ethical living through our business. We are to foster business and work that doesn't involve harming others e.g., selling weapons or substances that harm. We also need to refrain from being dishonest, cheating, deceiving, and behaving in harmful ways.

Right effort is the continued focus and practice of ethical living. We must take full responsibility for our thinking, speaking, and acting to cultivate a persistent ethical way of life. Remove the negative ways to uncover and free the positive ways, with the ongoing vigilance of right effort.

Right mindfulness is the focused awareness toward our body, feelings, thoughts, and mind. By training ourselves to be aware of these aspects of self we foster mindfulness and stop ourselves from slipping into negative harmful ways to self and others.

Right concentration is the application of right effort and right mindfulness. A concentrated state that allows us to experience single pointedness so we can see things as they really are. We are no longer distracted by the sideshows of life; we rest in a state of true awareness.

In Buddhism these eightfold factors of the eightfold path are grouped into three stages: right view and right thinking are grouped in Wisdom (panna). Right speech, right action and right livelihood are grouped in morality (sila), and right effort, right mindfulness, and right concentration in concentration (Samadhi). It is through wisdom, morality, and concentration that we can walk the eightfold path and foster ethical and non-violent forms of living and relating.

In relation to Buddhist writings, teachings, conversations, text, and Sutras that all relate to Buddha's wisdom, knowledge and practice, there are three main forms of classification for students and practitioners to learn from. These are known as the *tipiṭaka* in Pali or *tripiṭaka* in Sanskrit, which translates into English as the three baskets.

The three baskets are further classified into:

1. Discourses or Sutta in Pali, Sutra in Sanskrit, which in essence are the teachings of Buddha. These consist mainly of conversations and teachings between Buddha and his followers, which were recorded for students and aspirants to learn from.

2. The Monastic Laws or Vinaya in both Pali and Sanskrit. These are the list of rules for monks and nuns to follow and practice, which also contain the structure and development of community life, engagement, and relationships.

3. Abhidhamma or Abhidharma in Sanskrit, which are summaries and analyses of Buddha's teachings as laid out in the discourses.

There are many teachings and Sutras available, which are presented in the three baskets/ *tripiṭaka,* for aspiring Buddhist students and aspirants to engage with and learn from, e.g., Lotus Sutra, Diamond Sutra, Amitabha, Vimalakirti, Jewel Heap, to name a few. If you are interested, I'd suggest looking at https://suttacentral.net as they offer an extensive range and break down of the Buddhist texts and teachings with excellent guides to study and reading of the Sutras.

One Sutra, I believe, stands out from the rest and is ultimately the core of Buddha's teachings is the Heart Sutra, if you don't engage with any other Sutra of the Buddha, this is a must...

The Heart Sutra, in Sanskrit is *Prajñāpāramitāhṛdaya,* which translates as The Heart of the Perfection of Wisdom. This is a famous sutra as it holds the grounding principle and statement, 'Form is emptiness (*śūnyatā*), emptiness is form', which is an important principle in Buddhism, especially within the Mahayana school. The conclusion of the sutra is then concentrated into the mantra: gate, gate, Pāragate, Pārasamgate, Bodhi Svāhā which translates into 'gone. gone, gone beyond, gone utterly beyond, Enlightenment/Awakening, so be it'. The sutra in my understanding is essentially a guide and practice to letting go of attachment to objects, understanding the process the body, mind and senses play in this and realising the duality of existence – once this is understood the practitioner begins to develop a gateway/bridge to the 'other shore' or essentially the non-dual reality of existence or Emptiness by transcending duality and attaining Enlightenment/Awakening. The gift or beauty of this teaching that the Lord Buddha shared with us is in essence in this one Sutra, the Heart of Buddha's teaching is the Heart Sutra. By mediating, reflecting, studying, and practicing the mantra daily your ability to attain and gain spiritual awakening and intuitive knowledge will be quickened.

The great Swami Sivananda said *'we must have synthesis of wisdom, love and action, the head, heart, and hand. The head of Sankara, the heart of Buddha, and the hand of Janaka'*. The Heart Sutra aids us in developing a heart of Buddha. It begins in mediation through the heart and by cultivating the heart of Buddha, we are creating the bridge to divine wisdom that then directs our actions. Buddha is saying to us, *'develop your hearts, open your hearts, through the guidance, knowledge and practice of the Heart sutra and the reciting of the concluding mantra: gate, gate, pāragate, pārasamgate, Bodhi Svāhā'*. Buddha is telling us to cultivate our hearts, if you do nothing else in this world, cultivate your heart – if we can cultivate our hearts then everything else will follow by its own accord – our hearts will guide our wisdom and our actions simultaneously – make your heart the foundation of your very existence – the grounding principle of your life – by doing so enlightenment and awakening will ultimately be yours, and the world in turn will be a far happier, peaceful and kinder place to be...

Jesus of Nazareth aka Christ

Probably the most historically famous human being that has ever lived, Jesus has been and still is a global phenomenon. If you ask people in the street, they will have heard of or know of Jesus the Christ. If you live in the Western world then you will have been brought up on or have been influenced at some stage of your life, by Christianity the religion that was created around the human being that was prophesised in the Hebrew Bible as the Messiah, Jesus the Christ.

In the UK and other Western countries, there is a tradition in schools that centres around the birth of Christ called the nativity at Christmas time. Children re-enact the story of Jesus's humble beginnings with his parents being turned away from Inns, homes, and places of human shelter, until Mary and Joseph - his parents - find solace in a stable where Jesus is then born with the Star of Bethlehem shining brightly over his place of birth. He is then visited my three wise men and shepherds bearing gifts for the chosen one, the Messiah.

Another significant aspect of Jesus was his conception, according to the New Testament Gospels, Mary Jesus' mother was a virgin when she gave birth to Jesus denoting that her conception of Jesus was immaculate through the Holy Spirit, freeing her of original sin and allowing her as a pregnant woman to be betrothed to Joseph, Jesus's adopted father.

Carrying on the story - Herod the Great, the Judea Roman king, hearing of Jesus's birth and fearing for the usurping of his kingdom, ordered the death of all male children under 2. Joseph being warned of this in a dream by the archangel Gabriel, took his wife Mary and son Jesus and fled to Egypt later to return to Nazareth when Jesus was older. Joseph continued work as a carpenter instructing Jesus and his brothers. There are no accounts of Jesus' childhood in any of the New Testament Gospels, the next we hear of Jesus he is a young man and seeking out John the Baptist, Jesus is then baptised in the river Jordan by John the Baptist. On receiving baptism, the Holy Spirit descends into Jesus, declaring him the son of God. Jesus then goes off into the wilderness to face Satan and his temptations, after conquering and overcoming the trails and temptations of Satan, Jesus then returns to start his teachings, gathers the twelve disciples and begins his ministry…

This above telling of the conception, birth and life of Jesus is taken from the New Testament Gospels, which most Christian schools and organisations follow and espouse as their foundation to the teachings and life of Jesus. If you are looking for alternative renderings of the life of Jesus, you may find the Gnostic Gospels, Nag Hammadi library, *The Christ of India,* and the *Aquarian Gospel of Jesus Christ* of interest. These are texts that give alternative interpretations of Jesus' education, spirituality and meaning of Christianity; of interest is *The Christ of India* and the *Aquarian Gospel of Jesus Christ* as these delve into and give possible accounts of Jesus' education in his childhood and teenage years, which the New Testament Gospels fail to mention. The Aquarian Gospel links

Jesus' education to strong prominent spiritual and scholarly schools that existed before and around the time of Jesus, linking to Hindu, Buddhist, Persian, Greek and Egyptian spiritualism, and philosophy. We don't know if this is historically factual but maybe on a symbolical level it raises further plausible questions to Jesus' early life. Given Jesus' divine status, spirituality and wisdom, his meeting and being educated through these established spiritual schools and philosophies has some credence, however, it's best to study and reflect on this knowledge yourself and come to your own conclusions regarding the man Jesus the Christ.

So, what did Jesus of Nazareth (Christ) teach us?

Jesus taught and spoke prolifically throughout his time, journeying to various places around the Judean province, notably in Galilee, Judea, Perea and ending in Jerusalem, where Jesus predicts his betrayal and death at the last supper. The New Testament Gospels document Jesus' teachings, sermons, and miracles he performed throughout his life. A significant period was in the early Galilee ministry when Jesus, according to the Gospel of Matthew, gave a Sermon on the Mount, which culminated into the Beatitudes, the Lord's Prayer, and the central tenets of discipleship. The Gospel of Matthew forms five discourses of Jesus' teachings and these tend to be the most widely quoted from the New Testament Bible: 1. The Sermon on the Mount (5-7); 2. Discipleship (10); 3. the parables (13); 4. faith community (18) & 5. future times or 'end times' (24-25).

Religious teachings have varied levels or meanings to them, so we can in some instances take the surface level or literal meaning of a religious teaching, but this does not denote the deeper spiritual meaning, the essence of the teaching. Jesus was a master spiritual teacher, if we are to believe the history that he was in fact the Christ, the Christ-ed One, that incarnated here to bring salvation to humanity, to teach humanity and to assist humanity through their next evolutional stage of existence, the symbolic expression of the Christ is more than apt. Like Shakyamuni Buddha before him, Jesus' mission was to bring the deeper mysteries of life, spiritual practice, and spiritual awakening to humanity. Jesus' incarnation into human was not only to teach a deeper ethical form of existence but also to bring a sense of unity and togetherness to all races of humanity. Jesus' teachings offered a real opportunity to challenge the violent and brutal infrastructures of his time, especially in relation to the powerful empires that were dominant e.g., Roman Empire. Jesus' teachings on love, harmony, and peace, were signalling a time of change, away from the pantheons of sacrificial practice, orgiastic rituals, and warmongering toward a greater sense of unity, love, Oneness, and monotheism. Jesus was foretelling of a new age.

The Sermon on the Mount was a turning point for Jesus, prior to this he was still establishing himself as a spiritual teacher, unifying his ministry and disciples, and consolidating his teachings. The Sermon on the Mount signals a significant culmination not only of Jesus' ethical teachings but his deeper spiritual teachings on spiritual practice and self-realisation (enlightenment).

The Beatitudes:

The Beatitudes can be found in the Gospel of Matthew 5: 3-12, they are based as a series of Blessings. I have introduced firstly the original eight beatitudes as they are written in the Gospel of Matthew to represent the surface level meaning and then this is followed with each beatitude separated individually with an italic interpretation of a deeper spiritual meaning relating to deeper spiritual practice. These are spiritual understandings that I present as one possible way of understanding the deeper spiritual meaning that could be linked to Buddhist, Hindu, and Yoga practices; practices I believe Jesus was taught and then personified and integrated into his teachings, which led to his enlightenment and Christ status.

A note on the Bible and Gospel versions: for the use of this book, I'm using the 21st Century King James version of the Bible for ease and uniformity.

Matthew 5: 3-12 – The Beatitudes:

- Blessed are the poor in spirit, for theirs is the kingdom of Heaven;
- Blessed are those who mourn, for they will be comforted;
- Blessed are the meek, for they will inherit the Earth;
- Blessed are those who hunger and thirst for righteousness, for they will be satisfied;
- Blessed are the merciful, for they will be shown mercy;
- Blessed are the pure of heart, for they will see God;

- Blessed are the peacemakers, for they will be called the sons of God;

- Blessed are those who are persecuted because of righteousness, for theirs is the kingdom of Heaven;

- Blessed are you when people insult you, persecute you and falsely say all kinds of evil against you because of me. Rejoice and be glad because great is your reward in heaven, for in the same way they persecuted the prophets who were before you...

So, there we have the surface level blessings as spoken by Jesus on his Sermon of the Mount. They seem somewhat straight forward, if you hold an attitude or process e.g., meekness or mercy, then you will in some way be blessed by God.

But do they stand-up with deeper analysis and reflection?

Are these blessings what Jesus was teaching us?

Spiritual interpretations of the Beatitudes:

❖ Blessed are the poor of spirit, for theirs is the kingdom of Heaven.

To be poor in spirit suggests that we are lacking, and not only to be lacking we will be blessed and own the kingdom of Heaven due to this lack. Can we really be poor in spirit if we are to have the kingdom of Heaven? In Buddhist, Hindu, and Yogic spiritual practice there is a fundamental premise of letting go, a renunciation of attachment to those things that hold us back from our spiritual growth and development. If we accumulate unnecessary attachments to objects, thoughts, feelings, behaviours, and relationships then our ability to spiritually grow will be arrested. We need to understand our cravings, hoardings, consuming and greed, our attachments to the unnecessary that are sabotaging our ability to grow spiritually and our enjoyment of a deeper sense of fulfilment in our lives. In essence we need to be poor of those attachments so we can grow spiritually, if we are poor of those unnecessary attachments and understand that nothing belongs to us, we can have Heaven. We can move toward an internal self-realisation that all is One and that in actuality we do not possess or own anything, as our egoistic sense of ownership and possession is simply a deluded illusion of mind.

❖ Blessed are those who mourn, for they will be comforted.

If we allow ourselves to mourn then comfort comes our way. When we mourn, we mourn a loss, a loss to that which prior we held of value, the greater the value the greater the sense of loss and feeling of mourning that loss. We mourn because our egoistic mind is holding onto an attachment that we give value judgement too. Our ego Is constantly craving and grabbing objects toward it out of desire, to feel good, to receive the pleasure hit...if we carry-on in the pleasure/pain cycle we will constantly be in a process of loss and mourning, constantly in a process of suffering. To recognise the root of our mourning and then through spiritual practice and commitment we transcend the pleasure/pain cycle and our egoistic perspective, to finally experience comfort, to finally experience freedom, the ultimate loss and mourning of ego of the little self... We then experience self-realisation and spiritually awaken.

❖ Blessed are the meek, for they will inherit the Earth.

If we are meek, humble, and righteous then we are grounded and close to the Earth, we are not lofted, arrogant or experience ourselves above the Earth; and if this is so we are blessed for it. If we delve deeper into this teaching and understand that Spirit and Divine Will form the basis of all existence, then our ability to stay close to this, stay humble to the enfolding of divine we will eventually transcend our ego perspective and connect universally with All that there is. Again, we are being taught that a process of letting go of ego-centred arrogance, vice, and vanity and by being humble to the omniscience and omnipotence of Consciousness/Spirit will assist us toward self-realisation and spiritual awakening. Spirit is the creator of All that there is, you and me, so to loft ourselves above Spirit is arrogance, vice and harmful to our spiritual development. Spirit's will, not Your will - be led by the Divine Plan.

❖ Blessed are those who hunger and thirst for righteousness, for they will be satisfied.

If we are truthful and strive for this, good things will happen, which is morally sound. However, righteousness or the 'right way' to be and do is synonymous with all forms of spiritual practice, which is stated in Buddhist, Hindu, and Yoga, e.g., Buddha's eightfold path.

156

By striving for truth through divine guidance and grace the righteous path of self-realisation, awakening and spiritual growth will be made clear for us. Ultimately, we are looking to connect to and create integration of Body/Mind/Spirit through Spirit's divine plan and will.

❖ Blessed are the merciful, for they will be shown mercy.

If we adopt mercy then according to the law of karma, mercy will come back to us, ethically sound and grounded in compassion. The development of compassion is ubiquitous to all forms of spiritual practice. To spiritually grow and realise self-awakening we need compassion and empathy as our means toward understanding and experiencing divine grace. We must develop compassion/empathy and strive to offer it to All that is through our relationship to self and the Other. Do onto those as you would have done to you. We are all Spirit – to hurt and judge others is to judge and hurt self.

❖ Blessed are the pure of heart, for they will see God.

How are we to purify the mind/body so we can experience God? Ignorance is the block to self-realisation and the divine. We must work tirelessly in our spiritual practice to remove all our vices, negativity, and egoistic practices to purify the Mind and Body. To do this is to purify ourselves and to experience realisation, awakening and spiritual growth leading to a deeper more profound and loving experience with Spirit – to become pure of heart. Oneness with the divine reality, once this is realised, we experience and see God in everything...

- ❖ Blessed are the peacemakers, for they will be called the sons of God.

If we are to keep the peace and support others in this process, then we will be closer to God. Again, on the surface a sound ethical principle. If we look deeper through the process of spiritual growth, as we develop universal love and connect to the divine Spirit we will be experiencing and radiating positivity, love, and positive qualities. These positive qualities not only enhance us individually bringing integration and a sense of peace/centredness to our being, but they also radiate out into and for the collective species, which in-turn supports and leads to greater advancement of humanity.

- ❖ Blessed are those who are persecuted because of righteousness, for theirs is the Kingdom of Heaven.

The 'merry-go-round' cycle of pleasure/pain is fundamental to human existence and causes suffering, this is a fundamental fact grounded in dualism and the Earth-bound realm. If we are then to suffer, if we are then persecuted then do so for a purpose to enhance our spiritual growth. The skilful and intelligent purpose of suffering is for spiritual development and growth. Take charge of your suffering through personal heroism to overcome the pleasure/pain cycle (ego-centric existence) and move toward joy and spiritual awakening – then yours is the Kingdom of Heaven.

- ❖ Blessed are you when people insult you, persecute you and falsely say all kinds of evil against you because of me. Rejoice and be glad because great is your reward in heaven, for in the same way they persecuted the prophets who were before you...

People are defensive, scared, frightened and sceptical of higher spiritual teachings as they challenge the very foundations of cultural existence, cultural perspectives and cultural values and ways of living. Spiritual teachings are asking something more of us, something greater than us, something that ultimately takes us away and changes our very existence and perspective on self, other and life in general. Spiritual teachings are asking us to question the very foundations of what we exist in, live in, communicate in, and experience daily and throughout our lives. So, for this very reason individuals, people, groups, and societies have persecuted, judged attacked, dismissed, and tried to eradicate spiritual teachings and guidance. They've especially persecuted those that offer this too.. The reason is due to their deep-seated ego-centric fear of losing what they think, belief and feel they own and exist in and what they think will keep them safe, secure, and content in their dream-like state of ignorance (pleasure/pain cycle), and so for this very reason they continue to revile, persecute, and judge. Spiritual teachings, Oneness, impermanence, Universality and Spirit challenge this to the very core.

The reward in heaven is so - Divine self is the reality – overcome ignorance (ego-centred existence). Individuality is anathema to this, individuality of ego-centred delusion results in negative properties, vices, and blocks to spiritual awakening. To receive our reward of

Heaven is to overcome the cycle of pleasure/pain suffering. It is to achieve Self-realisation. It is to achieve spiritual awakening.

The Beatitudes occur naturally in a perfected mind – a self-realised personality – in an enlightened one. For an aspirant/student they must be nurtured and manifested through daily practice and commitment so the aspirant can achieve enlightenment and self-realisation. I believe this was and is the deeper spiritual teaching that Jesus the Christ was communicating to us. In these Beatitudes Jesus was communicating and offering a deeper spiritual guidance and pathway toward achieving self-realisation and spiritual awakening. Like Buddha's eightfold path, Jesus presented a structured spiritual pathway of knowledge and practice that could lead the aspirant, disciple, and student to attaining spiritual growth and spiritual awakening. If we are to believe that Jesus of Nazareth was indeed the Christ, the Messiah of the Hebrew prophecy then why would this great, divine spiritual teacher convey only a basic surface level teaching at such a pinnacle time in his ministry…why would this divine spiritual teacher withhold such knowledge and practice, when his mission like Shakyamuni Buddhas before him was to bring unity, universality and spiritual awakening to humanity…

The Lord's Prayer:

Another significant aspect of the Sermon on the Mount was Jesus' teaching on the power and use of prayer. Prayer had been a substantial element of religious practice for all forms of religion prior to Jesus' teachings – to ask your God for mercy, love, prosperity, security, bounty and survival were fundamental features of all the major religions of the time and still are to this day…how many of us when we are in that desperate hour of need, call out to a God or our God to deliver us from our pain and suffering and beg for it to be taken away?

So, what was so different with Jesus' teaching on prayer?

The Lord's Prayer as it's officially known can be found again in the Gospel of Matthew (6) and a shorter version in the Gospel of Luke (11). For the purposes of this discussion, I shall be referring to the Matthew version as this is the more well known and used throughout Christian teachings.

Matthew 6: The Lord's Prayer

Our Father who art in Heaven, hallowed be Thy name.

Thy Kingdom come. Thy will be done on earth, as it is in Heaven.

Give us this day our daily bread.

And forgive us our debts, as we forgive our debtors.

And lead us not into temptation but deliver us from evil.

For Thine is the Kingdom, and the power and the glory for ever. Amen.

Again, as with the Beatitudes, there are deeper levels of teachings that exist within the lord's prayer. I shall present the surface level teachings followed again in italics with a deeper spiritual interpretation. Jesus according to the Gospel of Matthew (6) gave clear guidance and understanding on how to pray and the significance of one's relationship to God using this prayer. From the start of Matthew (6) until we reach Matthew (6:9) Jesus' reputes the old archaic practice of prayer through certain Hebrew traditions, and signals to a new way of relating to God and how God's omniscience and omnipotence does not require the vainglory and ostentatiousness of public acts of prayer and almsgiving that looks for reward based in vanity. Jesus points toward a deeper more personal relationship to God that requires humility, privacy, and intimacy – a tender and knowing God - Matthew (6:8) *for your Father knoweth what things ye have need of before ye ask Him.* Jesus is asking us to relate more deeply to God, the nurturing guardian, who requires only our ability to accept the Source of All more deeply and closely.

Spiritual interpretation of the Lord's Prayer:

❖ Our Father who art in Heaven, hallowed be Thy name

To connect more deeply and profoundly to Spirit, we first need to focus and invite in – we need to invoke through our Invocation of the hallowed, Holy presence of All that there is, moving toward a presence of divine love, and infinite care that nurtures us. We do this through our personal and private act of sincerity of feeling and expression - even if our words are limited – Spirit hears us and responds with unconditional love and grace.

- ❖ Thy Kingdom come. Thy will be done on earth, as it is in Heaven

Self-realisation, enlightenment, and spiritual awakening are our purpose of being our raison d'etre. We learn and understand that self is no more than a manifestation of Spirit/All that there is, and this can be accomplished on Earth, as self is the self-realised non-dualistic expression of Spirit on Earth. Heaven is the internalised self-realisation that transcends time and space – heaven cannot be bounded by time and space. It is not a materialistic expression of riches or wealth. The spiritually awakened person is of non-duality of consciousness that transcends time and space incarnated on the Earth realm.

- ❖ Give us this day our daily bread

Holding self-realisation as your ideal, confront your present so past and future does not exist – live in the present. Divine will and grace that exists behind everything, the everything of daily life, the perceived mundane, the daily trials and tribulations of work to live, to exist, to survive, your daily bread. We are being asked to train the mind to find joy in whatever we do because divine expression of Spirit is in everything. Whatever Spirit gives of this day (your daily bread) you accept with graciousness living in the present. Whatever developments we experience in our day-to-day lives is the divine nurturing bread that feeds our soul, which feeds us infinitely – make spiritual practice your daily bread.

- ❖ And forgive us our debts, as we forgive our debtors

To achieve purity of mind, we must remove and balance all our debts, we must settle our karma. If we wish to be forgiven for our errors and unskilful ignorance that leads to illusion and delusion of separation of Spirit, then we must forgive others too, the law of Karma. Practice compassion, empathy, and truthfulness - if we want kindness then we must give kindness – settle our debts, find balance.

- ❖ And lead us not into temptation, but deliver us from evil

We are asking God to support our development away from egoism, delusion, illusion and craving the pleasure hit – the evil temptations. Help us to develop the virtues of life and remove the vices – expand the mind toward harmony, full integration, and non-duality to achieve spiritual awakening.

- ❖ For Thine is the Kingdom, and the power and the glory for ever. Amen

Prayer is the vehicle toward enlightenment – enthusiastic daily spiritual practice toward the divine presence where your karma is removed, and self-realisation is achieved - this is the goal and aim of human existence to achieve spiritual awakening toward enlightenment – this is your power and glory.

For the rest of Matthew (6) after the Lord's Prayer, Jesus expounds and focuses on the natural law of karma and how this relates to God and the natural world. If we are connected to and stay connected to the Source of All through our committed spiritual practice and prayer, then God, the divine will provide for us in the same way it is reflected in the natural world through the eco-systems in which incarnated life exists on the Earth. By knowing and understanding our place in the world through the natural order of divine existence, we come to a place of righteousness, truth, harmony, and sustainability. Jesus warns us in Matthew (6:12) that there are two paths we can take, the Divine path to God or the Base path to carnal pleasure seeking and materialism, if we follow the righteous path to God (spiritual practice) then we will achieve spiritual growth, nurturing and fulfilment, if we choose the Base path then this leads to suffering and an unfulfilled life. The Lord's prayer, the gift of Jesus, is therefore a prayer, mantra, vehicle, practice, and meditation toward Body/Mind purification. It's a spiritual practice we can actively engage in, in fact Jesus is asking us to engage with it and being the spiritual master and teacher that he is, knows that the continued active participation in this form of spiritual practice (Prayer/meditation) will lead us toward self-realisation and spiritual awakening.

The Parables:

According to the Oxford Leaner's dictionary (2023), a parable: *is a short story that teaches a moral or spiritual lesson, especially one of those told by Jesus as recorded in the Bible.* The parables of Jesus are to be found in the New Testament in the Gospels of Matthew, Mark and Luke and number around thirty-eight in total. If you research the parables of Jesus, you will find agreeing and contrasting viewpoints on them, either in number, understanding or meaning; for the continuity of this discussion, I shall be focusing on the thirty-eight parables of the New Testament Gospels of Matthew, Mark, and Luke. The parables tend to fall into five themes that focus on Love and forgiveness, the Kingdom of Heaven, Loss and Redemption, Eschatology (end of days) and Prayer. As with all of Jesus' teachings there are varying levels of meaning, and this is even told in the Gospel of Matthew (13:10-11):

[10] And the disciples came and said unto Him, "Why speakest Thou unto them in parables?"

[11] He answered and said unto them, "Because it is given unto you to know the mysteries of the Kingdom of Heaven, but to them it is not given.

Again, what we see highlighted, is Jesus' profound and masterful ability to convey the teachings to various levels of spiritual practitioners, from the novice to the intermediate to the advanced. His parable teachings give us a basic level understanding of ethical and virtuous understanding, conduct and behaviour, which all levels of spiritual aspirants and students can learn to integrate, whilst opening the door to the more intermediate and advanced practitioner through deeper experiential meditative *mysteries* and training. I will not cover all the parables of Jesus; I will take two of the more well-known to discuss. The parables are the timeless essence that one can experience through ongoing study at the various stages and levels of one's own spiritual development. Dependent on where you are along your own spiritual journey will determine the message, understanding and learning you get from the parables and any other form of spiritual teaching. The joy and fulfilment are the continued study and deeper meditative experience of the teachings…

The Parable of the Sower - Matthew (13:3-9) – Theme – Kingdom of Heaven

3 And He spoke many things unto them in parables, saying, "Behold, a sower went forth to sow.

4 And when he sowed, some seeds fell by the wayside; and the fowls came and devoured them up.

5 Some fell upon stony places where they had not much earth; and forthwith they sprang up, because they had no deepness of earth.

6 And when the sun was up they were scorched, and because they had no root they withered away.

7 And some fell among thorns; and the thorns sprang up and choked them.

8 But others fell into good ground and brought forth fruit, some a hundredfold, some sixtyfold, some thirtyfold.

9 Who hath ears to hear, let him hear."

The surface level teaching of the parable of the Sower is somewhat simplistic and refers to seeding, growth and nurturing, if you were a farmer of the time, this parable wouldn't be news to you…

However, Jesus himself, according to Matthew (13:18-23), expounds the meaning of the parable for us and explains to his disciples the point:

18 "Hear ye therefore the parable of the sower:

19 When any one heareth the Word of the Kingdom and understandeth it not, then cometh the wicked one and catcheth away that which was sown in his heart. This is he that received seed by the wayside.

20 But he that received the seed into stony places, the same is he that heareth the Word and at once with joy receiveth it;

21 yet hath he not root in himself, but endureth for a while. For when tribulation or persecution ariseth because of the Word, by and by he loses faith.

22 He also that received the seed among the thorns is he that heareth the Word; and the cares of this world and the deceitfulness of riches choke the Word, and he becometh unfruitful.

23 But he that received seed into the good ground is he that heareth the Word and understandeth it, who also beareth fruit and bringeth forth, some a hundredfold, some sixty, some thirty."

So, what is this parable telling us?

On one level we are hearing the words of Jesus extolling the need for single-pointedness and committed faith. If you receive the word of God into your heart (on good ground) and nurture and stay true to God, then you will be fruitful and good things will happen. Good advice and a clear starting point for the spiritual aspirant. On a deeper level we are hearing the words of Jesus, warn us of the dangers of materialism and the pleasure/pain cycle (*the deceitfulness of riches choke the Word, and he becometh unfruitful*) and explains to overcome these, to become the master of these, we need the ongoing practice, focus, concentration and skilful intelligence that is needed to be practiced vigilantly throughout one's spiritual journey, that is needed if we are to achieve self-realisation.

To achieve the purity of mind (*heareth the Word and understandeth it*) and the removal of vice (*the wicked one and catcheth away that which was sown in his heart*), we must be rooted, we must be grounded in our practice, and nothing must uproot this (*he not root in himself, but endureth for a while. For when tribulation or persecution ariseth because of the Word, by and by he loses faith*), be strong in your practice and trust in Spirit, and with committed practice you will achieve purity of mind and spiritual awakening (*received seed into the good ground is he that heareth the Word and understandeth it; who also beareth fruit and bringeth forth, some a hundredfold, some sixty, some thirty*).

The Parable of the Prodigal Son – Luke (15:11-32) – Loss & Redemption

[11] *And He said, "A certain man had two sons.*

12 And the younger of them said to his father, 'Father, give me the portion of goods that falleth to me.' And he divided unto them his estate.

13 And not many days after, the younger son gathered all together and took his journey into a far country, and there wasted his substance with riotous living.

14 And when he had spent all, there arose a mighty famine in that land, and he began to be in want.

15 And he went and joined himself to a citizen of that country, who sent him into his fields to feed swine.

16 And he would fain have filled his belly with the husks that the swine ate, and no man gave unto him.

17 And when he came to himself, he said, 'How many hired servants of my fathers have bread enough and to spare, and I perish with hunger!

18 I will arise and go to my father and will say unto him, "Father, I have sinned against Heaven and before thee,

19 and am no more worthy to be called thy son. Make me as one of thy hired servants."'

20 And he arose and came to his father. But when he was yet a great way off, his father saw him and had compassion, and ran and fell on his neck and kissed him.

²¹ And the son said unto him, 'Father, I have sinned against Heaven and in thy sight, and am no more worthy to be called thy son.'

²² But the father said to his servants, 'Bring forth the best robe and put it on him and put a ring on his hand and shoes on his feet.

²³ And bring hither the fatted calf and kill it, and let us eat and be merry;

²⁴ for this my son was dead, and is alive again; he was lost, and is found.' And they began to be merry.

²⁵ "Now his elder son was in the field; and as he came and drew nigh to the house, he heard music and dancing.

²⁶ And he called one of the servants and asked what these things meant.

²⁷ And he said unto him, 'Thy brother is come, and thy father hath killed the fatted calf, because he hath received him safe and sound.'

²⁸ And he was angry and would not go in; therefore, came his father out and entreated him.

²⁹ And he answering said to his father, 'Lo, these many years have I served thee, neither transgressed I at any time thy commandment, and yet thou never gavest me a kid, that I might make merry with my friends.

³⁰ But as soon as this thy son was come who hath devoured thy living with harlots, thou hast killed for him the fatted calf.'

[31]And he said unto him, 'Son, thou art ever with me, and all that I have is thine.

[32]It was meet that we should make merry and be glad; for this thy brother was dead, and is alive again; and was lost, and is found.'"

The prodigal son is one of Jesus' well-known parables. The idea of redemption, rejoicing the found which was lost, bringing home to the fold that which had lost its way, are common themes in Christianity and bible study. The focus on the wayward son that was seduced by material gains and pleasure seeking are again common threads in Christian teachings. One must practice the virtues and stay steadfast to the faith if we are to receive the Kingdom of Heaven and stay in favour with God.

However, is this what the parable of the prodigal son is saying?

There are varying levels to this parable, on the surface we are reminded to not wander from the Christian faith because if we do, we will come to ruin (*there wasted his substance with riotous living.[14] And when he had spent all, there arose a mighty famine in that land, and he began to be in want*). If, we turn away from God toward materialism and pleasure seeking we will eventually suffer. Though, our suffering doesn't have to remain, if we turn back to God and repent, God will be merciful and not only merciful, will rejoice and celebrate our return (*[22]But the father said to his servants, 'Bring forth the best robe and put it on him, and put a ring on his hand and shoes on his feet.[23] And bring hither the fatted calf and kill it, and let us eat and be merry; [24]for this my son was dead, and is*

alive again; he was lost, and is found.' And they began to be merry.)
So, we are shown that God is forever giving, loving, and nurturing.

Yet, on a deeper spiritual level Jesus is asking other things of us as
spiritual aspirants. Yes, he is telling us that we must hold the virtues
and not get sucked into negative ways i.e., jealousy and anger
(*[28] And he was angry and would not go in; therefore, came his father
out and entreated him.[29] And he answering said to his father, 'Lo,
these many years have I served thee, neither transgressed I at any
time thy commandment; and yet thou never gavest me a kid, that I
might make merry with my friends.*) He is also warning against
materialism and pleasure seeking and the dangers of this. However,
on a deeper level Jesus is saying to us that no matter what path we
choose, be it a righteous (Staying with the Father) or non-righteous
path (leaving the Father), that the ability to be challenged by vice,
negativity and woes are to be found on either path. What Jesus is
saying to us, is that the path we choose be it the 'good path or bad
path' will always be the right path because it is our path. The
experiences we experience are right and correct for us, which is
dependent on our spiritual development; and the glory of either path
is this – that both paths lead to spiritual development and eventually
self-realisation... The spiritual aspirant will eventually learn and
understand this when the time is right – the prodigal son (*[18] I will
arise and go to my father and will say unto him, "Father, I have
sinned against Heaven and before thee.*), the Eldest Son (*[31] And he
said unto him, 'Son, thou art ever with me, and all that I have is
thine.*) – the deeper lesson here, is knowing when to ask God,
ultimately our higher self, for what we need when we need it, and

not to be blinded by our own ignorance or negativity, so our higher self can answer and provide what we need to enhance and support our spiritual growth when the time is right…

Internal teachings and External teachings

Matthew (7:6)

[6] "Give not that which is holy unto the dogs, neither cast ye your pearls before swine, lest they trample them under their feet, and turn again and rend you.

Matthew (13:10-11):

[10] And the disciples came and said unto Him, "Why speakest Thou unto them in parables?"

[11] He answered and said unto them, "Because it is given unto you to know the mysteries of the Kingdom of Heaven, but to them it is not given.

Matthew (13:34-35)

[34] All these things spoke Jesus unto the multitude in parables; and without a parable spoke He not unto them,

[35] that it might be fulfilled which was spoken by the prophet, saying, "I will open My mouth in parables; I will utter things which have been kept secret from the foundation of the world."

Mark (4:11-12)

[11] And He said unto them, "Unto you it is given to know the mystery of the Kingdom of God; but unto them that are without, all these things are done in parables,

[12] that, 'seeing they may see, and not perceive, and hearing they may hear, and not understand; lest at any time they should be converted, and their sins should be forgiven them.'"

There are two forms of teachings within most schools of religion and spirituality. These two forms comprise of the external (ethical) teaching, which we see in parables, fables, moral instruction and codes of conduct, which are given to the populace, laypeople and the general public; and then there are the internal teachings (mysteries) or a form of spiritual practice that is only made available to spiritual aspirants/students that are working closely and are of the inner ministry of the spiritual teacher. I will use Shakyamuni Buddha and Jesus of Nazareth as examples, the inner ministry or circle would be the spiritual master's students e.g. For Buddha are Buddhist monks and nuns, and for Jesus the Disciples, twelve apostles.

So, we understand from the above quotes in Matthew (7:6, 13:10-11, 13:34-35) and Mark (4:11-12), that what is being communicated to Jesus' disciples by Jesus are the two forms of teachings. Jesus is saying that the mysteries (Internal teachings) are only made available to his disciples, and the external teachings (ethics) are made available to both, his disciples, and the laypeople *("Because*

175

it is given unto you to know the mysteries of the Kingdom of Heaven, but to them it is not given.)

In Matthew (7:6), Jesus gives an analogy to explain this:

[6] *"Give not that which is holy unto the dogs, neither cast ye your pearls before swine, lest they trample them under their feet, and turn again and rend you.*

Jesus here makes an even clearer distinction and gives a clear reason why there are two forms of teachings. He makes a comparison and analogy to dogs and swine…but who are the dogs and who are the swine?

In today's culture it would seem somewhat discriminatory and insulting to compare humans to animals but given the time and culture that Jesus lived, this analogy would have been perfectly acceptable, albeit still insulting I imagine. The dogs that Jesus is referring to are those humans that are loving, loyal and obedient to the ethical teachings but do not have the education, ability or understanding at this stage of their development to comprehend the deeper spiritual practice of the (mysteries) the internal teachings, so for this reason they are not given them. You wouldn't expect a 6-year child to understand moral philosophy or quantum physics…

The swine are those humans that are living non-virtuous, base existences in vice and negativity. Humans that have no desire or want to live a virtuous, non-violent, or ethical existence. The pearls are the holy internal teachings, which would be cast aside, dismissed, or ridiculed, so for this reason the teachings are not given

– only the external teachings are given with hope that the individuals can listen and decide to change their immoral ways for more moral and ethical ways of living.

So, we have two very clear distinctions laid out here by a spiritual master and two rationales that underpin a teaching method that we see generally used throughout our general education systems and religious systems today. The education and religious systems deliver age and ability appropriate knowledge and instruction, which is also dependent on the student's desire and committed focus on developing their own education.

What is different now about the age in which we live compared to the time of Jesus, is that today the general populace and layperson is far more educated and has a greater level of general knowledge, understanding and comprehension of knowledge than the average person back in Jesus' time. With the development of technology, we have experienced since the post-war era from the 1950s to now is quite incredible. The rapid increase of knowledge and access to knowledge through the Internet and online media has changed our understanding of ourselves and experience of ourselves exponentially. Our ability to engage with, learn and assimilate information is greater now than it has ever been, resulting in the average person being able to absorb and understand knowledge quicker than ever before. We are in a new age, the 21st century is an age of knowledge and information access, the average person is no longer the 'dogs' of Jesus' age. In fact, I'd go so far as to say that the average person today, far exceeds the learned class of Jesus' age and the disciples of his time. Yes, there are still people in our time that live non-virtuous and violent lives, but the general education of the average person far greater. I wonder from an eschatological perspective that the future time of the 2nd coming of Christ is now in our time. I do not mean that there will be another messiah coming down to save us all, but again, let's look at the non-literal deeper meaning of Jesus' teachings, that the 2nd coming of Christ or Self-realisation/spiritual awakening is now to be experienced in our time by the masses that now have access, information, ability and means to achieve this. The 2nd coming isn't one person, the 2nd coming is us as a species achieving and working toward what only a small number (his disciples) were able to achieve back in Jesus' time...

So, how do we do this? What are these Internal teachings that we can all experience now?

To understand these internal teachings, we need to look at two forms of knowledge and practice – Yoga and the Kabbalah. Firstly, Yoga - today but also throughout history the practice and knowledge of Yoga has been integral within Eastern cultures and traditions. In modern times Yoga, especially within the West, is seen and practiced as a form of exercise to condition the body and promote wellbeing in the practitioner. If you google Yoga, you'll find many links to practitioners, websites, classes, and courses available to you. Ask the average person in the street what Yoga is, and they'll probably have no problem giving you a knowledgeable answer, in fact they may have even tried it or know someone that does it...

Medline Plus (2023), first link on Google search, define Yoga as:

Yoga is a practice that connects the body, breath, and mind. It uses physical postures, breathing exercises, and meditation to improve overall health. Yoga was developed as a spiritual practice thousands of years ago. Today most Westerners who do yoga do it for exercise or to reduce stress.

When we discuss the origin of Yoga, there are no definitive texts or links that give the exact origin of Yoga, but we do know that it has been practiced for thousands of years in Eastern cultures, linking to Hindu, Buddhist and Vedic spirituality, practice, and philosophy. At this point in time, there are a many different forms of Yoga that one can practice. These range from:

- **Ashtanga or power yoga**. This type of yoga offers a more demanding workout. In these classes, you quickly move from one posture to another.

- **Bikram or hot yoga**. You do a series of 26 poses in a room heated to 95°F to 100°F (35°C to 37.8°C). The goal is to warm and stretch the muscles, ligaments, and tendons, and to purify the body through sweat.

- **Hatha yoga**. This is sometimes a general term for yoga. It most often includes both breathing exercises and postures.

- **Integral**. A gentle type of yoga that may include breathing exercises, chanting, and meditation.

- **Iyengar**. A style that pays great attention to the precise alignment of the body. You may also hold poses for long periods of time.

- **Kundalini**. Emphasizes the effects of breath on the postures. The goal is to free energy in the lower body so it can move upward.

- **Viniyoga**. This style adapts postures to each person's needs and abilities, and coordinates breath and postures. (Medline Plus, 2023)

Even though we now have different forms of Yoga, especially in the West which tend to be more exercise focused, the traditional focus of Yoga and the four different paths of Yoga (1. Karma Yoga, 2. Bhakti Yoga, 3. Raja Yoga & 4. Jnana Yoga) were all practiced for the same goal – enlightenment and self-realisation. Again, this is still prevalent in certain Eastern schools e.g., Yoga Research Foundation and Sivananda Yoga, but is less understood or found in Western schools.

A classical form of the four paths of Yoga that still links to this deeper spiritual practice is Raja Yoga, the path of self-control. Raja Yoga is a traditional practice of Yoga that is a meditative form of spiritual attainment that involves a deeper understanding of your Self, the Body and Mind. It is through this deeper understanding and disciplined meditative practice that the practitioner can access the body's energy systems to connect to the higher spiritual levels, with the goal of *Samadhi*, enlightenment/spiritual awakening which is attained through the experiencing of *non-duality*.

Throughout Christian teachings and texts of the Bible we see inference and reference to processes and signifiers that link to this deep spiritual form of practice – the texts of the bible make claim to the human body and the process of divinity that can be experienced through spiritual engagement.

Romans (12:2)

I beseech you therefore, brethren, by the mercies of God, that ye present your bodies a living sacrifice, holy, acceptable unto God, which is your reasonable service.

[2] And be not conformed to this world but be ye transformed by the renewing of your mind, that ye may prove what is that good and acceptable and perfect will of God.

1 Corinthians (3:26-27)

[16] Know ye not that ye are the temple of God, and that the Spirit of God dwelleth in you?

[17] If any man defiles the temple of God, him shall God destroy. For the temple of God is holy, and ye are that temple.

1 Corinthians (6:19-20)

[19] What? Know ye not that your body is the temple of the Holy Ghost which is in you and which ye have from God, and that ye are not your own?

20 For ye are bought with a price. Therefore, glorify God in your body and in your spirit, which are God's.

1 Corinthians (12:25-27)

25 that there should be no schism in the body, but that the members should have the same care one for another.

26 And whenever one member suffers, all the members suffer with it; or when one member is honoured, all the members rejoice with it.

27 Now ye are the body of Christ, and members in particular.

Matthew (6:22)

22 "The light of the body is the eye. If therefore thine eye be single, thy whole body shall be full of light.

In Corinthians and Romans, Paul the apostle of Jesus, exclaims the need of the body to be a holy temple and vehicle of God. He explains the need to keep the body clean, non-defiled, so we can not only honour God but *glorify God in your body.* He tells us that we are the body of Christ.

Matthew, also, communicates God as the *light of the body* through a single eye and if we can achieve this, then our *whole body shall be full of light.*

Although, we don't necessarily take the literal meaning of spiritual teachings generally, due to the *mysteries* of the internal teachings, we can take elements of the literal – for in the blatantly obvious hides the inner truth – therefore to hide in plain sight. When we interpret these teachings from a Yoga perspective, we see a use of the body that links directly to the meditative form of Raja Yoga. In Yoga, the process 'to yoke' or bring together 'Union' to use the literal translation, we engage in an embodied physical practice that brings union and purification to the Body/Mind through the attainment of Spirit. In Corinthians (12:25) Paul is telling us that the body should be whole, the union of all parts. In Romans (12:1-2) Paul is telling us that our Body needs to be a *living sacrifice*, therefore alive and not dead, which we give over to Spirit (sacrifice to Spirit); he also tells us that the Mind needs to be renewed, therefore purified; if we can accomplish this with the Body and Mind then we can experience God, spiritual awakening. In Corinthians (6:19-20) Pauls explicitly tells us that God - the Holy Spirit - resides in us, within our Body and due to this our Body is the temple of God. Matthew (6:22) also tells us that when we experience God '*the light*', we do this through the single eye and the body being whole – in Yogic practice it is renown that when spiritual awakening and Self-realisation is experienced there is an internal flooding of bliss through the single eye (the third eye), which are experienced through the ajna chakra located in the pineal gland in the brain and the forehead chakra (the third eye), which is then experienced throughout the whole body.

I shall go into more in-depth discussion and presentation surrounding the actual practice and knowledge of the internal teachings in section three, but now let us move onto the other aspect of the internal teachings the Kabbalah.

Kabbalah, according to Rabbi Shaul Youdkevitch, the founder of the Live Kabbalah site which belongs to Universal Kabbalah Communities (2023) *'is a process of remembering knowledge already engraved on our souls'*. It's an ancient knowledge and practice that followers embrace as the Soul of Judaism, which underpins all aspects of knowledge ranging from the Bible, traditions, rituals, and stories.

Throughout history, Kabbalah was referred to as
"The mother of all Wisdoms" (Youdkevitch, 2023)

It's believed that Kabbalah was in fact the first knowledge of humanity, passed down by God to Adam through Adam's partaking of knowledge – the tree of life – that was then disseminated through Adam's line of heritage and family to Noah and his sons to Abram/Abraham and his sons, etc... If we go to the Bible, we see this presented in the book of Genesis. It's believed and discussed through the teachings and knowledge of Kabbalah (www.LiveKabbalah. org) that Abraham *the Patriarch*, over 4000 years ago, was in fact the first Kabbalist in history to pass on the knowledge in the form as we know it today. Not only did he pass on the knowledge but also established monotheism – the One God. Again, this is not the superficial Christian idea of one God sitting in Heaven ruling over but that All that there is, All that exists is One. Everything we know, every flower, plant, animal, human, life form organic and non-organic is All one – time and space All one – Heaven and Earth All one – we all came from One so therefore we are All One, we are All connected. Again, we experience separation, 'disconnection' in the Earth realm (dualism) but in fact this is an illusion that we need to overcome to experience Oneness. Abraham was one of the first spiritual teachers that experienced and asserted this, '*and which is expressed in every Kabbalah book, that evil is an illusion and that the origin of the Creation, and the world is good. Everything is an Image of God*' (livekabbalah, 2023).

Sound familiar?

This Universal knowledge, this universal 'knowing' is always the same irrespective of what culture, group, race, gender, class, and time/space of the person that experiences it. This Universal knowledge/experience – this spiritual awakening - is ubiquitous to all aspirants, students and disciples that achieve it, irrespective of what culture, group, or sect they belong to. Spiritual awakening is not dependent on one's social culture, race, class, or gender – it's dependent on one's spiritual development. The Universal Knowledge that is presented in Kabbalah is also found in Yoga, Buddhism, Hinduism, Sufism and Christianity yes, it gets presented in a particular way that is relevant to the language and culture of the time but the internal teachings – the inner knowledge – is always the same...

In Christianity we see this passed on from Moses, who presented this through the 'Ten Commandments, or as its stated in Kabbalah the 'Ten Utterances', who Moses got from Abraham's lineage, which made its way through Moses's lineage, which was passed onto the line of David, and which eventually found its way to Jesus of Nazareth (Christ). Jesus, one could argue (See Paul Kolberg

185

'Jesus & Kabbalah' & Migene Gonzalez-Whippler *'Jesus & the Mystic Kabbalah'*), was in fact a Kabbalist and the knowledge and practice he passed onto his disciples was his form of the Kabbalah. Now we don't know this for definite, but one can infer from Jesus' teachings, analysis of religious text including the Old and New Testament Bibles, the Gnostic Gospels, and the Nag Hammadi library and of course his Hebrew lineage that Jesus was bringing his own way of doing spirituality and religion to the masses. Let us not forget that Jesus was Jewish, so Jesus would have been taught and he lived within the knowledge and traditions of Judaism. We know from the New Testament texts that Jesus challenged and questioned the old traditions and ways of his religious heritage. In Mark (7, 11:27-33 & 15), Luke (20:1-8) and Matthew (15:1-20 & 21:23-27) we hear Jesus standing against religious authority and questioning his Elder's practices. However, Jesus states that he wasn't turning against Moses' teachings, in Matthew (17:3) and Luke (9:30) Jesus communes with the Spirit of the great prophets Moses and Elijah. What Jesus was doing was bringing a newer understanding that the masses (Jews and Non-Jews) were now ready for, and the Old structured forms of exclusivity, ritual, instruction and tradition were in need of 'refreshing', which Jesus was doing for the new age and times ahead...as Jesus said (Matthew 5:17) [17] *"Think not that I am come to destroy the Law or the Prophets. I am not come to destroy, but to fulfil.*

So, how was Jesus going to fulfil?

If, we are to believe that Jesus was a Kabbalist, and he incarnated to fulfil God's message, what was this actual message…what was Jesus the Kabbalist going to fulfil? What was the 'good news'?

In Kabbalah there is a deeper knowing, a deeper wisdom, that if connected to can bring awareness to and give answers to the deeper spiritual questions that humans have been asking since time immemorial. What is enlightening (that which shines a light on) about Kabbalah is that this knowledge, this understanding has always been with us – it's always been there *within* us.

Jesus, according to the Gospels of Matthew (4:17) and Mark (1:15), is telling us that there is a new time ahead and this time is God's Kingdom; and he (Jesus) is here to fulfil it, and all God is asking of you to receive this Kingdom is to repent.

> *Thou shalt love the Lord thy God with all thy heart, and*
> *with all thy soul, and with all thy mind. This is the first*
> *and greatest commandment. And the second is like unto*
> *it: Thou shalt love thy neighbour as thyself. On these*
> *two commandments hang all the laws and the prophets.*
> *Matthew 22: 36— 40*

That's it the 'be all and end all' of Jesus' teachings. To receive God's kingdom, repent your old ways and accept God and all will be well! How easy it that…

Well, that's the whole point, it is not as easy as that, and that's why we as humans struggle so much to understand the teaching, let alone receive the teaching and integrate it into our lives.

The ancient wisdom of Kabbalah, received by Adam and passed onto humanity is asking of us the same message Jesus taught all those lifetimes ago. The same message the ancient spiritual masters taught, that Buddha taught, that Rumi taught, that Dogen Zenji taught, that Juliana of Norwich taught, that Swami Vivekananda taught, that is still taught in certain Buddhist, Yoga, and Kabbalah centres today - that the way to spiritual awakening, self-realisation and enlightenment – the way to connect to our universal source of energy, *the Light*, God, All that there is – is through spiritual knowledge and spiritual practice of self-realisation – to know thyself.

To quote Robert Detzler, the founder of SRT (Spiritual Response Therapy):

> *Jesus, the great psychologist, fully understood the nature of being human as a being of consciousness...Jesus used parables to present the principles by which humans can direct their own lives with wisdom and understanding. The basic premise of all of Jesus' teachings is that we as beings of consciousness, are constantly receiving impressions from Spirit.*

Interestingly, Robert Detzler calls Jesus *'the great psychologist'*, and as beings of consciousness, therefore self-awareness, we are being given signs and markers *'receiving impressions'* from Spirit (Divine Source/God) to help us live a better life. Calling Jesus, a *psychologist* is very apt in our current age, given our age is an age of self-development, self-identity, and self-focus. In the West it's very common to visit a psychologist, psychiatrist, counsellor, or psychotherapist when things are not going so well; this might include relationship break-ups, bullying, bereavement, loss of job or identity and extreme forms of mental distress (psychosis), etc. It's very acceptable in today's culture to visit a therapist to help with all forms of mental ill-health. So, to call upon someone that can help you move from a state of incongruence, from psychological and emotional tension, from a place of distress, helplessness/hopelessness, from a place of *'darkness'* to a place of *'Light'* is very much a part of our current Western world. If you can move toward a deeper understanding of your feelings, thinking and behaviour to a place of *'knowing'*, in the psychological sense you are moving into a place of greater self-awareness, authenticity, congruence to a place of *knowing thyself.*

So, could Jesus' message be as simple as psychologically and emotionally knowing how we think, feel, and behave with the experience of being One with All, One with 'God-ness'... is this not Self-realisation...is this not spiritual enlightenment?

The wisdom of Kabbalah is that human beings need to take responsibility for their selves, it's written in the Zohar, a central Kabbalah text. As humans, if we are to fulfil our full potentials and achieve greatness, we must take time to examine ourselves and we must change our ways from self-centred egoistic living to more non-egoistic, harmonious, caring, other-centred ways of living, and so by doing we can achieve and experience our connection to the great source of our existence, we can experience *'the Light'*. To use a very

189

basic analogy, if the source of all existence is the main power supply and we are the light bulb, then we need to make sure that our circuitry to source, the power supply is not blocked, dirty, encumbered, or damaged in any way and to do this we need to examine it and maintain it. If it is damaged or dirty in some way, then we will not get a clean source of energy and the bulb won't shine to its maximum capacity. So, if we compare this to us, we need to make sure that the body and mind are clean from damage and dirt on a physical, psychological and emotional level, if we can keep them clean (free from impurities) then we'll be able to receive and have a strong connection to our live source, our ultimate energy source, therefore to *the Light*, God, All that there is, to Divine Consciousness – this is what Jesus was teaching and this is what the Kabbalah teaches too.

Kabbalah, in our current time, has had a welcomed resurgence, so I'd suggest looking further into this ancient knowledge and practice by visiting www.livekabbalah.org which is founded by the spiritual teacher Rabbi Shaul Youdkevitch. For those in the UK please visit the London Kabbalah Centre www.kabbalah.com founded by Rav Berg and continued through Yehuda, Michael, and Monica Berg.

Jalāl ad-Dīn Muḥammad Rūmī, aka Rumi

When we think of poetry, especially in the West, we perhaps think of Wordsworth, Keats, Shakespeare, Walt Whitman, Shelley, Rossetti and maybe even Chaucer, great poets that conveyed depth, mystery, passion, pathos, imagery, thought, rhythm, and tone.

But how many of us think outside of our 20th Century Western culture?

Yes, you may be familiar with, or know of, historic European poets like Homer, Dante, Goethe, or Baudelaire, but how many of you have heard of Li Bai, Omar Kayyam or Matsuo Bashō? Unless, you have a deep interest in poetry or poets, I don't imagine you would have...I didn't know who these poets were until I started researching them. However, I did know of one 12th century poet from outside the modern Western world, and I'm wondering if you have also heard of him too? Yes, I'm talking about Rumi or to give him his full name Jalāl ad-Dīn Muḥammad Rūmī.

Probably, the most famous mystic and Sufi poet of all time, Rumi was born on the 30th of September 1207 in Wakhsh (modern Tajikistan) under the Balkh administration on the Eastern Persian Empire. His family was of learned scholars and theologians who travelled around the Muslim lands until they settled in Konya, capital of the Turkish Selijuq dynasty, in 1228, after a pilgrimage to Mecca and extensive journeys around the country. Rumi's father Bahā' al-Dīn was offered a position at one of the learned theological schools, whom Rumi, at age 24, succeeded after the death of his father in 1231. Ten years later, Rumi, confirmed his position as 'king of religious scholars' taking the mantle from his father and being fully embraced and accepted by the learned and lay communities alike.

Rumi's beliefs and practice, like his father's, were based in Muslim law and ideology but Rumi's focus and main practice lay within Sufism, the mystical and ascetic practice of experiencing God.

> Chittick (2005) states: Sufism is the most universal manifestation of the inner dimension of Islam; it is the way by which man transcends his own individual self and reaches God.

It is thought that Rumi had many experiences with Sufi spiritual teachers, but it wasn't until he met the wandering Sufi Shams al-Dīn of Tabriz, in 1244 at the age of 37, that Rumi's life would change forever.

There are many stories around the relationship between Rumi and Shams the wandering Sufi dervish, but the overarching consensus is that Shams had a profound and life changing effect on Rumi. After their meeting Rumi's focus changed from the scholarly preaching of theology to the mystical and poetic. It is said that Shams and Rumi would Sufi-dance and sing for hours in states of ecstasy in the streets embracing and connecting to the divine love of God. We don't know for certain what Shams taught Rumi, if he taught him anything at all, but Shams did break the religious dogma of the time through his passionate belief in the power of Love over everything – according to Shams love was the ultimate expression of the source of All and the foundation of life itself. It was their relationship that sparked the divine connection and helped Rumi's flourishing and prolific output of divine poetry, prose, and spiritual teachings, which is still held to high regard today.

It is said that Rumi and Shams spent many months together, to the exclusion and possible abandonment of Rumi's students and family, which left a bitter rift and much animosity toward Shams, finally causing Shams to move to Syria in February 1246. This of cause, as one could imagine, left Rumi in a state of grief and deep sadness, missing his brotherhood, friendship, and spiritual connection with Shams, he was lost and heartbroken...Rumi's son, Sultan Walad, seeing the distress and pain his father was in finally got reprieve for Shams and brought him back from Syria. However, the family's and Rumi's disciples' prejudice and jealousy, could not be abated and one-night Shams disappeared in 1247, never to be seen again. Rumour has it that Shams was probably murdered by Rumi's disciples, but there is no written documentation or evidence of this officially.

For the rest of Rumi's life, he spent composing, writing, and teaching. His grief for Shams was profound and resulted in a major work 'Divan-i Shams-i Tabrizi' (The works of Shams) made up of over 40,000 verses and 3,000 ghazals, the themes of love, longing, and the divine connection so key to Rumi's works, are worked throughout 'Divan-I Shams-I Trabizi' as they are in his other major texts. A notable aspect of the composition of the ghazals (odes) is linked to the Sufi-dance, or 'whirling dervish' that Rumi engaged in to connect to the Divine through the meditative trance-like state of spinning. His other major works consist of his six-book epic poem 'Masnavi' or 'Mathnawi' that also looks at love, longing and the Divine but we also experience deeper teachings on mysticism, Sufism, and ethics. His third major work is Fihi ma fihi (It is what it is) a collection of lectures, sermons, and conversations Rumi had with his disciples, which were compiled and written down by his disciples, for Rumi didn't write this collection himself.

Rumi died on 16th December 1273 and following his death the order of Mevlevi was founded by his most fervent and trusted disciples. The order, over 750 years old, remains today and Rumi is celebrated and honoured throughout their practice but most markedly in the annual weeklong Sema, or Sama ceremony, where the order engage in dance, music and singing to connect to the Divine presence, and remember their founding father, Jalāl ad-Dīn Muḥammad Rūmī.

So, what can we learn from Rumi and his prolific writing and teachings?

To understand Rumi, we first need to look at his spiritual practice, Sufism.

According to Dr, Ahmadi (2023):

> *Sufism is based on the notions of self-purification, abstinence, discovery of truth through spiritual training, and reliance on self-control. At this stage heart is purified from all forms of turbidity, and the*

Divine light, by way of emanation, is reflected in one's being, and the invisible becomes visible in the immediate spiritual experience and all the veils are removed... Sufism is neither a specific religion nor a system of thought separable from all the other systems of thought. It may be said that its basis is pure monotheism and the notion that everyone can communicate with God as it has been said:

الطرق إلى الله بعدد نفوس الخلائق.

The ways to God are as many as the number of human beings. In other words, every heart opens an avenue leading to God.

So, from the offset we can begin to understand that Sufism, the practice of Rumi, is based within a process of purification, self-discipline, and a continued commitment to spiritual training. Like Yoga, one could argue, is the ultimate desired outcome of unification with God. What is also notable is the realisation of God, of the Divine light is through the embodied experience of the practitioner, and as Dr. Ahmadi states *the 'invisible becomes visible in the immediate spiritual experience and all the veils are removed'.* We see a similar understanding within Kabbalah, by overcoming one's ego-states, God *the Divine Light*, can be experienced. However, what is beautifully concluded with Dr. Ahmadi's understanding is the embracing and pointing toward the inclusivity, uniqueness of individual experience and the uniqueness of the spiritual student's personal returning to God; yet the doorway to the

Divine Light to God is universally the same for all – through the opening of our hearts.

If we look at this further there are three aspects to Sufism and the process of Sufi-training and spiritual practice: Shari'ah, Tariqah and Haqiqah.

> *Shari'ah as a term means the religious commands conveyed by God through the Prophet (S) to his people, by his words or actions, to properly regulate and manage their affairs in this world and the Hereafter…Since the Shari`ah is a manifestation of God's benevolence, which is common to all, God Almighty has benefited the entire humanity by sending His messengers to all of them…According to Sharh-e gulshan-e raz, the Shari `ah comprises the Law governing outward behaviour and serves as the outer shell.* (Ahmadi, 2023)

So, Shari'ah are the external laws of God that were passed down to the Prophet for the benefit and affairs of humanity. Shari'ah are the exoteric (outer) aspects of Islamic law and require the follower to accept and submit to these laws by verbal declaration. The other aspect is the esoteric (inner), which is first accompanied by the exoteric, that is the unique and individualised experiencing of God through one's open heart and embodied experience which forms true reality.

The basis of Shari'ah is the identification of the (absolute) truth, which is only possible through self-realization: (one who knows his own self also acquires the knowledge of God). One of the traditions in al-hadith al-Qudsi states:

كنت كنزا مخفياً فأحببت أن أعرف فخلقت الخلق لكى أعرف

I (God) was a hidden treasure, and I desired to be known. I, therefore, resorted to the act of creation, so that I may be known. (Ahmadi, 2023)

If Shari'ah is the beginning of the student's spiritual journey, the acknowledgment of the path, then Tariqah is the walking of the path, the practice that is undertaken by the trainee Sufi toward attainment of self-realisation.

A disciple who resorts to remembrance of God by the way of worship, prepares himself to rise to the next stage called Tariqah, or the Sufi Path. The Quran declares:

وَالَّذِينَ جَاهَدُوا فِينَا لَنَهْدِيَنَّهُمْ سُبُلَنَا

As for those who strive in Us, We surely guide them to Our paths ..(29:69)

The conditions essential for Shari'ah are sincerity (ikhlas) and true faith (Iman); those who reach this stage are ready to move on to the path of spiritual progress (sayr wa suluk) and are able to attain

197

spiritual and moral purification. The condition for advancing on this path is to have a guide, as the poet says:

طی این مرحله بی همرهی خضر مکن

ظلمات است بترس از خطر

Do not go on this path without the companionship of Khidr (guide). For it is a dark region; Beware of the danger of getting lost. (Ahmadi, 2023)

Here, as in other spiritual schools e.g., Buddhism, Yoga, Kabbalah, we are warned that the spiritual path, is not an easy path. The path of the spiritual aspirant is fraught with challenges and hardships, so having a guide, a spiritual master to assist and support along the way is essential if we are to succeed. If we have the support, fortitude, belief, and commitment then our destination is Haqiqah, self-realisation and experiencing of the Divine.

> *Shari `ah is the recognition of the path towards God, whereas Tariqah is treading that path through self-purification and by traversing the stages of detachment (tahhliyah), adornment (tahliyah), and enlightenment (tajliyah), and consequently crossing the `seven valleys,' viz. yearning (talab), love (`ishq), gnosis (`irfan), contentment (istighna'), Divine Unity (tawhid), perplexity (hayrah), and poverty and self-annihilation (faqr wa fana').*

Haqiqah or realization of the Absolute Truth is arrival at the ultimate destination, which is nearness to God and vision of His rububiyyah (Lordship). According to al-Lahiji, Haqiqah is the unveiled manifestation of the Divine Essence, achieved after disappearance of the mists of all distinctions and false plurality by the light emanating from the Divine Essence.

It is said that the first stage of Haqiqah is shuhud (witnessing of the Divine Reality), and its last stage is annihilation of the finite self in God (fana' fi Allah). Thereafter comes the stage of attaining eternity with God (baqa' bi Allah). In the same way as the Words of God are unlimited, so also the stages of realization of Haqiqah. (Ahmadi, 2023)

This is the ultimate teaching and message that Rumi is sharing with us. For we must not forget, yes Rumi was inclusive and accepting of many differences in race and religion, but first and foremost Rumi was a Muslim who devoutly followed Islam and the words of the Prophet; so, to overlook this, to miss this is to miss Rumi and the deep love and expression of God that is Islam. What Rumi was sharing through the beauty, depth and wonder of his poetry, prose, and teachings, is that we must accept and follow Shari'ah, we must walk and practice Tariqah, and then finally as Rumi himself experienced, achieve the ultimate destination of Haqiqah, the lifting of the veil of darkness to experience the oneness with the Divine through nonduality. We can experience the *Divine Light*, as Shams (his beloved) so profoundly realised the experience that is Universal Love.

Juliana of Norwich

There is not much written or known about the life, education, or family of Juliana of Norwich before she took anchorage. We know she was born in 1343 and lived in the city of Norwich, an important city of the time, second only to London in respect to commerce, religion, and culture. In 1348-1350 Norwich, the Medieval city of England, suffered terribly from the bubonic plague or 'Black-Death', which caused high death rates and devastation to villages, towns, and cities; we know that Juliana of Norwich would have witnessed and lived through this terrible pandemic. We know that in 1373, at the age of 30, Juliana was taken very ill, she and others were convinced that she would surely die from the illness. However, this is where the life of Juliana of Norwich changes forever. On her deathbed, Juliana, experienced a succession of visions, or as she would call them 'shewings', over a period of a few hours in one night, and the last one being a day later, of Jesus the Christ. These consisted of sixteen visions or 'shewings' of the passion of Jesus Christ through his crucifixion and his sufferings. These 'shewings' profoundly changed Juliana, not only did she fully recover from her illness but from that point forward she vowed to take anchorage (withdrawing from ordinary secular life) into a small monastic cell, next to the Church of St Julian, to devote her services to God and to Jesus Christ through prayer and ascetism.

So, what can we learn from Juliana of Norwich?

There are many lessons we can take from the lifestyle and experiences of Juliana of Norwich, even before we delve into her book the *'Revelations of Divine Love'*. The first example that Juliana presents to us is the power and presence of spirituality, of a powerful divinity that can be experienced by the human being, and not only experienced but a healing power, a power to right what is being wronged. Juliana of Norwich was at death's door at the age of 30, she was close to receiving her final rights by the clergyman; yet something happened, something intervened that infused her body and mind with great healing, something far greater than her corporeal being...from her visions or 'shewings' a divine presence engaged with Juliana through which she experienced the healing of her body and mind. She tells us of her experience through her 'divine revelations' how God through the appearance of Christ's passion opened her eyes, her body, her mind, her heart to an experience of divine power. How she, a mortal woman, felt, sensed, experienced, and lived the presence of Divine being through the sixteen 'shewings', the sixteen-experiential lived 'embodied experiences' of Juliana of Norwich connecting to a higher power, the power of her eternal God, the son Jesus Christ, and the Holy Spirit – the Trinity.

How can we believe this experience?

It can be hard to accept and appreciate the religious and spiritual experiences of a single person, especially in our current age where evidence based scientific proof and research dominates. To take on face value the experiences or 'shewings' of a 14th century person does require us to suspend 'rational belief' but perhaps that is the whole point, and why Juliana of Norwich's *'Revelations of Divine Love'* is so relevant today where the mystical, the mysterious, the spiritual has lost its wonder, its power, its healing to a superficial commodity that gets bought and sold through the media of our global markets…

Through her experience Juliana of Norwich is telling us that God/Divine Presence is alive and not only is God alive, but God is also alive in every single one of us. Juliana is 'shewing' us that this power, this presence is not a thing to be bought and sold, it's not a superficial commodity that should be taken lightly. Juliana's experience through God's divine presence, an extra-ordinary experience that can heal, that can change our existence and life forever, is to be revered, respected but ultimately loved. The experience and the power of the divine can reunite us, re-integrate us with all that is good in ourselves and the world, and is available to us all. I'm not talking of resurrection in the physical sense or prolonging life. Physical death through divine providence is our time to die when it is our time to die. Existentially we are all born to die, this is our inevitability, this is the gift of birth; yet due to our sense of disconnection from the Divine we spend most of lives trying to avoid, distort or delude ourselves from our divine providence of accepting the finiteness of our body and mind that we cling to so tightly. Juliana of Norwich is telling us otherwise. Juliana of Norwich is telling us, is 'shewing' us, that our death is not dependent on our belief in the mortal finite realm, our death is Divine providence, as the passion of Christ shows us. Our death, our mortal sense of death (the death of the body and mind) is dependent on the Source of All, that source we all originated from, and that omnipresent, omniscient, and omnipotent source of All exists and is the essence of all of us.

Why should we fear death? Why should we fear the death of the body and mind?

What are we so afraid of?

Juliana is telling us, is 'shewing us' through her visions, that death is transitory; yes, the body and mind will die but what is left after the organic body stops and the associated mind platform is switched off, is the essence of who we are - this is who we really are. God, Divine Love, helped Juliana of Norwich, facilitate her ability to heal, bringing her back from her mortal death's door to deliver this message. A message that reminds us of who we truly are. If we are to understand the *'Resurrection'*, the *'Passion of Christ'*, if we are to grasp the process and meaning of the *'Resurrection'*, and the *'Passion'* which is associated with the death of Jesus the Christ; we are to believe that Jesus came back to life after dying through crucifixion on the cross, and then to be seen three days later by some of his disciples. Again, let us not get side-tracked and hood-winked by the literal meaning of the teaching, we are looking for the deeper symbolic meaning here…

The symbolic process *of 'resurrection'* of *'Christ's passion'* is quite simply this…through the process of spiritual growth we understand that the body, the mind is not who we really are…when we are able to transcend the carnal egoistic association with the body/mind (corporeal existence) through our *'travail'* , our passionate work, our spiritual practice then we lift the veil of illusion, our darkness goes and we experience our connection to All that there is, the Light – we remember who we really are. Juliana of Norwich is 'shewing' us this through her 'revelations of Divine Love', to remember who we truly are, to remember that our Source, our Home is Love and is eternal. Juliana is reminding us of this, she is asking us to remember this through the example of her experience but also the example of the great spiritual master Jesus too. The spiritual path is not an easy path, it is bitter at the start, it takes work, commitment, courage, and passion but is always sweet at the end. The carnal egoistic path feels sweet at the start but is always bitter at the end…how many people in our worlds follow the egoistic paths only to feel 'hungrier', more 'lost', more 'isolated', more in pain…as they constantly go round and round the 'pleasure/pain' cycle of their lives falling deeper into 'darkness' and 'delusion' as their body suffers, as their mental health suffers…

Juliana is not asking you to become an ascetic monk or to take hermitage isolating yourself from the rest of the world. Even though in practice Dame Juliana did this, she never turned away from those

204

that sort her guidance, her counsel, her love. She opened her heart to all those that needed her and she did this through her spiritual role, the religious pathway that was available to her at the time. Who knows if she'd been alive today, if the essence of Juliana of Norwich is alive today incarnated as another, she may be doing this in a very different way. What we learn from Juliana of Norwich and her teachings is that ultimately our spiritual essence, God, Divine Presence, Our Source of All, call it what you will, never leaves us and in our times of despair, pain and deep suffering is there for us if we can but only ask for help and support. If we can call unto ourselves, our true Being will answer us, will 'shew' us the way forward.

Swami Vivekananda

Born as Narendranath Datta on the 12th of July 1863 to an aristocratic Bengali family in Calcutta; Swami Vivekananda was one of the most influence and prominent figures in the religious and secular world of his time.

His talents started at an early age, and it wasn't long before he was impressing and bringing attention to his scholarly, musical, and physical prowess. This was first evident, in 1879, as he was the only student to achieve first-division marks in the Presidency College entrance exam. His reading ability astonished his teachers, and he had a ferocious appetite for many subjects including religion, philosophy, social sciences, history, literature, art, and music; not excluding Hindu scriptures. In 1881, he passed a fine arts exam and achieved a Bachelor of Arts degree in 1884 studying Western logic, Western philosophy, and European history at the General Assembly's Institute.

From the natural outgrowth of his study and learning, Vivekananda finally came to the question that had been slowly percolating behind his ferocious desire for knowledge – how to experience God? After asking prominent religious figures in and around Calcutta and not being satisfied with an answer, it wasn't until he met the mystic Ramakrishna that he felt he was getting closer. The pursuing years between 1881 and 1884, were challenging times resulting in dissatisfaction, tension, and loss for Vivekananda. His religious beliefs were challenged by Ramakrishna and his economic and family stability was challenged by the loss of his father and their financial welfare. After a visit to pray at the temple of Kali, by suggestion of Ramakrishna, Vivekananda found himself not praying for material welfare but for ultimate knowledge, truth, and Godly devotion, which signalled the adoption of Ramakrishna as his spiritual guru. His spiritual education continued with Vivekananda and Ramakrishna's other disciples finally achieving samadhi, resulting in the acceptance of their ochre robes and the founding of Ramakrishna's monastic order. In 1885 Ramakrishna developed throat cancer and sadly died in August 1886, leaving his monastic order to the leadership of Vivekananda by request, after instructing Vivekananda to look after his disciples. On the Christmas eve of 1886, after Ramakrishna's death, Vivekananda and eight other disciples, took formal monastic vows.

From 1888 to 1893 Vivekananda took the life of a wandering monk and travelled extensively around India, meeting with rajas (Kings and royalty), government officials, academics, Hindus, Muslims, Christians, Dewans, people from high, middle, and low caste…He met with religious and lay people from all walks of life challenging the existing social caste system he had been brought up in. A significant meeting that developed into a close friendship was with Ajit Singh of Khetri, ruler of the Shekhawat estate. Ajit Singh, after their first meeting in 1891, became a disciple of Vivekananda and financially supported his family and religious prowess in India and in the West. It was Ajit Singh that first suggested that Vivekananda go to Chicago America to speak at the Parliament of the world's religions in 1893. It was also Ajit Singh that proposed that the then Narendranath change his name to 'Swami Vivekananda' (the bliss of discerning wisdom) before he left for Chicago.

On the 11[th of] September 1893 Vivekananda made his first step onto the Western stage at the Parliament of world religions in Chicago America and was an instant success. The American press praised and acclaimed Vivekananda for his knowledge, presence, oratory, and representation of the theme of universal acceptance and inclusivity. From that point forward he proved himself in the West, lecturing around America and Europe, and founding the first Vedanta Society in New York in 1894. Returning to India in 1897, he was hailed for his global success and founded the Ramakrishna mission and met with leading religious scholars, teaching and working tirelessly. He made one more trip to the West in 1889 until he retired Back in India in 1900, finally settling in Belur Math to continue the work of the Ramakrishna mission. Sadly in 1901 due to declining health, he was unable to attend the 1901 Congress of religions in Japan, yet still presented a ferocious verve for life and religion, forever sharing his passion and desire to aid other's growth and development through his work and pilgrimages. This was no more evident than with his disciples and pupils at the Belur monastery. Yet physical incarnation was to be short for Vivekananda, an intensely bright light that burnt briefly. After a day of teaching, Vivekananda retired to his room in the evening for meditation and then died of a brain bleed on the 4th ^{of} July 1902. It is said that his disciples believed that Vivekananda had finally achieved *Mahāsamādhi,* the great and final *samādhi* that a yogi master realises by exiting his body and attaining enlightenment at the moment of the body's death. Vivekananda was 39 years old.

So, what can we learn from this great yogi master?

At the heart of Swami Vivekananda was religion, not an organised, bureaucratic, administrative system of hierarchy that tries to govern the populace but an ethical, transcendental, personal and universal way of existing that not only supports and constitutes a progressive way of life but also that unites and brings joy, wisdom, courage, and peace. Swami Vivekananda proposed a compelling argument for religion and for spiritual life, as the foundation of human individuality, knowledge, and society. The end of the 19th century and the beginning of the 20th century was seeing the age of modernism, objective thinking, and the sciences to assist humanity's development and happiness. Swami Vivekananda was asking the people of the time to consider religion as a science, as the greatest and healthiest scientific exercise of the human mind based in human knowledge, experience, and practice. If the pursuit of happiness and pleasure from the utilitarian perspective is humanity's goal, then religion/spirituality is the highest attainment of this goal. For Swami Vivekananda the search for the infinite, the Oneness of the Absolute is the highest attainment of the human experience, so therefore his argument for religion, if grounded in this utilitarian pursuit founded on scientific means, seems obvious and necessary by cultivating religious and spiritual thought, knowledge, and exercise for the individual and society to achieve.

Yet, how is one to do this?

Swami Vivekananda was a yogi master. His religion, his spirituality, his knowledge, his intellect, his practiced is based, is grounded within Hindu philosophy and religion and yoga philosophy and practice.

> *According to Yoga philosophy, it is through ignorance that the soul has been joined with nature. The aim is to get rid of nature's control over us. That is the goal of all religions. Each soul is potentially divine. The goal is to manifest this Divinity within, by controlling nature, external and internal. Do this either by work, or worship, or psychic control, or philosophy — by one or more or all of these — and be free. This is the whole of religion. Doctrines, or dogmas, or rituals, or books, or temples, or forms, are but secondary details.*

The above quote in essence sums up the whole of Swami Vivekananda's approach to spirituality and religion. He advocated through his teachings the various levels of religion and spirituality as outlined in the Hindu scriptures, yoga philosophy and how to achieve Self-realisation. He wrote and lectured extensively on the four main pathways of yoga: Karma (work), Raja (self-control), Jnana (philosophy) and Bhakti (devotion). He understood the value of and the learning that could be gained from religious scriptures, books, rituals, and temples but ultimately, he saw these as a means to an end - the end being self-realisation - and not the end in themselves as some dogmatic religious groups preach, evangelise and enforce through their religions in Temples, Mosques and Churches.

What stands out for those that engage and read his works and what we but get a secondary glimpse of, is his self-belief, presence, authority, and love. His ability to understand, interpret, analyse, synthesise, and then deliver the teachings to all that are willing to open their hearts is testament to his devotion to humanity. Swami Vivekananda was a tireless worker, philosopher, worshipper, practitioner, and teacher. His admirers, disciples and students can only speak of great praise of their spiritual teacher. In his day, the East and the West loved him equally, and hailed him a great yogi.

Although Swami Vivekananda has been praised and recognised as one of India's most influential social reformers, he has been criticised by scholars, religious leaders, and socio-political modern

Indian reformers. He has been labelled as a neo-Vedanta, neo-Hinduist, Hindu-Universalist and has been criticised for Westernising the Hindu religion and not acknowledging British colonialism. In our current times, these criticisms and arguments are easily qualified and are valued points in any progression of social development. However, some of these criticisms and arguments are based in philosophical and religious fundamentalism and fanaticism. This book is not a platform for academic and religious discussion per say, or a supporter of fundamentalism and fanaticism, if you wish to look further into these criticisms, discussions, and areas of fanaticism and socio-political reformation, I'd suggest doing your own research but please engage with caution, discernment and with a critical objective mindset. Fundamentalism and fanaticism in any name, shape, and form only harbours exclusion, suffering and hatred. This sadly is the shadow-side of ideology, philosophy, and religion, which is based in fear, disguised as love but delivers an exclusive blow of hate. The complete opposite and antithesis of the heart of all the great religions of this world.

Like all the great spiritual teachers before him, Swami Vivekananda stood and expressed from a position of tolerance, inclusivity, and love. His passion, knowledge, and vitality for life shines through clearly and coherently in all his works, and his ability to engage and communicate to people from all walks of life again signifies his place among the great spiritual teachers of the past. He came to 'fulfil' the Universal message and to show that once again there are many roads to the Universal, the Source, God, All that there is, and it is through our committed work, our committed devotion, our developing knowledge and our committed building of character that we will realise Self/Brahman.

The Dalai Lama – number 14:

The Dalai Lamas are believed by Tibetan Buddhists to be manifestations of Avalokiteshvara or Chenrezig, the Bodhisattva of Compassion and the patron saint of Tibet. Bodhisattvas are realized beings, inspired by the wish to attain complete enlightenment, who have vowed to be reborn in the world to help all living beings.

www.dalialama.com

The current Dalia Lama is Tenzin Gyatso. Who was born on the 6th of July 1935 at a small village in Taktser in northeast Tibet, to a local farming family. He is the 14th reincarnation of the Dalia Lama and precedes the 13th Dalai Lama, Thubten Gyatso. The tradition of recognition and manifestation of the Dalai Lama officially began in the 15th century with Gedun Gyatso being accepted and confirmed as the reincarnation of Gedun Drub, this established the institution and we have seen continued reincarnations since. It wasn't until the third, Sonam Gyatso, was recognised that the official name of Dalia Lama was accepted. The Dalai Lamas have both functioned as the spiritual and political leader of Tibet, which was created in 1642 by

212

the fifth, Dalai Lama, Ngawang Lobsang Gyatso. However, on 14th March 2011, Tenzin Gyatso, his 14th Holiness, changed this tradition with the retirement of political office and recognition of the Dalai Lama taking this political role, breaking a 368-year tradition.

> *After coming into exile, I have made sincere efforts to establish a democratic system of governance in the last more than 30 years. The Tibetans in exile say, "our democracy is a gift from His Holiness the Dalai Lama." Ten years ago, the system of electing Kalon Tripa through democratic elections was introduced rather than nomination of the candidate by the Dalai Lama, which was not correct. Since the direct election of Kalon Tripa, the system of the institution of Gaden Phodrang of the Dalai Lama as both the spiritual and temporal authority has ended. Since then, I described myself as in semi-retired position.*

> *Dalai Lama*

To resolve any concerns and fears that the Tibet institute of Goden Phodrang would be ending imminently with the handing over of the political position, His Holiness comforts:

> *Those of you from Tibet when you return and if there are people to whom you can confide then tell this to them. This may also be broadcast on the radio as well. I have made this decision to retire after giving thorough thought over it for years and years and for*

213

the ultimate benefit of Tibet. There is no reason at all for you to be disheartened. On the other hand, Ganden Phodrang is not being shut down. Ganden Phodrang is the institution of the Dalai Lamas and as long as I live, I will need a small institution. So, this Ganden Phodrang will still remain. What is happening is that Ganden Phodrang is relinquishing its political responsibilities.

This decision marked a landmark point in the responsibilities and governance of the role of the Dalai Lama, changing his position from a political and spiritual leader to focusing only on the spiritual leadership role. The handing over to a democratic government was an egalitarian and utilitarian process of peace that is believed to help all Tibetan people bringing stability, security, and power to the general people – keeping in-line with Buddhist non-violent values and ethical beliefs.

There are considered three main commitments of being the Dalai Lama:

1. The first is the promotion of a humanitarian belief in happiness and living a good life. Helping people understand secular ethics and universal values and how these translate into the need to develop compassion, peace, understanding, tolerance, forgiveness for self and others through the focused self-discipline of self-development.

2. Secondly, through his being a Buddhist monk, he is advocating and presenting a committed belief to universal

harmony, unity, and inclusivity. He recognises that at the heart of all religions is the universal source to help humans to become better humans and promotes acceptance and collaboration of all religious groups and traditions to promote and support this process.

3. Thirdly, as a Tibetan citizen, the Dalai Lama wishes and supports his fellow Tibetan's welfare, culture, heritage, language, and trust. This commitment to his fellow Tibetan's is unquestioned and serves as a primary role of his spiritual and humanitarian office.

Most recently, the Dalia Lama has promoted a renewed interest into Indian philosophical traditions and practice. He believes that the ancient traditions focusing on meditation, mental, emotional, and physical training have a huge benefit to everyday society. If this is incorporated into academic and modern educational systems, it can enhance wellbeing and benefit the contemporary social world. A belief I whole-heartedly share and promote through my own study, work, and day-to-day practice.

So, what can we learn from the Dalai Lama?

Like all Buddhist monks and followers of Buddhism, there is a strong advocacy and belief in living a non-violent life of compassion, acceptance and understanding of the human and non-human experience We are being shown a way, we are being given an example of how to live a more harmonious, caring, loving and compassionate existence. If we work hard at developing, embodying, and living the universal ethics Buddhism promotes, we not only have the possibility to live a good personal life, but we can promote and develop a good harmonious social world as well. The Dalai Lama is the embodied human advocate of this as realised through Chenrezig, the Boddhisatva of compassion.

In 1989, the Dalai Lama was awarded the Noble Peace prize. His tireless efforts and commitment to promoting the non-violence of Buddhism, especially relating to the liberation of his home country Tibet. Again, highlighting the example the Dalai Lama sets before us. Although primarily a religious/spiritual leader, we can also learn from his ability like all great spiritual teachers, to transcend different disciplines and traditions to unite, advocate and collaborate for the good of humanity. This is clear through the dialogues, discussions, and research that the Dalai Lama has engaged with in the sciences, academia, the medical world, and social sciences.

So, what is unique about the Dalai Lama in this lifetime?

The difference that comes with this Dalai Lama and spiritual teacher, is that he is alive and embodied in our current time. We have first-hand opportunity to engage with this great spiritual advocate. He has a website, he has written many, many books, he's on social media, he has a press office, he has live webcasts – he even has a twitter account and is active on it most days. How good is that! We have the possibility to engage with him, read his actual words, listen to his voice, see him in action, a uniqueness and luxury that isn't afforded with some of the past spiritual teachers. You can go to his website now and click on his schedule and see where he's teaching next. He is here in our times, for us right now...so, why not take the chance and opportunity to engage with this great teacher, to hear and experience what he has to offer and share while he is still with us...

Will he be the last Dalai Lama?

When asked this question, his Holiness replied with uncertainty. He said that the next Dalai Lama depends solely on the decision of the Tibetan people. Back in 1969, he was presenting the idea that democracy was the way forward for Tibet regarding politics and for the institution of the Dalai Lama. He said in interview:

> *If I were to die today, I think the Tibetan people would choose to have another Dalai Lama. In the future, if the Dalai Lama's institution is no longer relevant or useful and our present situation changes, then the Dalai Lama's institution will cease to exist. Personally, I feel the institution of the Dalai Lama has served its purpose.*

Whatever the future for the institution of the Dalai Lama, we have among us today a leader of great spiritual worth. A leader that promotes peace, love, understanding and compassion to all, and like all great spiritual teachers he offers us an example of how better to live in our world.

Master Choa Kok Sui

On the 15th of August 1952, Choa Kok Sui, was born to a wealthy business orientated Chinese family in Cebu city in the southern district of the Philippines. Not one to play with toys or hang out with other children of his age, he was always found with his head in a book digesting all the knowledge he could get his hands on and learning as much as he could about spirituality, science, and healing. This desire and engagement with study and learning lasted throughout his whole life and accumulated into the current global business and healing organisation, Master Choa developed, known as Pranic healing, with the accompanied synthesised form of practice and philosophy of Arhatic yoga.

For the last 30 years, Master Choa, has written and published over 27 books worldwide, worked tirelessly in researching his pranic healing systems, and supported thousands of people around the globe. His vision and focus have been to unify and bring together Eastern and Western disciplines, philosophy, science and healing to offer a scientifically valid form of healing that can be used and practiced worldwide. Master Choa's teachings and healing systems are continued on through the World Pranic Healing Foundation (WPHF), Institute of Inner Studies, Pranic Healing associations around the world and through all the thousands of pranic healers and practitioners that work around the globe. On March 19th, 2007, Master Choa Kok Sui, left his physical body and passed, leaving a wonderful legacy and healing system for us all.

Today Grand Master Choa Kok Sui's Pranic Healing®
and Spiritual Workshops circle the globe in the United
States, Central and South America, India, Western and
Eastern Europe, Asia, Africa, Middle East, Canada,
Australia and elsewhere and are touching people's
lives resulting in the "will to do good" and formation
of Pranic Healing® Centers, Foundations and
Institutes with thousands of teachers and tens of
thousands of Pranic Healers and Arhatic Yoga
practitioners. The validity of Grand Master Choa's
teachings is attested to by graduates everywhere, men
and women from every walk of life, who have
successfully improved their health and well-being as
well as their spiritual growth.

www.thepranichealers.com

So, what can we learn from Master Choa Kok Sui?

Master Choa Kok Sui had an ability to traverse the social world and its many forms of communication, business, disciplines, knowledge, healing, and spiritual practices. His ability to translate the hidden ubiquitous spiritual meanings and practices within the world's main religions also shows a depth of human ability and profound spiritual insight and development. This was a human being in his own lifetime that showed a limitless drive to actualise all the possible potentialities that was Choa Kok Sui. Therefore, he fully engaged, actualised, and completed his Master Plan in his own lifetime. He did what he came here to do…

So, what did he leave for us?

The two areas of Maser Choa Kok Sui's work are the development and system of pranic healing and the spiritual practice and system of Arhatic yoga.

Pranic healing is the utilisation of prana, ki, or life energy to heal the human physical body. Its origins stem back to an ancient science and art form within human cultures that believe Prana or ki is the source of life, which keeps the body alive and healthy. In Eastern cultures it's known as prana, ki, chi. In Greek it is called pneuma, in Polynesian mana, and in Hebrew ruah, which means 'breath of life'. Master Choa states that the three main sources of prana are solar prana from the sun, air prana from the air we breathe, and Earth prana from the ground, which we absorb through our feet. The healer connects with the prana, which is found in these three main sources and projects the life energy to the patient, clearing negative energy, and replacing it with positive life energy/prana. The healing works on two basic principles of life: 1. that human's self-heal/recover and the body's ability to do this, 2. the principle of prana or life energy is fundamental to existence. The pranic healing works on these two basic principles of life by increasing the body's natural ability to heal/recover by utilising prana or life energy to do this through the pranic healer.

What we call miraculous healing is nothing more than increasing the rate of self-recovery of the body. There is nothing supernatural or paranormal about pranic

220

healing. It is simply based on natural laws that most people are not aware of.

Master Chao Kok Sui

Arhatic yoga is a system of yoga, like all classical systems of yoga, which aid the student and spiritual seeker to achieve oneness with Divine Spirit. The uniqueness to Maser Choa's system is the integration of seven forms of yoga practice: Karma yoga, Raja yoga, Jnana yoga, Bhakti yoga, Kundalini yoga, Mantra yoga and Hatha yoga, which have been structured into a system of levels. The process and synthesis of the different yoga forms is to help accelerate and focus spiritual development through safe and easy techniques that have been tried and assessed over many years of practice and attuning by Master Choa and his students. When walking the spiritual path, as all of us are if we choose to like it or not, comes with degrees and approaches, and like all forms of practice we must take the approach that is best suited for us at our current stage of development. If we take on too much or engage with a level that isn't appropriate for us it can result in disappointment, loss of motivation and harm us emotionally, psychologically, and even physically. Arhatic yoga gives the student a progressive method and approach that is individually suited to the student's stage of spirituality and spiritual development.

For further information and study of pranic healing and Arhatic yoga, I'd recommend going to www.thepranichealers.com and/or reading Master Choa Kok Sui's books: *Miracles through Pranic*

221

Healing and/or *The Origin of Modern Pranic Healing & Arhatic Yoga.*

I hope you have found the introduction to the great spiritual teachers of interest and informative, perhaps it's even sparked an interest into delving further into our rich history of religious and spiritual knowledge and practice. Of course, there are more influential spiritual teachers among us past and present that I have been unable to share with you within the bounds of this book. Currently among us we have the representatives of the great Yoga and Vedanta traditions of India, carrying on the teachings and heritage of Sri Ramakrishna and Swami Sivananda in the East and West. We have the great traditions of Buddhism in its three main forms: Theravāda, Mahāyāna and Vajrayāna, that can be found and are practiced all over the world. We have great spiritual teachers in Christianity, Islam, Judaism, and non-religious secular traditions among us too. However, when we look closely at these spiritual teachings, whatever form they are presented or communicated, they all deliver the same point.

> *Ekam Sat Vipra Bahudha Vadanti – Truth is one but Sages speak of it in different ways*
>
> The Vedas

At the heart of all spiritual teachings is the same message and the same desired outcome – to achieve Oneness with Spirit/Divinity/God/Allah/Universality/All that there is. To manifest and 'lift the veil' so we can experience our true essence…and be One with our Divine Self and Source of All.

Revisiting the Art of Listening

The Art of listening is your in-road, skill, and instrument to delving deeper into accessing your Master Plan and stepping out of Victim. The engaging of empathy, compassion and your growing self-awareness will move you ever closer to a deeper understanding and knowledge of self and others. To know oneself is the key to accessing your Master Plan and living a more fulfilling life. The enhancement of yourself, your relationships, and the connection to the world in which you live must be your main goal and focus if you wish to live a fulfilling life. The Body/Mind/Spirit process and integration is the only way to achieve this – our religious and spiritual heritages, histories and practices attest to this. There is nothing new in this book that hasn't been said many times before. You will never find ultimate contentment, peace, happiness, bliss, and self-realisation in the material world of ego and vice, it is just not possible – it never has been and never will be. To step out of Victim is to know true liberation, is to be truly free. We are working toward *jivanmukia* to be liberated while we are still living. The great spiritual masters, sages, saints, and teachers all share the universal teaching/truth – they offer us a shining example of what we can be and what we truly are...

Do not be defeated by what may seem a mammoth task to emulate and follow in their examples. We can only do what we can do right here and now – and that is more than good enough. The key to their example is in the striving, in the committed focus and in the desired belief that we all want to be the 'best versions of ourselves' and that is our motivation, that is our goal. A saying that is common to therapists is 'trust the process' – all is as it should be – so do not despair, do not feel hopeless, hand over your pain, your struggle, your suffering to that higher-Self, that aspect of yourself that is far greater, more profound, and infinitely more than you could ever possibly imagine – let them do their job...

Further reading:

Earth Medicine Wheel – Sunbear & Wabun (2006) The Medicine Wheel: Earth Astrology. New York: Fireside Books

Four Noble Truths https://www.theravada.gr/en/about-buddhism/the-four-noble-truths/

Gayatri Yantra https://www.rudraksha-ratna.com/articles/gayatriyantra

Goddess Spirituality
https://journeyingtothegoddess.wordpress.com/

Jodo Shinshu Buddhism
http://bschawaii.org/shindharmanet/course/

Number symbolism https://www.numerology.com/

Sacred Geometry
https://www.gaia.com/search?q=Sacred%20Geometry%20&%20Empowered%20Action

Shin Buddhism https://www.buddhistchurchesofamerica.org/shin-buddhism

Spiritual Symbols 60 spiritual symbols and their meanings (full guide) - The Monk Life https://themonklife.net/spiritual-symbols/

Section 3. – Integrating Practice

Section three is how we as individuals, practitioners and professionals use our current practice in our daily lives, work contexts, therapeutic environments, and personal life. It is how we as practitioners, irrespective of what context we are in, can learn to integrate different forms of practice for the benefit of ourselves and the people we are working with.

A note on terminology:

Practice is used as a general term for anyone that practices an exercise, form, protocol, procedure, and/or framework e.g., yoga, meditation, walking, listening, mindfulness, medical intervention, etc.

Practitioner is used as the general term for anyone that performs or undertakes a practice.

Professional is used to mean anyone that has a professional role within a working context e.g., teacher, nurse, therapist, GP, etc.

Client is used to denote the general recipient or collaborator within the dyad relationship of practitioner and the person coming to and engaging with the service offered by the practitioner. For example, in counselling/psychotherapy context it's therapist and client, in the medical context it's doctor and patient, in the education context it's teacher and student.

Professional practice is used to mean a professional that uses their practice in their designated role. At the back of the book, you will also find a glossary of terms with explanations to assist you with understanding terminology further.

Integration of Practice

On a basic level:

> Integration is quite simply the combining of two or
> more things in an effective way

Cambridge University Press, 2023

Personal Integration:

When we look at this in relation to personal practice, we are considering different forms that already exist, with a focus in combining these to produce an effective outcome. So, for instance you might have a favourite breathing exercise you use or stretching technique that works well for you, but you are looking to develop more mental focus or awareness of body feelings – so you decide to take your existing stretching and breathing exercises and combine them with mindfulness practice. Through the integration of breathing, stretching and mindfulness, your Body/Mind connection and development starts to progress further as you are consciously integrating these three methods, which in-turn gives a better Body/Mind connection leading to a deeper sense of wellbeing.

Another example - you enjoy and use yoga for exercise, body flexibility and to minimise stress/anxiety in your life, but you want to develop a deeper connection with the natural world. So, you take your practice outdoors into your garden, a local park, woodlands, or countryside; through the integration of yoga in the natural world you are allowing yourself to do yoga and at the same time being open and allowing yourself to develop a deeper relationship with the natural world around you. A win, win.

A final example might be combining your daily walk with a spiritual mantra or spiritual focus on a sacred symbol or phrase. You quite simple hold the image in your mind or say the mantra under your breath or aloud (depending on where you are) whilst walking in your favourite spot. You are gaining the exercise of walking for the Body/Mind connection and at the same time you are developing a spiritual connection through your desired focus i.e., sacred symbol and/or mantra.

These examples might seem obvious and simple, and in effect that is the point, they are supposed to be. There is nothing difficult about this, it's about what you decide to do, that's the fun of it, you can do almost anything. You will get naturally drawn to and begin to use certain methods and practices that 'feel right' for you, and again this is another integral aspect of you accessing your Master Plan and stepping out of Victim. In time and through the practice of different methods you will begin to 'know what feels right'. You will begin to trust yourself, your judgement and decision making around what works and doesn't work. This is a foundational premise of your journey into self-discovery, self-understanding, and self-development. Through this process of trying things out, eventually you will decide and know what feels and what works best for you. What this fosters and nurtures within in you is the deeper connection and developing relationship to really trust You and your decisions.

Professional integration:

I will be looking at professional integration of practice briefly from a counselling/psychotherapy perspective, as this is my background. What you'll soon see and appreciate, is that even though I'm focusing on counselling/psychotherapy, as practitioners you'll soon see similarities with other forms of practice and disciplines as well. What we are looking at within professional integration from a therapy perspective are common factors akin to the therapeutic relationship that the practitioner offers and creates with the client and service user generally.

Stricker (2001) states:

> Although there is no fixed established list of common factors, consensus suggests that such a list would include: a therapeutic alliance; exposure of the client to prior difficulties followed by a new corrective emotional experience; expectations by the therapist and the client for positive change; beneficial therapist qualities, such as attention, empathy, and positive

regard; and the provision to the client of a rationale for problems.

Therefore, the practitioner, be it a counsellor, energy healer, nurse, etc. is 1. developing and creating an environment conducive for positive therapeutic change for the client, 2. an explanation of how this can be achieved and 3. the offering and embodying of certain qualities that will help achieve this e.g., empathy, compassion, and authenticity. This suggests that the key to any form of therapeutic integration lies primarily with the practitioner. The practitioner must have the knowledge and means to apply integration to make it work.

If we take an example of psychotherapy and Spiritual Response Therapy (SRT) as the two forms of therapy to integrate; initially the practitioner must have sufficient knowledge of both approaches, have sufficient understanding of application of both approaches and have the necessary and sufficient means in applying an integration.

To consider an integration of therapy/practice the therapist needs to assess the client's needs and issues; in effect we need to know why they've come to therapy and what the issues are. To do this we create what is known as a formulation with the client.

A **formulation** consists of three main questions that focus and underpin the therapy structure:

1. what has caused the client's problems?

2. what factors are maintaining the client's problems?

3. what might facilitate change?

Integrative therapy is sometimes referred to as holistic therapy because it aspires to consider an individual's mental, physical, and emotional health in a unified way. Ideally, therapist and client will work together to understand the sources of the latter's anxiety, unhappiness, physical discomfort, or unhealthy behaviour patterns.

Psychology Today

For integration to take place the practitioner must know how they are going to implement this holistic approach and the rationales behind how and why they are doing it that way. The formulation gives the therapist/practitioner the structure, framework and means to gather the necessary information and then with the collaboration of the client to devise an effective therapeutic plan that best suits the client.

For effective integration to take place, we must be focused on collaborating with the client holistically i.e., emotionally, psychologically, physically, and spiritually – body/mind/spirit. The key here is not to dismiss something at first sight because we think that there is no place for it. The existing practitioner may have accumulated hours of experience in their approach and generally in life within different contexts e.g., being a student, being a service lead, being a volunteer, being a parent, being a therapist, so, to dismiss and disregard all this experience seems somewhat shortsighted and disingenuous. For example, the practitioner may have established solid ways of engaging, understanding, and communicating with the people they work with – an established skill set. To dismiss and disregard this could possibly deskill the practitioner, prevent them working effectively and prevent positive outcomes.

Section one of the book covered each aspect of Body/Mind/Spirit. In section three of the book, we are going to focus on integration of these three key elements in relation to practice. I will introduce you to a few that I feel are coherent, structured and that offer excellent outcomes. Through examples and case studies I will show how these different forms of therapy, practice and methods can be integrated and used by practitioners and professionals alike.

Spiritual Response Therapy (SRT)

Spiritual Response Therapy (SRT) is a quick and accurate spiritual healing technique that helps you remove blocks that prevent you from living a happier life. SRT works on a spiritual level to help eliminate spiritual, mental, emotional, and physical challenges. Although a spiritual healing method it can enhance all areas of life.

SRT is a system of researching the subconscious mind and soul records to quickly find and release the discordant, limiting ideas and replace them with loving, supportive ideas, and beliefs. SRT provides an exacting, powerful, virtually painless, and accurate way of changing the landscape of our inner and outer lives, enabling us to live our lives more freely. This "research," which is accomplished with the help of higher guidance (your "High Self"), includes finding past life energies, subconscious blocks, and negative soul programming. Once identified, these blocks and negative energies can be cleared from the subconscious, soul (Akashic) records, allowing you to heal yourself on all levels. SRT was developed by Robert E. Detzler and has been used by thousands of students since 1988.

Spiritual Response Association

This is the official definition from the Spiritual Response association website. The association was founded by Robert Detzler and his wife Mary-Ann back in 1990 as the springboard and founding association for SRT. Since its start it has been growing and developing throughout the world, where it is home for many practitioners worldwide.

Let's begin by having a more detailed look at the definition and exploring the basic concepts and processes involved in this therapy:

1. It's spiritual, you respond to it and it's a form of therapy – as the name suggests. However, what is being spiritual? Is your spirituality the same as mine? Where does religion fit into this? Isn't this about believing in something and following that belief?

Spirituality/being spiritual is many things to many people on many different levels be it emotional, psychological, physical, and beyond, as we've previously discussed in section one and two. SRT is a form of being spiritual, engaging with spiritual processes and a system of being spiritual that helps us understand ourselves better and heal ourselves for the good of ourselves and the good of all. This premise is important and is the underpinning ethic that runs through the whole process of SRT – **for the good of ourselves and for the good of all.** By working on our own wellbeing, healing, and spiritual growth, we are also benefiting everyone else. It's like the ripple effect on a pond, throw a small pebble into a pond and then watch how the ripples expand and grow, connecting and engaging with everything in its path. SRT is the same, as we clear blocks, negative energies, and programs from our mind, body, and spirit, we also ripple out in a positive way connecting to all those around us.

Do I have to believe in the SRT system for it to work?

No, what you do have to believe in, and this is true for all forms of therapy, is the belief in your own healing. If you do not wish to heal, resolve, and enhance your wellbeing then you won't. Healing, growth, enhancement, development, call it what you will, will only take place once you start to believe in yourself. There are no magic wands, magic pills, magic potions, or magic practitioners that will 'save you', 'heal you', and/or take away all your pain, suffering, fear, worry, doubt, and disillusionment. I've been a healthcare practitioner for many years and in all that time the only people that get better are the ones that want to and believe they will. This is the truth of the matter but also the beginning of your healing, growth, enhancement, and development. Understanding this basic premise of life is the turning-point and the foundation to you living and developing the life you've always dreamed of. You create this, you are this and SRT is a therapeutic system that can help you discover and become this life. You step out of **Victim** and into **Believer**.

SRT – How we do it and use it:

As stated by the SRT association:

> SRT is a system of researching the subconscious mind and soul records to quickly find and release the discordant limiting ideas and replace them with loving, supportive ideas, and beliefs.

This is where we identify and research our current life and past lives using SRT charts to clear the negative blocks, programs and negative energies that prevent us from enhancing our wellbeing and spiritual development. How this is achieved is through higher levels of consciousness that exist within us all and are our throughline connection to our original source Spirit. If we go back to spiritual principle one, it's stated that separation from Spirit/Source is an illusion, therefore we are primarily connected to Spirit/Source. FEAR comes into play to create this separation, which we use for our development.

SRT helps you to realise this illusion of separation from Spirit/Source by helping remove the negative blocks that are preventing you experiencing the connection to Spirit/Source. It's like dialling up and having distortion, interference and crackling on the phone line; only in this case it's become so distorted that you think you've lost connection altogether and can't hear the person on the line at all – in fact you believe they've hung up…

SRT helps by removing the distortion and interference, the more blocks we remove the clearer the phone line and the easier it is to hear what the other person is saying.

As the SRT association state:

> *SRT provides an exacting, powerful, virtually painless, and accurate way of changing the landscape of our inner and outer lives, enabling us to live our lives more freely. This "research," which is accomplished with the help of higher guidance (your "High Self"), includes finding past life energies, subconscious blocks, and negative soul programming. Once identified, these blocks and negative energies can be*

cleared from the subconscious, soul (Akashic) records, allowing you to heal yourself on all levels.

And this healing opens us up to a clearer connection to our original source Spirit and our 'High Self'.

So, what is this higher guidance? What is the 'High Self'?

Spiritual principle two:

> 2. As spiritual beings, we have access to higher spiritual guidance in the form of High Self. High Self works with the Soul to research and clear programs.

The 'High Self' is a higher level of consciousness of You. As we said previously regarding the light and dark process, the closer we get to Source/Spirit the lighter/higher our level of consciousness becomes. The further away from Source/Spirit the denser/darker our level of consciousness becomes. So, the 'High Self' is You but You at a higher level of consciousness. If we go back to our phone line analogy – Spirit is at the highest level (at one end) and we on planet Earth as spiritual beings having a human existence are dialling Spirit up. Your 'High Self' is the operator the 'go between' that helps connect you to Source/Spirit and download the necessary information to help you develop and enhance your wellbeing. Due to your 'High Self' existing at this higher level of consciousness, you therefore have access to You at a higher level and therefore access to more information, knowledge, guidance, support and help that you can't directly access here on planet Earth. Remember, it's the distortions and blocks that prevent you gaining direct access to this, so we use SRT and your 'High Self' to clear these blocks, negative energies, and distortions.

We are the orchestrators of our own existence – spiritual principle four:

4.   The Soul is ultimately in charge of its own healing. Nothing happens that is not planned for or allowed by the Soul. As divine beings creating our own reality, we cannot be victims.

And this is the *raison d'etre* of our being – the reason we are here. It's a simple or as difficult as that. We are here to develop and grow spiritually. Nothing happens that we haven't planned for. We decided what we needed to learn and designed our life before we were born into this human body…All the highs and all the lows and everything in between was your design – your Master Plan. You decided it. You planned it. You wanted it! Because the Soul/You knew that to gain and develop spiritually these were and are the experiences, relationships, and situations You needed/need to achieve it – your Master Plan. Just like driving that car – if I want to learn to drive that car, first I need a car to practice in, then I need knowledge and time to practice and possibly a good teacher to help me. You find these, you practice and then with time you succeed at learning to drive a car…that was your choice, your decision, your time, you planned it, you wanted it – therefore You are responsible for it.

So, how on 'Earth' can we be Victims…you designed your own Master Plan.

Integrating therapies

This is where it can get interesting and there are no set rules in relation to how integrating therapies and practice can be done. Although, integration is led by two overarching factors:

1. the client's presenting problems and issues,

2. the development of the therapist.

Both factors are fundamental to the benefit of the client's outcome. The second factor of therapist development is led by either an intrinsic motivation to focus on personally developing self and practice and/or extrinsically motivated by focusing on the client's presentation. Both are equally valid and constitute a comprehensive approach to integration. I shall explore both factors with examples to illustrate the points further.

1. The client's presenting problems and issues:

Through the formulation and initial assessment with the client, we begin to understand and identify the client's presenting issues and what's maintaining the issues, so we can collaborate with the client to design and implement a therapeutic plan. It is the therapeutic plan that consists of the interventions, structure, timeframe and aims of therapy that will underpin and be utilised throughout the ongoing therapeutic relationship. As previously said, all competent styles of therapy, approaches, modalities, and practices will have a coherent theoretical methodology that has appropriate methods to achieve a desired outcome. In effect, we have a coherent theory that has coherent rationales that support and give reasoned arguments for the methods that are being used in the approach to achieve the desired outcome.

CBT: using Cognitive Behavioural therapy (CBT) as an example:

1. the theory that underpins CBT is founded in cognitive and behavioural psychology,

2. the methods that are utilised are based within a skill set that can apply the theory and a collaborative relationship between the therapist and client is created to use the skill set,

3. the desired outcome is for the client to change from a negative cognitive and behavioural process to a positive one – to change from negative ways of thinking and behaving to positive ways of thinking and behaving,

4. the rationales for this are based in theory and application, which show that when this desired outcome is achieved a person's quality of life enhances and their sense of wellbeing improves.

In the CBT example above, we can see how this form of therapy fits a clear methodology relating to theory and practice. There is a logical reasoned point to its theory and application. So, when we create the formulation with the client, we must have coherent reasoned arguments and rationales as to why we are designing and using the specific therapeutic plan we've created. The integrating of therapies must align and fit these rationales and reasoned arguments within the therapeutic design, hence the factors that dictate the therapeutic design are the client's presenting issues/problems. This also relates and links directly to good practice, competency, and ethics. Through the upholding of this framework through a collaborative approach, you are delivering good practice, showing competency, and grounding your practice ethically. So even though I said at the beginning of this section there are no set rules per say, whatever the approach you take to integrating therapies and practice there must be a coherent framework, therapeutic relationship, and reasoned arguments for the 'how and why' to the approaches you've chosen to use. If you do not apply this coherent reasoned framework to your approaches and integration, your practice and application becomes ungrounded, incoherent, unreasoned, and unethical.

Now that we've established the framework that underpins our practice and integration, we are ready to consult with the client and create an appropriate therapeutic plan that will meet the client's needs and assist them in achieving a positive outcome in therapy.

2. The development of the therapist:

Integration from the therapist perspective or intrinsic motivation, constitutes a process of learning, practicing, and integrating different forms of practice, skills, theory, etc. into the embodied thinking, feeling, and behaving of the individual – into your very core. When we learn, study, practice and apply our new learning, we begin to embody and shape our Body/Mind connection and relationship. Like learning to drive a car example, at first, we are all fingers and thumbs, uncoordinated, nonflowing, consciously aware of what our feet and head is doing, etc. but with time and practice we slowly and surely become proficient, and we stop thinking what to do, we just do it automatically. The neural pathways get created so we can stop consciously thinking about what to do and allow ourselves to just do it. Integration from the therapist perspective is the same process, we develop the practice intrinsically, which has a twofold benefit: 1. Personal development of the therapist, and 2. A wider skill set and competency to offer when working with clients. This also creates a broader and wider client base to work with. Due to the development of your skill set, theory, application, and practice, you are increasing the range and diversity of client presentations you can work with.

For example: your basic training could be in Humanistic counselling, but post training you decide to study and integrate Mindfulness for your own personal development but also as a skill set to offer clients. You might decide that you want to work with more severe forms of mental ill-health, trauma, and psychopathology, which your basic training didn't cover, so you decide to study and qualify in a trauma -focused approach e.g. EMDR (Eye Movement Desensitization and Reprocessing). If you wish to bring more spirituality into your life, you might start to practice Sivananda Yoga and begin to feel the benefits of this and start to see that you are beginning to relate to yourself more spiritually, which in-turn gets naturally reflected into the therapist/client relationship. Connecting to the natural world and nature is having a positive effect on your life, so you decide to do an eco-therapy course, again which can be shared with clients to help them connect and benefit from too, assisting them in experiencing the positive benefits of developing a relationship with the natural world.

Integrating SRT into your Current Practice

Now that we've identified the two main factors underpinning the integration of practice. We will go back to SRT therapy and look further into how this can be integrated. The integration and assimilation of SRT and the practice of SRT is to support, enhance and take your current practice to another level. This next level being the level of higher consciousness and clearing of energy blocks and programs that are getting in the way of you achieving the desired positive outcomes. In a way we can see it as an upgrade to our existing way of doing things – removing those viruses, bugs, discordant processes that are getting in the way of our practice and daily living. We remove these bugs out of the system – the system being You - and clean it up, making it run more efficiently, smoothly, and effectively. So, by doing this we are functioning better to aid, support and facilitate those we are working with.

An example would be a counsellor e.g., a Humanistic counsellor or CBT (Cognitive Behavioural Therapy) therapist. They help people find answers, solutions, acceptance and understanding in their current life situations. The clients will come into therapy feeling uncertain about a current life issue and hopefully with the help from the therapist, will leave counselling/therapy feeling better and more able to resolve that issue. The case study of Tara Fig. 5 shows a classical form of Humanistic psychotherapy to illustrate this point.

Figure 5 Case Study 1 Tara:

Tara is a black 35-year-old woman and working as a Solicitor for a private firm. Tara identifies as non-binary gender (using the pronouns of Them/They/Theirs) and has recently ended a four-year relationship with a woman. Due to their workload and stresses of their personal relationship with their partner, Tara has been experiencing anxiety attacks and feelings of extreme low mood, which has resulted in their taking leave at work. Tara has been to their GP and has been signed off work with depression and anxiety.

Case illustration: Tara – a therapy extract

Tara: I don't understand it; I've never experienced panic attacks before.

Therapist: So, this feels alien to you…

Tara: Yeah, like it's just not me, I'm usually so confident with who I am.

Therapist: So confident normally but this isn't you.

Tara: That's it, this isn't me, but why do I feel so scared and anxious...

Therapist: A sense of fear.

Tara: Absolutely, fear, dread, Mum, and Dad said I should never fear who I am.

Therapist: So, they were clear, you should not be scared and be strong...

Tara: Yeah, be strong too, don't worry about stuff, always be able to cope and get on...be proud of who I am.

Therapist: That feels like a lot of pressure.

Tara: If I'm honest it was...I'd always be expected to get the grades, not to get stressed and be able to cope with anything.

Therapist: No room for vulnerability or help?

Tara: Yeah, kind of, needing to be grounded on my own two feet.

Therapist: Be strong on your own.

Tara: Yes, no room for weakness.

Therapist: Expectations from your parents...

Tara: Yes, both of them, they were pretty united, whatever they said went. I just wanted to make them proud.

Therapist: Their approval was key.

Tara: Like you wouldn't believe.

Therapist: And you still need it…

Tara: Well, no, of course not I'm a grown woman now…(pause)…they'd struggle to see me like this.

Therapist: Vulnerable.

Tara: Not coping…I haven't told them I've gone off sick.

Therapist: You can't ask them for help or let them see you like this?

Tara: No, they wouldn't approve, they'd be ashamed.

Therapist: Feels like a strong condition on your relationship with them.

Tara: It is, how could they still love me if they saw me like this?

Therapist: Feels like their love is conditional on you being strong and coping with anything.

Tara: (Client's eyes begin to water).

Therapist: Feels sensitive for you

Tara: I just want them to love all of me, even the scared and frightened me.

Therapist: Even the scared and frighten you.

Tara: Yeah.

Therapist: It feels like a door has been opened?

Tara: Yeah, I never realised how much I still depended on their approval

Therapist: It's different now?

Tara: Yeah, still uncomfortable but not so scary anymore, feels like I know now.

Therapist: So, you'll be able to acknowledge and accept that more vulnerable side of you, and maybe share that more?

Tara: (Client smiles) we'll see.

The above case study, Sims (2022), is a classical form of counselling, it's akin to humanistic therapy, but the general feel and application could be seen in many forms of counselling. The desired outcome for the client, is to get more clarity and understanding of their relational dynamics and conditional aspects with their parents. These conditions show how the client (Tara) has been shaped and guided throughout their life by the parental conditions and how they are still impacting their current situation.

SRT Approach:

If we are working with the case study (Tara) from solely an SRT perspective, we would frame this situation in pretty much the same way as a presenting problem. However, we would collaborate differently with it from a practice perspective. As previously said, there are a series of charts that the SRT system uses to find and then clear the necessary blocks, programs and negative energies that have attributed to and caused the conditional aspects to the client's parental relationship. Using the charts we would find and then clear these negative energies with the help of the 'High self' and the supporting higher levels of consciousness that work with the SRT system, practitioner, and client. Once these negative energies, programs and blocks have been cleared, this would then have a positive effect on the parental relationship and the client (Tara) would be free of these conditions. This would allow Tara to live more freely with the knowledge that these blocks have been cleared on a body/mind/spirit level.

These are two quite different ways of working: 1, Psychotherapy, and 2, SRT therapy. Both have a theoretical underpinning, skill set to use, and both are looking for a desired outcome for the client. So, how do we integrate these two systems, so they work efficiently, effectively for both the practitioner and the client? Again, this is dependent on the client's presentation and issues. Case study 1.2, will illustrate the point as we look further into Tara's issues and her relationship with her parents:

Figure 6 Case Study 1.2 Tara

At the end of case study 1, Tara the client has gained greater self-awareness around her conditional relationships with their parents and how these have shaped and influenced Tara in their life. Even though Tara has gained this self-awareness on a body/mind level there is nothing to say this has changed on a spiritual level. In further sessions Tara discloses that their parents are devout Catholics and regularly attend their local church. Tara explores in their therapy that they have never really been religious and finds it difficult to be involved with a religious institution that doesn't recognise or accept Tara's sexuality and sexual identity. Over the years this has caused tension in the family home between Tara's parent's religious beliefs and values and Tara's more secular non-religious beliefs and values.

Tara explains in therapy that they love their parents dearly and would love to be able to accept and find common ground and deeper acceptance of them even though Tara's values/beliefs and their parent's values/beliefs are in tension and conflict. Now that Tara has presented this new information and aim of therapy – the therapist reviews the current therapy with Tara considering this new aim and discusses the possible ways forward in helping Tara achieve this new aim. The therapist goes back to the original contract of therapy, and Tara and the

Therapist collaborate on a new formulation (the therapeutic plan).

Formulation:

1. what has caused the client's problems? The conflict between Tara's parents and Tara's values/beliefs.

2. what factors are maintaining the client's problems? Tara's and Tara's parent's struggle to find resolve and acceptance around the difference in each other's values/beliefs.

3. what might facilitate change? Working with interventions that address deeper relational dynamics around self-acceptance and acceptance of others – looking more closely at the connection between Body/Mind/Spirit within the client.

Tara and the therapist now discuss the formulation questions in therapy to help Tara achieve their new aim. The new aim for Tara is to be able to accept and find common ground with deeper acceptance of Tara's parents even though Tara's values/beliefs and Tara's parent's values/beliefs are in tension and conflict.

Therapeutic Discussion:

The therapist and Tara explore the possible options for Tara considering their new aim of therapy. The Therapist explains that as individuals we cannot or should not expect change from the other people involved in a relationship which is causing tension and/or conflict. Therefore, Tara can't or should not expect their parents to change their views or position, to do so is unrealistic and could be experienced as coercive and manipulative by Tara's parents creating greater tension and a defence. The therapist explains that the best outcome we can wish to achieve is from working on ourselves and hopefully being able to change our viewpoint, perspective, position and dynamic in the current relationship. If this is achieved by the client it may in turn create greater self-acceptance, confidence, agency, increased positive mood and a general sense of feeling 'OK' about themselves and the relationship, therefore achieving greater self-worth and becoming more self-empowered. If we look at this in an extreme case, for example domestic violence, it may assist the victim/client to gain greater self-worth, develop greater courage and have more agency to leave the abusive relationship and perpetrator.

Options for therapy and interventions:

Tara and the therapist now explore what options are available for Tara given the therapist's qualifications and skill set.

Working holistically from a Body/Mind/Spirit perspective the therapist explains that she can work from a Humanistic, CBT, existential, ecotherapy, and spiritual position. Discussing the possible strategies, techniques, and therapeutic options available for Tara to engage with given the therapist's qualifications and skill set. Tara explains that although they are not religious, Tara is spiritual and has a close connection to nature and the natural world and likes the ideas based around Buddhism and mindfulness.

The therapist offers a combination of walk and talk ecotherapy in the outdoors connecting to nature to explore the ongoing relationship with their self and their parents with moments to engage in mindfulness; and SRT to look deeply at the intergenerational and past life connections with Tara's parents to see what underlying blocks and negative programs could be influencing and impacting their current relationship.

New therapeutic contract:

Tara likes the idea of the new therapeutic plan, and the therapist creates a new therapeutic contract with Tara incorporating the new therapies and interventions. The new contract consists of SRT and eco-therapy 'walk and talk'. The SRT consists of two clearings: 1. A full clearing to begin with in the first week and, 2. a second clearing focusing on the relational dynamics between Tara and their parents in the third week. The eco-therapy is for 6 more sessions weekly with an open ongoing review depending on Tara's needs.

The above example of SRT and therapy integration is one example but hopefully as you're seeing the combinations and options are many. You can be as creative and scientific as you choose, depending on the client's presentation, your own personal interest and development, and the context you are practicing in. In the following sections I will introduce several types of practice that are grounded within the Body/Mind/Spirt framework that can be used but also can be utilised for integration with other practices.

Yoga

I briefly touched on yoga in section two when looking at the spiritual teachings and spiritual masters, now I'll go into more depth around the philosophy of yoga and how the practical application of yoga can be integrated into one's life and professional practice.

From a modern Western perspective yoga is mostly understood as a form of exercise and body conditioning. It is offered and promoted in community centres, leisure centres, gyms, and health studios in the West, marketed as a form of exercise like Pilates and is understood as a series of postures that can promote good physical wellbeing, toning, stretching, and strengthening of the body. I appreciate this is a generalised view of yoga and there are many institutions and practitioners within the West that practice and understand yoga as so much more...interestingly when yoga was first introduced to the West back in the late 19th Century and early 20th Century the idea of balanced exercise was very much a secondary concept. On experiencing and practising yoga through the poses (Asanas), people from the West were journeying to India in search of gurus and spiritual teachers to help with a deeper philosophical and practical understanding of the benefits of yoga and the philosophy.

It wasn't until the mid-20th Century when practitioners from outside the West started to come to America that yoga, and what we now call Hatha yoga, began to establish itself and become publicly available. Shri Yogendri and Paramahansa Yogananda were the first to really start the introduction and practice of yoga in the West and from their lineages and followers we have what we know of as Hatha yoga today. There are many different forms of Hatha yoga that have grown from those early roots including: Iyengar yoga, Bikram (Hot yoga), Ashtanga yoga, Power yoga, Kundalini yoga, Restorative yoga, Vinyasa yoga and Yin yoga.

Yet is yoga just about asanas postures and body conditioning?

If we turn to the ancient Hindu scriptures and texts of The Vedas, The Upanishads, The Bhagavad Gita, and the Sutras of Patanjali we find the deeper philosophy, the paths, and the practical methods to achieve the ultimate outcome of yoga – to find union with the Divine - by fully experiencing and realising the Self/God/All That There is/Brahman. Yoga in its different forms/paths gives us practical methods to achieve Self-realisation and Oneness with the Divine and to experience our true essence - our Divine-Self. So, yoga in essence is the ultimate Body/Mind/Spirit vehicle to full integration of the human being by achieving the goal of becoming a fully realised human

How do we do this and what are the paths?

Initially yoga was a form of meditation that was prescribed in The Vedas through focused repetition of mantras or *Japa* either sung or mentally intoned, which was carried through into The Upanishads. This was a fundamental practice that proved with time and continual application that the student could and would eventually achieve Self-realisation. This is and has always been the foundational practice and still is the best form of practice, which will be discussed later. However, it wasn't until The Bhagavad Gita or Song of God that three other forms of yoga were introduced:

1. Karma yoga
2. Jnana yoga
3. Bhakti yoga

1, Karma Yoga (yoga of action) is the path of service or servitude, it may seem a somewhat severe word to use 'servitude', but this is the goal of Karma yoga. Karma yoga is to devote every single thought, every single feeling, and every single action to the service of the Divine/God through your selfless service to others in the world. Do not become attached to any of your actions, do not take any pride or pleasure in your actions, be disinterested, be dispassionate, be selfless. Your aim is to be in complete servitude to God and through this process of serving up everything you think, feel, or do, to God through your selfless service to others, you will eventually achieve complete subjugation of egoistic desire, thought, feeling and action and experience your true essence and God-realisation. Ego will be transcended and Oneness with your fully realised Self will be achieved.

2, Jnana Yoga (yoga of knowledge) is the pursuit of self-realisation through the process of thinking, discussing, meditating, and studying with oneself, a guru, and other students. Through reflecting and studying on the metaphysical questions such as 'Who am I?' 'What am I?' 'What is God?', etc...one begins to establish a greater sense of self and self-awareness culminating and being cultivated into the final answer and experientially realised attainment of the 'knowing' or 'knowledge' of this fundamental question. Students will study and discuss the ancient Hindu texts and scriptures, they will immerse themselves in yoga philosophy, metaphysical, religious, and existential discussion, they will thrash out intellectual debate until Braham/God/Self is truly experienced. Self-realisation is achieved once the student has gained the ultimate knowledge through lived experienced of the very nature of oneself, therefore you have become a fully realised Self and 'know this'.

3, Bhakti yoga (yoga of devotion) considered to be the 'crowning glory' of all paths of yoga, is the spiritual path of complete devotion to your God. What is quintessentially glories about the Bhakti path is that we all become the Bhakti yogi on attainment of Self-realisation and Oneness with the Divine. Self-realisation fundamentally is the realisation that God/Self is most glorious, sublime and bliss, so once this is realised our ignorance and veils of darkness are lifted and we experience the Universal Love that is God/Self, and one's devotion, one's complete selfless love is personified into the Bhakti yogi. Although, considered in some ways as an easy path to follow, all you need to do is focus on your God, worship, devote time and praise and glorify your god, the darker side can lead to fanaticism and fundamentalism and many religious wars, fighting and atrocities have been performed in the name, worship and devotion to certain Gods and sadly still are…however, if the student is grounded in the universal belief of Ahimsa/non-violence and cultivates strong ethical practice in one's life, the Bhakti path can be a most wonderful and glories path to follow. The path of the Bhakti is one of love. We begin our journey with love, we walk the path of love and when we reach the end, we find the most glorious love of All - Self-realisation/God-realisation/Oneness/Cosmic Love/Universal Love.

The Yoga Sutras of Patanjali:

In the early centuries CE, some scholars say around 400CE, others say 200 CE but generally around 2500 years ago, a yogi of the name *Patañjali* compiled and wrote down 196 aphorisms structured in four chapters about the philosophy and practice of yoga, known collectively as the Yoga Sutras. The yoga sutras are given high precedence and tend to be the foundational blocks for modern yoga today. *Patañjali* in some ways is considered the godfather of yoga and one of the most prominent aspects of his theory and practice is found in chapter two, where he expounds the practice and theory of the eight limbs of yoga (ashtanga yoga), which is also understood as Raja yoga (the yoga of self-control).

The four chapters (padas) of the yoga sutras are structured as:

1. Samadhi pada (Self-realisation) – consists of 51 sutras that explain and layout the philosophy of yoga, what it is, its point, the reasons for practice and the possible obstacles that can get in the way of the ultimate goal of samadhi.

2. Sadhana pada (the path of yoga) – consists of 55 sutras that explain the practice/method of yoga – the how to, and what to do process to achieve the outcome of chapter one. Here we find the 8 limbs of ashtanga yoga:
    1. Yama – restraints/ethical behaviours
    2. Niyama – observances/practices
    3. Asana – postures
    4. Pranayama – breath control
    5. Pratyahara – withdrawal of the senses
    6. Dharana – concentration
    7. Dhyana – meditation
    8. Samadhi – absorption/oneness

3. Vibhuti pada (manifestation) – consists of 56 sutras that assist the practitioner in staying on the path and cultivating greater self-discipline and focus. Through the refined cultivation of limb six, Dharana (concentration) and limb seven, Dhyana (meditation) we can get closer to achieving the last limb eight, samadhi (absorption/Oneness).

4. Kaivalya pada (Isolation from the mind) – consists of 34 sutras that explain the liberation of the practitioner from the mind, the role of karma and perception, and the state and attainment of Self-realisation.

The eight limbs of Ashtanga Yoga

Ashtanga Yoga, as expounded by Patanjali, is the foundation and development of certain practices, restraints, and observances that the student must follow to achieve the ultimate goal of yoga – Self-realisation. By following and practicing the eight limbs of ashtanga yoga the student is not only developing and grounding an ethical existence they are creating and building foundational blocks to wellbeing, increasing physical and mental health, developing greater self-awareness, connecting to higher levels of spirituality, and integrating the Body/Mind/Spirit system. This in-turn creates a happier and more fulfilling inner and outer life experience with oneself and others in the world. The eight limbs of yoga are structured as progressive building blocks and can be perceived in this manner, but to do so is to miss the fundamental independent and inter-relational aspect of each limb. This is a framework, and each element is a foundational element that structures and supports the whole system, take one element away and the ability to achieve the final goal, limb eight, will be inhibited. Yet we mustn't be deluded and fall into the illusion that limb eight exists and comes into existence because of the other seven limbs – limb eight samadhi is Consciousness that we all exist from, existence in its purest form –

limb eight samadhi is the experience or realisation of our Divine essence that is Self-realisation – the other seven limbs create an environment, a practice, a method for the yoga practitioner to experience Oneness, Divine Source and therefore Self-realisation through.

Yama limb one:

The yamas or restraints/ethical behaviours consist of five Don'ts that underpin and ground the practice and life of the student:

1. Ahimsa/Non-violence/harmlessness – this yama is the foundational block of the whole system of yoga and is the fundamental ethical practice that grounds the student's existence, and we see this also advocated in many other forms of spiritual and religious philosophy and ideology e.g., Buddhism, Jainism, Sufism, some Christian groups and secular forms of ecology, animal rights (PETA) and civil rights movements. The practice of non-violence is a core belief and practice whereby the individual restrains from harming/injuring any living creature through non-violent thought, speech, and action. If a human being aspires for only one quality of character – let it be Ahimsa.

2. Satya/Truthfulness – the second yama is truthfulness/honesty – to think, speak and to act one's truth is one of the greatest qualities a human can aspire to – connecting to one's deeper sense of Self and understanding how one is formed and exists

in their relationships and world. However, Satya is not a free for all letting go of one's frustrations, anger, pain, suffering, hurt, pride and negative thoughts and feelings – this is not Satya or in any way one's truth – no this is ego. If we consider the highest attainment of truth is Self-realisation/God-realisation through the lived experienced of the human being then our expression of truth is grounded in love, kindness, understanding and compassion to ourselves and to others. Satya is the expression of the living truth of our deeper essence, our greater Self/Higher Self. Remember our grounding principle is Ahimsa/Non-violence, so our truth must be communicated and grounded in this primary principle, if it is not then what we perceive or believe to be our truth is non-other than our own egoistic, self-centred, selfish deluded thought, speech, and action.

3. Asteya/non-stealing/non-misappropriation – the third yama again is a good ethical principle that seems to be a general quality that is passed down in our institutions, schools, families, etc…yet do we really understand this quality or aspect of character that we are instructed to develop. If we look at our government systems, our administrative systems, our institutional systems, economic systems within our world can we experience or see this quality being acted out? Fundamentally this principle aligns with the concept of non-attachment. When we become attached, we apply a value to the object of attachment. The greater the attachment the greater the value and then due to the cycle of pleasure/pain Samsara we

261

want the object or objects more and more to satisfy the never-ending highs/lows of the cycle we are trapped in. Asteya is the de-attachment from this cycle, the arresting of our passion, our desire to get more. To begin with this must be learnt and we must discipline ourselves to outwardly not take, acquire, and demand what we believe is ours through our egoistic want/desire. Non-stealing is practiced through thought, speech, and action to transcend the desire to steal that which is not ours.

4. Brahmacharya/Continence – this originally was based in control or abstinence of one's sexual desire and/or activity. When we engage in sexual activity our ability to release and deplete our energy system is greatly increased, so the control and managing of this system is vital to the student of yoga and anyone in life. If we want to achieve our goals and aims in life, we need to apply energy through our thinking, feeling, and acting, so any unnecessary depletion of this will inhibit our ability to achieve our set goals. This isn't to say we can't engage in loving, mutually positive and wholesome sexual activity with our partners, we just need to raise this sexual connecting from the base/lower egoistic level to a higher spiritual level, which then enhances the people involved by sending and cultivating a greater positive charge. Brahmacharya is also the control of our feelings and emotions in our day-to-day life through the cultivation of positive thinking, feeling, and acting – processes that enhance and expand the individual through, love, kindness, compassion, generosity, and charity, and not those negative processes of

anger, greed, envy, pride, hate, fear, anxiety, and depression that deplete the person.

5. Aparigraha/non-grasping/non-possessiveness/non-hoarding like Asteya/non-stealing, is based in the principle of non-attachment. It is the arresting of the desire to attach but also understanding the illusionary belief that we 'need' the thing we own or 'grasp for'. This illusionary 'need' drives our desire to acquire the thing we want with the delusional belief it will make us feel 'better' or make our life more fulfilling, yet all it does is create an unhealthy attachment to the object and we become slaves to our illusional 'needs/desires', right back into Victim.

Niyama limb two:

The Niyamas consist of five Do's or observances that underpin right development of thought, speech, and action, which work cohesively with the five yamas to ground the student in a strong foundation of positive qualities and practice constituted into positive character building:

1. Saucha/Cleanliness/Purity – the first niyama is centred on the student cultivating a lifestyle that upholds and constitutes clean thinking, speaking, and acting. This is reflected in the cleanliness of the body through diet, hygiene, and appearance, in the mind through learning and information input/consumption and our environment through lifestyle, living spaces, work and our relationships to Others. We are

what we consume, so be mindful of only consuming positive wholesome and enhancing forms of energy...if you exist in Vice, you become vicious – if you exist in Virtue, you become virtuous.

2. Santosha/Contentment/Gratitude – the second niyama is contentment/peacefulness, which is the lived experience of happiness, joy, 'OK-ness' that one genuinely feels and experiences in their life. This is a natural outcome of the practicing of the yamas, as these become grounded and constituted within our body and mind, we begin to experience life in more spontaneously whole-some and contented way. We look through the lens of gratitude for everything that is at hand and that comes our way...

3. Tapas/Self-discipline – this is the 'doing of' or practical application of working toward a goal or aim. Tapas generally means 'heat', so tapas in yoga is the use of action and application, the generation of this, the 'heated energy' to transform and transmute our baseness into higher levels of spirituality – egoism to Self-realisation – darkness to light – transmute old negative ways into new positive ways.

4. Swadhyaya/Self-study/Self-reflection – this is the active engagement with self-reflection, self-enquiry and turning the gaze inward toward oneself. The ability to go deep within oneself and discover the inner workings and processes that make us think, feel, and act in certain ways is swadhaya – to know oneself. It's the develop of self-awareness – yes, we can

engage with appropriate texts, scriptures, philosophy, and knowledge that assist us but ultimately swadhyaya is to trust and know the inner workings of Self.

5. Ishwarapranidhana/Devotion/Faith – the final niyama is one's devote offering of our self to our Source of existence. Everything that manifests as the person we give wholeheartedly to our God. Through our Bhakti our God with divine grace blesses our continual love and devotion by supporting and aiding us through our spiritual growth and personal development as a spiritual being having a human experience.

Asana limb three:

This limb is focused on the posture of yoga and initially this is based in the meditation postures that can be used to ground the body. In modern day Hatha yoga, the postures are the poses that the student uses to move through the different movements of yoga, what you see in a modern-day yoga class. However, originally, and still used today in meditation yoga the posture is the seated position we adopt to ground our body and prepare it for the successive limbs: 4, 5, 6, 7 & 8.

Regarding the seated pose, we are instructed to seat in a comfortable position with our back straight, hands on our knees or thighs resting on each other or in our lap, and our head held 3-5 inches away from our chin. Our eyes will be closed gently, and our breathing will be natural. This posture is to aid the natural energy flow of our body and mind and allow us to sit comfortably without falling asleep. The official seated positions used by students are:

- Sukhasana -Easy pose-crossed legged,
- Vajrasana - Hero pose-seated on our heels
- Siddhasana – Adept pose
- Ardha Padmasana – Half Lotus
- Padmasana – Lotus

The above seated postures are particularly good to use, however, sitting in a chair, on a cushion and even standing can work just as well. The key is to find the most comfortable position and posture for you, that allows you to practice in a relaxed manner, keeps you awake and fits around your body type, flexibility, and any injuries you may have.

Pranayama limb four:

Pranayama is concerned with two aspects: 1. Prana – life force or energy & 2. Yama – 'control of', so we have pranayama - control of our life energy. How we do this through the process of breathing, as prana can be managed through one's breathing and breathing gives us the fundamental energy exchange throughout our body and fuels our mind. By controlling our breath/prana through breathing exercises/techniques we can control our body and our mind, which is needed to develop and experience limbs 5, 6, 7 and 8 of Patanjali's ashtanga yoga.

Pratyahara limb five:

Limb five is withdrawing inward away from our senses. It is our senses that crave the external stimulus of our outside world. The senses want to attach and engage with sound, smell, taste, touch, and sight to play in the playground of the mind through our connection to our external world. Pratyahara is to turn away from these senses and outside stimuli and focus on our inner world, our inner Self, our heart, the core of our Being. Limb five is also the bridge, the connecting space, between the foundational outer limbs of 1, 2, 3 and 4, and paves the way for development of the inner limbs of 6, 7 to finally realise limb 8.

Dharana limb six:

Dharana is concentration or 'single pointedness'. It is the ability to focus on one object or point through our yoga practice. This focus could be on a mantra, visual object, or image – see section two on sacred symbols for examples.

Dhyana limb seven:

Limb six is the meditative state of continual flow of being. Through the concentration/Dharana we move into a continuous flow of breathing and awareness of our inner consciousness of dhyana. We are detached from external stimuli, and our mental focus is softened and flows freely through a continual pulse in meditation, like the sounds of the sea on the shoreline continually moving back and forth in a natural congruent flow of energy.

Samadhi limb eight:

Oneness, complete absorption, realisation of Self, Unification of Body/Mind/Spirit, Non-duality, these are just a few names for the process of Samadhi. This is the final limb of Patanjali's eight limbs and is the pinnacle experience of all the other limbs leading to this final experience of Oneness. Here we experience the complete merging of the inner and outer worlds, our experience is one of love, togetherness, completeness, bliss, which is experienced throughout our whole Being or integration of Body/Mind/Spirit. From a Hindu perspective there are three forms of Samadhi:

1. Laja samadhi – which is a feeling of peace experienced through a deeper meditative trance like state.
2. Savikalpa samadhi – whereby peace and bliss are experienced within the meditative process, but complete absorption is not experienced; however, you do have the ability to control one's thoughts freely without attachment.
3. Nirvikalpa samadhi – this is complete absorption into Oneness, where distinction between body, mind and spirit is not experienced, only a complete Divine state of enlightenment.

In Buddhism we have four stages or Jhanas that can be achieved through higher states of meditation:

1. First Jhana – you experience detachment from external stimuli and feelings of calmness and a sense of joy.
2. Second Jhana – this is very much like the first jhana but more concentrated and sustained.
3. Third Jhana – your experience of joy begins to diminish into a greater sustained process of overall calmness and peace.
4. Fourth Jhana – this is the complete and deep state of equanimity.

When reflecting on Samadhi from the perspective of Patanjali's eight limbs of yoga, the above states as presented in Hinduism and Buddhism respectfully, will be dependent on the practitioner and their spiritual development and practice. However, to experience samadhi is a profound and life-changing process, so I wouldn't get too hung up on what state of samadhi you experience – to do so will arrest and inhibit your ability to realise it...

Yoga is more than just a series of postures and exercises (Hatha yoga). To engage in Yoga, as expounded by the ancient Hindu and Yoga scriptures, and that is promoted in our world through the lineages, schools, ashrams, and disciples of the great Yogis of the past and present, is to engage in a process of living that can and will fundamentally change your life. Yoga is the ultimate Body/Mind/Spirit method and the way to integrate and fulfil these three main aspects of our existence.

A note on gurus: There have and there are still many promoters of Yoga in the West and many, many so called gurus and mystics that are willing to take your money and create an unhealthy dependency on them through the offering of enlightenment, answers to life after death, salvation, redemption, happiness, and eternal existence. We saw a great surgency of this in the 1960s, 1970s and 1980s with the rise of the cult leaders, false prophets and mystic gurus praying on vulnerable people desperately looking for belonging, friendship, closeness and love but often coming to dire ends through the control, suffering, financial ruin and even death at the cult leaders hands...please approach with caution and please evaluate with a critical eye and with considered discernment.

Yoga is a system of living, a philosophy, a practice, and a method that is free to all. No one holds the monopoly on Yoga, no one controls the means to this wonderful divine system that has been handed down to us generation by generation. Yoga belongs to you, and it can be your way to fulfil and become the person that is You...to begin with maybe try a Hatha yoga class and see how that works, no pressure, no judgement, or maybe pick up an intro book and/or do your own research on the internet...

Vegetarianism & Veganism

You may at first be wondering why I've included a dietary approach in this section on spiritual practice…how is being a vegetarian or vegan a spiritual practice?

In section one, we investigated the three realms of how humans exist in the world – the Body/Mind/Spirit - and when integrated positively these three factors of human existence, when nurtured with a positive approach to living can enhance our sense of wellbeing and enhance our relationships to ourselves and others. We also investigated the negative/harmful elements and how these impact and block us experiencing a good life.

The Body and Mind exist and are fuelled by three main substances: Sunlight, Air and Food. It is these three energy forms that constitute and supply our Body and Mind with the necessary energy/fuel, so we can use the Body and Mind to navigate, exist in and do the think/feel/behave processes of being human. Without sunlight, air, and food (inclusive of liquids, e.g., water) the body will eventually die, and the mind will shut down, and our time here on Earth will be over…so food is of paramount importance and probably constitutes the main source of energy and energy conversion to sustain the Body and Mind to function at optimum levels. Yes, we could probably exist for a while just on sunlight and air but without food the Body and Mind will eventual be unable to repair and our ability to function will eventual fail leading to the death of Body and Mind.

So, with the high importance of food to our functioning and existing, one must question: what is the relevance to this food? Does it matter what type of foods we use?

In 2021 a research study was conducted by Hargreaves, Raposo, Saraiva and Zandonadi, giving and *'an overview of the vegetarian diet through the perspective of Quality-of-Life domains'*. The Quality-of-Life domains (QoL), according to WHO (World health Organisation):

> QoL is a multifactorial concept that includes the following domains: physical (physical state), psychological (affective and cognitive state), social (interpersonal relationships and social roles in the lives of individuals) and environmental (quality of the environment in which individuals live).

So, with QoL we are looking at the overall biopsychosocial factors that go into the life of a human and how they are constituted. What the study found was that overall, a vegetarian diet had a positive impact and influence on all four of the domains: including better overall health and lower rates of diseases on the physical domain. Positive wellbeing and feelings relating to the individual's psychology and the group's social psychology; and a positive lower impact overall on the environmental domain.

The study did also highlight possible negative effects: possible nutritional deficiencies, possible stigma, and rejection due to being a part of a minority group and how these could in turn influence and impact mental health if not supported. However, the overarching consensus was that the positive impact to one's wellbeing and life by adopting a well-managed vegetarian diet, far outweighed the potential negative effects, which could be easily mitigated if the vegetarian diet was nutritionally managed and adopted correctly. Other studies and articles highlighting research by Brazier (2020) and Weller (2022) also highlight the positive impacts of adopting a vegetarian diet including reduced risk of cancers, heart disease, diabetes, obesity, ecological sustainability, and ethical ways of living. So, overall, the research and the continued research is all advocating the positive influence and impact we can experience when we become a vegetarian or vegan. However, don't take my word for it, go out there do your research or better yet test it out…if you are considering vegetarianism or veganism, or are just curious to experience the health benefits, why not try it out…it's reported that within as little as 7-10 days you will begin to feel better, look better and experience positive outcomes purely from a Body/Mind perspective alone.

So, great for the Body and Mind but how is this a spiritual practice?

In section one we looked at the concept and practice of spirituality, if we take from this, that the general consensus, is that spirituality is the search, connecting and experiencing of that which is greater than us, beyond our Body/Mind processes and encompasses an experience of higher consciousness, and divinity, then any process, any practice that supports or enhances our ability to achieve this, is a spiritual practice in and of itself…therefore being a vegetarian or vegan constitutes and does this very thing.

By adopting a vegetarian or vegan diet we are stepping into and advocating from a position of non-violence/Ahimsa, the foundational premise of all spiritual practice. To advocate non-violence through our relationship to our Body/Mind and practicing this lifestyle, belief and value through the acquisition, relationship and consumption of the very substance that sustains our existence is by rights and virtue a spiritual act. We are consecrating our food stuff - vegetarian diet - by the rejection and abstaining of taking, advocating, and supporting the slaughtering and killing of an animal's life for our own gastronomic, apparel and stylistic pleasures and greed. We are by virtue promoting and adopting non-violence towards farming, butchering, slaughtering and the consuming of all animal products, and to do so is to perform a spiritual act.

There is the old age argument from non-vegetarians that claim that isn't the vegetarian killing and consuming plant life. Yes, the vegetarian is killing and consuming plant life, which is a valid point, but the vegetarian is not killing or consuming animal life. In the incarnational realm of Earth humans have not developed or evolved at this current time to exist without food completely, who knows maybe one day in the long-distant future, but right now we haven't. However, what we have evolved is the ability to sustain our lives through a purely vegetarian diet, which supports us and allows us to stop killing, slaughtering, and consuming animals. We as a species no longer need to (if we ever really did need to) kill and consume animal flesh to survive and live on Earth. We just don't need to do it, and if we are honest with ourselves as a species we never really did need to. Planet Earth, our wonderful Mother Earth, provides and sustains us through the growth and production of plant life including grains, wheats, pulses, herbs, seeds, vegetables in all their wonderful forms and liquid. We have everything we need, and if you've got the space, you can even grow your own, believe me they are a lot tastier than the mass-produced stuff you find in the superstores. We were never really meant to consume flesh, and if you research and delve into all the spiritual teachings, texts, scriptures, and studies of the past and present, they all say the same thing – if you want to get closer to your true essence, to achieve Self-realisation, enlightenment, and experience Wholeness – don't eat meat.

Energy Healing

AKA Prana Healing, Spiritual Healing, Bioenergy Healing:

There are many different names that describe the above form of healing, but ultimately the process of healing is all the same. Within the human body, and in every single form of life, there is believed to be a 'life force' that is fundamental to one's very existence. Without this 'life force' all of creation and all life forms, including humans, would cease to exist. In fact, it is due to this 'life force' that planet Earth exists also, and so does the Solar System, the Stars, the Galaxies and even the very Universe. Depending on what religion, spiritual practice, and philosophy this 'life force' is attributed to, will depend on the name this 'life force' is given.

People that exist within Eastern cultures and adopt Eastern frameworks, associated with Eastern medicines, martial arts, cultural and religious practices will be well versed with the concept and practical application of working with this 'life force'. It will be either known as 'Ki', 'Chi', or 'Prana', which we see associated with practices of qiqong, tai chi, pranic healing, ayurveda, karate, kung fu, aikido, acupuncture, acupressure, herbal medicines, reiki, hatha yoga and meditation. In the Hebrew traditions it is known as 'ruah', the ancient Greek traditions as 'pneuma', Polynesian traditions 'mana', and in some indigenousness traditions 'Great Spirit'. Unfortunately, within Western cultures this concept and practice of working with this 'energy/life force' seems to have been lost, although we can still find it in some Pagan, Wiccan, and Western Mysticism traditions, where it is either understood from a non-religious perspective as 'Mother Earth's presence' the power of 'Nature' or from a more religious or spiritual perspective as 'God's Grace', 'Holy Spirit', 'Fire of Pentecost' or just 'Spirit'. Whatever the name that is given to it, depending on tradition, it is all the same and constitutes as the 'breath of life'.

So, what do we do with this life force?

Depending on the form of practice will determine how the practitioner utilises the energy/life force for the purpose at hand...if you are coming from a healing perspective, for example prana healing or reiki, you will utilise the energy to assist your healing

276

practice and aid the person you are working with. If you are coming from a martial arts, spiritual exercise or systemised form/kata perspective, for example tai chi, hatha yoga and aikido you utilise the energy/life force through your body/mind/spirit system to optimise efficient, controlled movements, postures and breath control to enhance and to complete the outcomes of your practice, which in turn will increase your overall sense of wellbeing, increase mental and physical health, and create a stronger/firmer grounding within your spirituality.

What is energy healing?

For the purposes of this section, I shall give you an overview of energy/spiritual/prana healing linking to the different types that are promoted and practiced, with general examples of how it's done and the possible ailments that it can be utilised to clear to assist healing. For further information on this style of healing I'd suggest reading Master Choa Kok Sui's books on pranic healing and visiting the websites associated with pranic healing in the East and the West, which you can easily find through 'google search'. Personally, I find Master Choa Kok Sui's system of prana healing to be the most comprehensive, structured, and scientifically proven through research and developing research. This is not to undermine any other forms of energy healing, which under the correct tutelage, guidance and teaching can be used effectively and productively to aid healing. If you are interested in practicing energy healing, it's important that you study and find the one that best 'fits' you, as you will be the one using it and you must be able to comprehend, feel, and be confident in how you use it…so if you are interested in practicing energy healing do your research and use your discernment.

How do we do energy healing?

The basic premise that underpins energy healing is the utilisation of 'life force/prana/Ki energy' to assist and speed up a person's natural healing process. Energy healing is a process where we examine the human energy system more closely, finding and working with any forms of depletion, congestion, degradation, illness, and disease, and assisting the process of healing by clearing negative/diseased energy and replenishing with positive/healing energy.

The practitioner uses their own physical and subtle/astral body to channel the energy/prana and direct it toward the person they are working with through their hands; first to remove any diseased energy or blocks by clearing this energy from the person's subtle/astral body and then to replenish and balance the energy systems of the person they are working with. It is understood and known within Eastern medicine systems that the human being is formed and 'made up' of, and for ease of understanding, three bodies and five different sheaths/layers:

Three Bodies:

1.   Physical/Gross Body – our physical form
2.   Astral/Subtle Body – our subtle or energy body where meridians and chakras exist
3.   Casual/Spiritual Body – our blueprint or master plan, where we experience Self-realisation.

Five sheaths/layers that are located within the three bodies that cover/encase our soul/divine Self:

1. Food sheath
2. Energy sheath
3. Mind sheath
4. Wisdom/Intellect sheath
5. Bliss/Ananda sheath.

When we are practicing energy/prana healing we are working with the person's first two bodies: the physical body and the subtle/astral body. The human has an aura or energy field that can be felt through the hands of the practitioner, and for those gifted with clairvoyancy it can be seen by the clairvoyant, also it has now been identified through Kirlian photography as well. It is the process of energy/prana healing that works to balance this aura and clear any diseased energy from it. Before a human gets physically ill or diseased in the physical body, the diseased energy will first manifest in the subtle/astral body of a person, and if it is not cleared from the subtle/astral body of a person it will then eventually manifest into the physical body, which is when most people first become aware of or notice they are feeling unwell or have a diseased area of their physical body.

The subtle/astral body like the physical body is constituted with a system of channels and organs that are used to circulate energy to keep the body alive and healthy. In the physical body we have nerve and blood systems that circulate energy and work with the organs of the body e.g., heart, liver, to keep the physical body functioning and alive; the subtle/astral body is no different, the energy channels in the subtle/astral body are known as nadis/meridians, and the organs are knowns as chakras/energy wheels that allow prana/energy to flow efficiently and effectively throughout the subtle/astral body to keep the person healthy and the subtle/astral body alive. When these channels and chakras in the subtle/astral body become blocked, depleted and/or diseased is when the person will first start to become ill. They may not become aware of this until it manifests in the physical body, but they may experience a sense of feeling lower in energy, tired, 'out of sorts', stiffness, or pain in certain areas, and/or anxious or depressed. The subtle/astral body, or the energy body as identified by Master Choa Kok Sui in his system of Pranic healing respectively, has eleven chakras/energy wheels that exist at different points in the subtle/astral body and can be placed in accordance to certain areas of the physical body, although the chakras do not exist in the physical body but manifest through the physical body constituted within the subtle/astral body. In other systems seven or nine chakras are identified and most forms of energy/prana healing can work effectively with the seven or nine chakra system. For ease and overview, I will show the seven and nine chakra systems.

Seven chakra system:

1. Base chakra – located at the base of the spine
2. Sacral chakra – located in the reproductive organs
3. Solar Plexus chakra – located at the solar plexus
4. Heart chakra – located at the heart
5. Throat chakra – located at the throat

6. Ajna chakra – located between the eyes
7. Crown chakra – located at top of the head or crown of the head.

Nine chakra system:

1. Base chakra – located at the base of the spine
2. Sacral chakra – located in the reproductive organs
3. Navel chakra – located at the navel
4. Solar Plexus chakra – located at the solar plexus
5. Heart chakra – located at the heart
6. Throat chakra – located at the throat
7. Ajna chakra – located between the eyes
8. Forehead chakra – located at the forehead
9. Crown chakra – located at top of the head or crown of the head.

Like the organs in the physical body, the chakras in the subtle/astral body have specific functions that correspond to the healthy functioning and constitution of the subtle/astral body that correspond directly to the healthy functioning and constitution of the physical body. It is due to the subtle/astral body that a manifested physical body even exists and functions. Without the subtle/astral body the physical body would never develop and grow and without it, it would cease to exist. When the physical body dies the withdrawal of energy from the physical body which causes death is due to the subtle/astral body in accordance with our time to physically die; the next process is the diminishing of the subtle/astral body and the continued journey of our causal/spiritual body into our next life. Although, we have investigated the process and connection of the physical body and subtle/astral body, their constitution only exists due to the underpinning of the spiritual/casual body, this is the seed/core form of our existence, this never dies and is eternal. This is carried through our many, many lifetimes and decides what physical form and life we will have through reincarnation – this is our connection to God/Divine our Divinity. So, we can see how prana healing is linked to and aids the spiritual development of the practitioner but also the person/client they are working with - to develop a deeper connection to the spiritual world and assisting a deeper understanding of the Body/Mind/Spirit integration.

If you are sensitive and aware of your subtle/astral body, and work to keep it healthy and the channels flowing freely and the chakras clear and balanced, the probability of you manifesting and experiencing physical 'illness/disease' will be greatly reduced, if not at all…if however, you are experiencing physical 'illness/disease' you may wish to visit a prana/energy healer to assist in the clearing and balancing of your subtle/astral body through the unblocking of the meridians and the clearing/balancing of the chakras, which in turn clears and balances your physical body.

Why do we get ill and experience disease and negative energy in our bodies?

If we look at disease and illness from the framework of energy/prana healing, the fundamental premise is based on the subtle/astral body and the resultant physical body experiencing negative forms of energy or diseased energy, which in turn has a negative/toxic impact on the subtle/astral body, which in turn then effects the positive balanced functioning of the physical body. When referring to the subtle/astral body, it is the inefficient flow and blocking of the chakras and meridians through either energy/prana congestion and depletion, which if not treated then manifests into a disease or ailment of the physical body, e.g., sore throat, viral infection or in more extreme cases cancer.

> *Through clairvoyant observations, a disease can be seen in the energy body* [subtle/astral body] *even before it manifests itself on the visible physical body. Non-clairvoyants may scan or feel that the inner aura of the affected part is either smaller or bigger than usual. For instance, before a person suffers from coughs and colds, the bioplasmic throat and lungs are pranically depleted and can be observed clairvoyantly as greyish. These areas when scanned can be felt as hollows in the inner aura. Another example: A person who is about to suffer from jaundice can be observed clairvoyantly as having a grey solar plexus and liver. Physical tests or diagnoses will show the patient as normal or healthy. Unless the patient is treated, the disease will manifest inevitably on the visible physical body.*

Master Choa Kok Sui, *Miracles Through Pranic Healing* (p. 55)

Master Choa Kok Sui highlights the intrinsic connection between the subtle/astral body and the physical body, and how certain ailments and conditions if not treated manifest directly into the physical body through the impairing of the chakras and flow of the meridians in the subtle/astral body. In effect the process of energy/prana healing, although effective when an illness is detected in the physical body, the main aim is one of preventative. So, ideally what we are looking to do is support a healthy subtle/astral body and keep this working efficiently and effectively before any diseased or negative manifestation is allowed to enter the physical body. The argument is: if you have regular 'check ups' through energy/prana healing, as you would do with say a GP or Doctor six monthly, then your risk of becoming physically ill would greatly reduce and accompanying this with regular mental health support and a positive healthy lifestyle of good exercise and diet, your life expectancy greatly increases too.

What are the probable causes of illness and disease?

There are three main factors to consider: 1, the Mind, 2, Internal factors and 3, External factors. These three factors connect to why and how we get ill.

The power of the Mind is not a new concept or practice. Humans have been harnessing the power of the mind since our first incarnations and historically and presently we see repeatedly how certain humans harness the power of the mind to achieve and succeed in all areas of life. So, how we use the Mind and how we create is vital to our health and our wellbeing. If you think negatively and are always in Victim, your lifestyle, your ability to achieve, your progress in life will be negatively impacted – the self-fulfilling prophecy – if you constantly believe and create negative thoughts around your health and wellbeing, eventually this will impact your astral/subtle body and if not cleared or worked through will eventually manifest into ill health in the physical body.

> *Anger and intense worry devitalize the whole energy body* [subtle/astral body] *so that the body becomes susceptible to all kinds of diseases. Negative emotions cause disturbances in the energy body so that the whole physical body becomes sick. You may have experienced that after intense anger or an altercation, you felt physically exhausted or became sick. This is because both the energy and visible physical bodies had been drained of prana or life energy and become susceptible to infection.*

Master Choa Kok, (p. 78)

So, the ability to stay positive and to foster positive thoughts and feelings in your life is essential to a positive healthy life. Sometimes it's not as easy as just thinking and feeling positive due to traumas and extreme negative impacts on a person's body and mind; if this is the case then working with a psychotherapist and an energy/prana healer can help support you through your healing and recovery, to be better able to think and feel more positively about yourself, your relationships, and your life.

Internal factors that affect our health can be understood, again as negative emotions, thoughts, and feelings that we ruminate on and give life to, that in turn impact our subtle/astral body by impairing our chakras and flow of energy through the meridians.

External factors can be understood as those external factors that exist 'outside' of us and/or we contribute to, for example bacteria, toxins, pollutants, viruses, germs, etc... but also our harmful lifestyle choices and decisions, for example smoking, drinking excessive alcohol, lack of balanced exercise, poor diet, toxic relationships to family members, partners, colleagues at work, addictions and lack of self-care and nurturing.

Internal factors and external factors are not necessarily separate and constitute an overall impact on the person effected, for example excessive smoking (external factor) and feeling negative about yourself (internal factor) weakens and toxifies the throat, heart and solar plexus chakras, which if not treated manifests into throat, lung and respiratory problems that could leave you open and vulnerable to bacteria or viral infections (external factor).

Another example could be you are constantly being bullied at work (external factor) and unable to express your own anger, sadness or frustration, while harbouring negative thoughts and feelings about yourself and the other person (internal factor), this leads to depleted energy in your subtle/astral body, which leaves you feeling more depressed and anxious having a negative impact on your heart, solar plexus and navel chakras; if not treated this could lead to mental health problems, IBS (Irritable Bowel Syndrome), digestive problems and/or respiratory problems and even heart conditions. So, the link between the mind, internal factors and external factors are important - advocating a good balanced lifestyle between all three of these factors is important. Of course, if there is an extreme external factor, for example, fatality to the physical body in whatever shape and form e.g., RTA (road traffic accident) then that is the end of your incarnation now, irrespective of how healthy your subtle/astral body is. Extreme internal factors, for example severe mental illness, are treatable as they are based within the mind and internal processes of the person, so can be supported through the body and mind.

What illnesses and diseases can energy/prana healing work with?

According to Master Choa Kok Sui in his book *Miracles through Pranic Healing* the scope of prana/energy healing is vast and wide. He claims that prana/energy healing can assist in the natural healing and recovery from a myriad of different, illnesses, complaints, and diseases, for example ranging from small cases of headaches, earaches, sore throats, muscle cramps, muscle stiffness, pimples, diarrhoea, constipation, sunburn, cuts and wounds, asthma, heart ailments, enlarged prostrate, skin complaints and mental health. In a 2019 study by Sabharwal Pooja, Naik Bibhu Prasad and Sharma Akanksha looked at the benefits of pranic healing for cancer patients and found positive benefits, and in a 2020 study by Nittur and Ganapathi, pranic healing was used on a female stage 4 breast cancer patient, after 6 weeks of treatment the cancer size was reduced and the spread decreased. Cancer Research UK also advocates alternative healing including prana, spiritual healing, etc, but they do state, '*There is no reliable scientific evidence to support its use as a cancer treatment'.* Agdal, Hjelmborg and Johannessen (2011) created a critical review on energy healing for cancer and concluded:

> The existing research does not allow conclusions regarding the efficacy or effectiveness of energy healing. Future studies should adhere to existing standards of research on the efficacy and effectiveness of a treatment, and given the complex character of potential outcomes, cross-disciplinary methodologies may be relevant. To extend the scope of clinical trials, psychosocial processes should be taken into account and explored, rather than dismissed as placebo.

So, the research is mixed and there needs to be further research and studies conducted before we can scientifically prove the effectiveness of energy/prana healing on cancer patients. However, Pranic Healing UK & Ireland state on their website that they are undertaking clinical trials at Kings College Hospital London looking at the effectiveness of pranic healing with patients, which is promising and could increase the overall scientific evidence base, alongside the work of Master Choa Kok Sui and the global pranic healing organisations around the world, and the PHRI (Pranic Healing Research Institute). Scientific evidence is a good place to start when personally researching treatments and looking for healing approaches that can help and enhance a person's wellbeing and general health; although, these are objective and subjective to those involved and presenting the research. The best person to make the judgement and try out these approaches is always You. Begin to trust your own reasoning, feelings and judgement by trying these approaches out personally, make up your own mind from the results you gain from your own experiential experience, step out of victim and begin to trust your own discernment, feelings and judgement...yes external guidance and help can be useful, yes objective and subjective experiences of others do have value but ultimately, they only lead and guide you to your own discernment, self-trust and development of your own integrity and self-worth.

Sex & Brahmacharya

Considered one of the most difficult yet fundamental spiritual practices that human can adopt and engage with, Brahmacharya is 'hailed' by those that are able to vow and practice it as the epitome of spirituality. It not only leads to greater forms of self-mastery, focused/concentrated energy cultivation, more profound spiritual experiences, and the anchor to and for all other spiritual practices but is also a quicker/faster road to enlightenment/Self-realisation.

So, what is this Brahmacharya?

When we break down this term it means literally 'to stay in conduct with your own sense of being or absolute reality'. Brahma referring to the concept of Brahman/God/Ultimate Self when relating to ancient Hindu and Yoga scriptures e.g., Vedas, and Charya meaning to be in conduct with or to behave in that way...so, it could again be loosely translated as 'to be in line or conduct with God'. When we refer to Patanjali's yoga sutras, brahmacharya is number four of the five yamas (the don'ts of yoga practice) and is understood traditionally as a vow of celibacy/continence. The student vows to abstain from all forms of sexual conduct through word, thought and deed for purity of spiritual practice and correct use of energy for Self-realisation. By making the vow of brahmacharya and living by this vow, the student is anchoring his spiritual practice away from all forms of base, carnal and egoistic thought, feeling and behaviour that will undermine and use up the powerful 'life force' energy, which needs to be cultivated for the path of spiritual development and enlightenment. Brahmacharya is more than abstaining from sexual intercourse, it is the committed spiritual vow to transcend all that is associated with the sex impulse, sex instinct, sexual desire, and lust, which holds the individual deeply within the bounds of the 'pleasure/pain cycle' through the orgiastic embodied pleasure 'hit' known as the orgasm.

It is the orgasm that releases a profound and all-encompassing physical, mental and emotional high that can hold the individual in a state of orgiastic greed and need, not only through the animal/carnal instinct to procreate but also through the desired lust and attraction of the physical body and overall image of the person…everything that is wrong with our world and has been throughout the ages is underpinned by the misdirected misuse of this powerful sex instinct and sexual drive in the human. If we link this to modernity and our current postmodern age, the human sex instinct and sexual drive has been and still is the ultimate gift for advertising, marketing and the selling of products and services in our global marketplaces. It's literally the consumeristic 'wet dream', if you will excuse my pun for organisations, companies and corporations selling and advertising products. The human sex instinct is their alpha and omega, the fundamental source of their power, and their winning lottery ticket that just keeps winning…

Reflective Task 10 - Sex:

I'd like you to take a moment (between 5-10 minutes) to reflect on your day-to-day lives and to consider your relationship to sex and the human sex instinct…think about your own sexuality…think about your own sexual practices, thoughts, feelings, and behaviours…how often do you think about sex or have sex? Are you aware of your attractions to other people? How important is sex to you - very important, take it or leave it, not important at all? Do you enjoy sex, or is it something you do for others? … think about the websites you visit daily…think about how you engage with social media…think about the products you buy, the advertising you see, the people and products that 'influence you'…think about the constant messages, words, images and sounds that stream through every aspect of your life…how much of this is using sex, sexual attraction and attractive images to 'turn you on' to their products, get your attention to buy a product, to influence your decisions making?

Thank you for taking the time to engage with this reflective task. I hope this task has given you further insight into how You as an individual relates to sex, sexuality and how sex is used within the global marketplaces. The sex instinct is a primordial force that exists within the human being that has a deep physical, emotional, and psychological influence on how we as humans exist in our relationships to ourselves, other people, and our environments, even if we allow ourselves to be aware of it or not...

So, if I want to live a spiritual life and work toward enlightenment, do I have to be celibate?

In our postmodern age, especially in the West, sex, sexual identity, sexual image, and sexuality have a strong currency among the general population. The post-war era of the 1950s leading into the 1960s and then into 1970s saw a huge surgent rise of sexuality, sexual identity, and sexual behaviour, which was highlighted through the 'sexual revolution', 'free love' and the countercultures that were challenging the existing establishments of conservatism and strict religious groups in the West. Music, fashion, activism, politics, anti-war, literature, socialism, civil rights movements and gender equality, were all working together to challenge the existing status quo and change the mindset and ethos of the mainstream societies and cultures that were predominating at the time...this has led and has been developed through the last fifty years, throughout the end of the 20th century into the beginning of the 21st century, now being integrated and presented through all forms of social media and the global markets of our present day. Therefore, to

292

practice brahmacharya or even consider the concept of celibacy in our current age, would appear as anathema to our current lifestyles and almost an impossible joke given the presence, power, and insidious nature of how the sex instinct is being used...sex is all around us, it's in everything we see to the point of being blind to it. How could anyone in their right mind want to or even be able to be celibate?

This is where individuals and even groups of people in Western culture and other global cultures do their usually classic human idiom:

> Let's bend the rules a little and reframe it a little
> so this thing can fit nicely within our current
> lifestyle or way of life, so I don't have to fully
> commit and make this thing work for me...

Humans have been doing this since our very beginnings and I can guarantee we'll happily keep doing it till the end of time. When the human being is presented with a concept, thought, idea or behaviour that in theory is sound and practical but the doing of it completely is just a bit too much of a commitment or sacrifice, the human mind steps in and justifies an alternative reason, belief, idea or way of doing it (distorts it) or even turns their back on it completely through avoidance (denies it). When we look at brahmacharya we see the same process applied. Brahmacharya can be conceded as a vow of celibacy through word, thought and deed, a middle-path, and /or a conservation of sexual energy but ultimately Brahmacharya 'is to *conduct oneself in the way of Spirit/God/Brahman'* – align oneself with God/Spirit/Brahman and fulfil one's existence in this way…

How does Brahmacharya work if I'm married and/or in a loving long-term relationship or partnership?

If you google brahmacharya you will find a mixed bag on what certain groups, individuals, websites, and businesses will have to say on the matter. Some will talk about celibacy, others about correct energy use, some about moderation, others about the middle ground or path to practice and others promoting a combination of the afore mentioned…for me I'd say these are all correct, to achieve brahmacharya all the afore mentioned must be practiced in one way, shape or form but ultimately brahmacharya is the cultivation, conservation and internal transmutation of one's sex instinct and sexual energy through correct spiritualised practice. Looking further into Brahmacharya from different perspectives, I'd suggest reading *The Practice of Brahmacharya* by Swami Sivananda, *The Benefits of Brahmacharya* by Swami Nirmalananda (Abbot George Burke), which is a compilation of essays and writings from great spiritual Swamis and teachers, and also engaging with Master Choa Kok Sui's writings on the sacred use of sex energy and kundalini yoga, which can be found in his books, *'Achieving Oneness with the Higher Soul'*, *'The Spiritual Essence of Man'*, and on the pranic-healers website.

But again, how does Brahmacharya work if I'm married and/or in a loving long-term relationship or partnership?

I personally believe no one can make any decision for anyone else regarding their own sense of body/mind/spirit. Brahmacharya is a personal relationship an individual has with their own body/mind and their spiritual beliefs and practice and higher power...if you are in a loving relationship and sex is a part of this relationship then brahmacharya is a decision that is between the two people involved. The physical union and sharing of love between two consenting adults can be a most wonderful and powerful experience; and when this physical union and sharing of love is spiritualised and transcended beyond the base carnal/egoistic desires of selfish lust, it can open a connection to a universal love and divine sense of being that fills the two people with an experience that is never forgotten. However, I question in our current times, how often, if ever do two people ever really experience a spiritualised experience of love making...that's not to say it doesn't happen or couples aren't working toward this but I think it's a rare experience...most of the time people are enjoying their own pleasurable sex hit either through the giving or receiving of sexual stimulation from the other person working up to the final orgasm...

The sex instinct is one of the most powerful drives that underpins the human being and the human condition. The drive to procreate in heterosexual unions is strong and there is also a powerful social conditioning that suggests we as a species should have children that goes with this drive. The pleasure of the orgasm and the pleasurable stimulation we can give and receive in sexual encounters is a very powerful heady potent force that gives us that 'feel good' all body/mind effect that makes us and stimulates our desire for more…just like the addicted person chasing the next high. Whatever decision you make regarding brahmacharya, the key is understanding how it serves you, understanding your relationship to the process of brahmacharya and being honest with yourself.

Meditation

Sitting with crossed legs, closing the eyes, focusing on the breath coming in and out, holding space in your mind and being aware of your thoughts as they come and go, this is the general understanding of meditation…a space to feel relaxed and to centre oneself…here is what others have to say:

> *Meditation is the practice of intentionally spending time with our mind. We take time out of our busy days to sit, breathe, and try to remain focused on our breath. Doing this helps us become more aware of our thoughts, act more compassionately toward ourselves and others, and connect with the present moment.*
>
> Headspace

> *Meditation is considered a type of mind-body complementary medicine. Meditation can produce a deep state of relaxation and a tranquil mind. During meditation, you focus your attention and eliminate the stream of jumbled thoughts that may be crowding your*

mind and causing stress. This process may result in enhanced physical and emotional well-being.

Mayo Clinic

By releasing physical tension held in the body, meditation can help us release worries buried in the mind, easing anxiety, stress, and low mood, and even helping you get deeper, more restful sleep. Meditation can also bring a sense of calm that enables us to respond to life events in a measured way, rather than reacting with our emotions. For the best results, try to build regular meditation into your daily routine.

NHS UK

The practice of meditation can bring many benefits: greater attention and awareness, the settling down of our emotional life, a growing sense of goodwill and kindness, and a desire to be of help in this world. The latest brain-imaging technology is showing what meditators have sensed for millennia—that the brain circuitry associated with relationships, compassion, attentiveness peace, and joy is all amplified in long-term meditators.

Mountain Cloud Zen Centre

In mindfulness meditation, we're learning how to pay attention to the breath as it goes in and out and notice when the mind wanders from this task. This practice of returning to the breath builds the muscles of attention and mindfulness. When we pay attention to our breath, we are learning how to return to, and remain in, the present moment—to anchor ourselves in the here and now on purpose, without judgement.

Mindful.org

Meditation has been around for an exceptionally long time. If we go back to the ancient texts and scriptures of Hindu and yoga traditions, meditation is a corner stone of their practice and philosophy. If we look at Buddhism in its three main forms Theravada, Mahayana, and Vajrayana, meditation is a foundation of their practice too. In fact, when you delve into different forms of Eastern religious/spiritual practice, I'd go so far as to say, there isn't an Eastern form of religion or practice that doesn't advocate or practice meditation…if we move into the West, we see meditation or meditations associated with Christianity, New Age movements, Religious Mysticism, Esoteric practice, and Paganism as well. Over the last thirty years, we've seen the rise of the Self-Help movements, helping people to live healthy lives, and offering ways to improve people's mental health. This is no more evident than in the development, practice, and popularity of Mindfulness, where you can even download an App on your phone to help you do this...

Meditation has become a highly valued currency in our current age, where people are suffering with overwhelm, anxiety and depression due to the constant pressures of life. Constantly images are being projected into our lives of how we should be living, how we should be looking, how we should be parenting, how we should be communicating, how we should be succeeding and if we are not they hang the noose of failure and disappointment over our heads, as we constantly compare ourselves to others, who are succeeding (well so it appears on social media), as we measure ourselves and our life against these false images, lifestyles, friendships and successes…So let's add one more ingredient to the mix, let's give you a coping strategy to help you with this Capitalist/Consumer overload…here have meditation, you can even use your phone to do it, so it can't be that bad, look you're still plugged-in…

It comes from a deep place of concern, so please excuse my satire, in no way am I condemning the use of meditation as a means and strategy to help individuals find a positive way forward. In my somewhat clumsy way, I'm striving to lift the veil of delusion or perhaps offering another critical way to help see the link and appropriation of a spiritual practice that has been capitalised, and is being sold as a product by the very system that is harming you and keeping you firmly in the position of Victim…I pose the question: do you really need to subscribe to a cooperation or organisation and pay a monthly fee to engage with a practice that has always been and will always be free? How can you really step out of Victim and get off the 'pleasure/pain' merry go round if you are dependent on an app or piece of software that insidiously and deceptively is telling you that you need it to practice meditation?

Meditation first is a spiritual practice and is available to you to assist you in your further physical, emotional, psychological, and spiritual development. When we meditate, we are giving ourselves an opportunity, space, and time to engage with our eternal sense of being, our Godhead, our eternal source, our greater Self. Meditation is our means to get closer to Self-realisation and the vehicle that enables us to finally experience Oneness- Samadhi. Again, I'm not telling you anything new here, we've known this throughout every generation and throughout our entire human history, and when you start to practice, it's no wonder you start to experience positive outcomes. You are moving closer to the Divine, to Universal love, to the Bliss that is all of us - Satchitananda – pure existence, consciousness, and bliss – that is why we meditate, and any positive outcome we experience from this is a wonderful secondary gift that allows us to live a greater positive existence.

So, what is the best way to meditate?

I believe for beginner and/or intermediate alike, the meditation on 'I AM Not' (see appendix 8) is a good starting point. Again, don't take my word for it, try it out...

How will I know when it's working?

The best way to know if it's working is to keep a diary or journal on your meditation journey. Write down your feelings before or after a meditation session. Be aware more of how you are engaging with yourself and others generally. Notice any changes in your thoughts, feelings and behaviours toward yourself and others. Observe and listen to how others receive you and are communicating to you. There are general positive markers that we experience when we practice meditation:

1. You'll start to feel calmer in your life.
2. You'll gain a sharper clarity of focus and understanding to your life.
3. You'll experience friendly and positive relationships in your life.
4. You'll be more patient and understanding of yourself and others.
5. You'll be more inclined to offer kindness to yourself and others.
6. You'll find you have a greater willingness to help others.
7. Your interests and lifestyle will change toward positive activities.

Meditation is a wonderful means to enhance our lives and it gives us a practical method to experience the greater spiritual core of who we really are Self/Divinity/Universal love – Satchitananda.

What if I can't meditate, and/or relax and my mind is always wandering?

This is a common question and concern for many of us when we start practicing meditation. The thought and practice of sitting still, focusing on our breathing with our eyes closed, feels almost impossible...The key to any form of practice, especially meditation is perseverance and skilful practice. To begin with start small. You don't have to go in there with an hour or two hours that's just not feasible or practical. Starting off with as little as 5 minutes is fine, and gradually with time and progress work up to longer periods – this is what we call skilful practice. Maybe just do 5 minutes a day for a week first to see how that goes, and if you are feeling confident and managing it, then try 10 minutes each day for the next week, and gradually build up this way until in a few months' time you are finding that you can comfortably meditate for 50-60 minutes - remember slow and steady wins the race. It's ok to be the tortoise in this race you don't want to be the Hare. With time, perseverance, and skilful practice you'll soon find that you'll become more adept and experienced. You'll be experiencing those positive markers, developing spiritually, and getting ever closer to enlightenment and Self-realisation.

Section 4. Science – Religion – Spirituality – the links

In this next section I want to introduce and look closer at the relationships between science, religion, and spirituality. In appendix 1,2,3,4, I've included diagrams/tables to give a visual illustration of the links and differences between science, religion and spirituality that illustrates how these disciplines sit within the Body/Mind/Spirit framework. These lists are by no means exhaustive and certainly not prescriptive but hopefully they will give an overview.

In the last hundred plus years science has taken centre stage and dominates a strong position of authority within our cultures and global markets. This is especially evident in Western culture and even more so with our fast-paced technological worlds of the internet, social media, and global markets…the worlds of marketing and advertising look closely to the sciences to validate and support their products and services. Research offers a strong scientific reason and rationale that supports the products reliability, use and validity. This can strongly influence the buyer and consumer of the product promoting an ease, security, consistency and positive feel and experience to the consumer...with the underlying idiom: *you'd be crazy and doing yourself out of pocket not to buy this*...we see this also in all areas of life not just in the business worlds. We see this in education, academia, economics, politics, finance, engineering, agriculture, law, the humanities and pretty much any 'ology' you can think of. Science and evidence-based research holds a strong value and 'trust' within our modern and postmodern cultures.

So, what is science?

According to the Berkeley University of California (first hit on the google search):

The word "science" probably brings to mind many different pictures: a fat textbook, white lab coats and microscopes, an astronomer peering through a telescope, a naturalist in the rainforest, Einstein's equations scribbled on a chalkboard, the launch of the space shuttle, bubbling beakers .... All of those images reflect some aspect of science. But none of them provides a full picture because science has so many facets:

- *Science is both a body of knowledge and a process. In school, science may sometimes seem like a collection of isolated and static facts listed in a textbook, but that's only a small part of the story. Just as importantly, science is also a process of discovery that allows us to link isolated facts into coherent and comprehensive understandings of the natural world.*

- *Science is exciting. Science is a way of discovering what's in the universe and how those things work today, how they worked in the past, and how they are likely to work in the future. Scientists are motivated by the thrill of seeing or figuring out something that no one has before.*

- **_Science is useful._** _The knowledge generated by science is **powerful and reliable.** It can be **used to develop** new technologies, treat diseases, and deal with many other sorts of problems._

- **_Science is ongoing._** _Science is continually refining and expanding our knowledge of the universe, and as it does, it **leads to new questions for future investigation.** Science will never be "finished."_

- **_Science is a global human endeavour._** _People all over the world participate in the process of science. And you can too!_

The above quote gives an excellent overview of what science is, how it's understood, what it can do and how it's used. If we look more closely at this definition, we can single out a few underpinning factors that give reason, structure, and purpose. I've **bolded** these factors to add clarity:

- Body of knowledge and process – the collection of reliable and valid 'facts' and outcomes that are constituted through rigorous scientific testing and observation.
- Process of discovery – scientifically testing and observing theories and hypothesis to gain reliable and valid outcomes and results
- Discovering something new – scientifically testing and observing theories and hypothesis to gain newly undiscovered reliable and valid outcomes and results.

- Understanding how 'things' work - scientifically testing and observing theories and hypothesis to gain reliable and valid insight and understanding of how 'things' work.

- Linking facts – the joining together of results and facts from scientific investigation to create reliable and valid theories and understanding.

- Useful, powerful, and reliable – the utility of scientific investigation and outcomes through reliable and valid testing and enquiry.

- Leads to new questions and future investigation – development of ongoing scientific investigation from the results and outcomes of previous scientific investigation.

- It's a Human global endeavour – science is a universal human process and activity.

We can quickly begin to understand that given the establishment of this scientific knowledge base that has been reliably discovered and understood through a rigorous valid process of enquiry and testing – it quickly becomes a valuable, useful, and powerful commodity. An example to elucidate this further, is applied science. This is how we use the scientific research and discoveries people make in the fields they are studying; for example, we see this in medicine (drugs and services), agriculture (food and sustainability), transport (logistics and invention), communication (internet and phones), manufacturing (plastics and commercial products), chemical engineering (food stuffs and detergents), and energy cultivation (solar, oil and electricity). It is from the research and discoveries of science that we can understand, use, and create advances in our physical worlds. So, it is due to scientific endeavour that we have all the things we have, which makes it such a powerful 'valid' commodity.

How does science relate to religion and spirituality?

Over the last hundred years or so, since the ongoing development and establishment of science, religion and spirituality has taken a step back from the strong centre stage position it once held. Religion and spirituality, if we look back into our histories, was a powerful force that gave meaning to human life and gave clear guidance on how humans should live their lives. Religion has many faces, so the structure, values, and beliefs of religion gave rise to different systems of belief, values, and practices. Humans in their egocentric existence became worried and distressed when faced with a belief system or ideology that didn't fit or was perceived as different from their own. This difference caused certain religious groups to become fearful of their own existence and the usurping of their religious belief system and 'way of life' by other religious groups...so, the religious groups generated armies and defence systems to protect and fight against these imposing other scary religious groups. Throwing politics, trade, territory, cultural difference, and economics into the mix as well, we have the potent and volatile ingredients for war. Our histories tell a sad and dark tale of human atrocity, death, and destruction underpinned by religious/spiritual belief systems and the human pursuit of power, dominance, and the appropriation of land/territory, for the control of wealth, resources,

307

and power. Religion, like science in our current times, held a strong powerful currency that leaders of territories and nations used for their political and economic gain. If you look at the dominate empires of our history, we see this in the Byzantine Empire (330-1453), Islamic Empires (esp. Umayyid/Abbasid (661-1258), Almohad (1140-1250), Almoravid (1050-1140)), Holy Roman Empire (1254-1835), Spanish Empire (1492-1898), Russian Empire/USSR (1552-1991), Dutch Empire (1660-1962), British Empire (1607-ca. 1980) and the French Empire (ca. 1611- ca. 1980). Each of these empires at certain points were underpinned by a powerful religious force that looked to gain power, wealth, and control of resources by overthrowing and converting people and nations to their existing religion...this is no more evident in the power and dominance that Catholicism and other forms of Christianity has held, and still does in certain countries...so we become aware, like science in our current age, that religion and spirituality holds a power base.

With the rise and fall of religion in the last few centuries, one could argue due to religion's misuse of power, control and resources, humanity especially in the modern and postmodern age became somewhat disillusioned and mistrusting of religion. Religion hasn't left a warming and caring legacy. It's left a shadowy/dark trail of violence, pain, destruction and suffering in its wake. Certain groups and nations have taken what was once a wonderful, glorious, and loving spiritual body of knowledge and practice and turned it into a violent, oppressive, and harmful system of control and rule. Sadly, even today we still see this being played out with certain fanatical and fundamentalist religious groups causing oppression, destruction, and harbouring war in the name of their religion. I'm not going to explicitly give examples other than to suggest you research the wars that have existed and played out in the last 20/25 years, and it will be very evident the role religion and religious beliefs have played and still do for certain groups on both sides…so we can see why science in the last hundred years has easily and securely filled the gap that religion has sadly and misguidedly opened up for another system to fill that offers a less harmful impact on humanity – and not only less harmful but offers technological advances and modernisation through manufacturing, medicine and health care, communication, business, education, agriculture and all the wonderful and helpful things science has had a hand in developing to make life better and easier. Let's not kid ourselves and give credit where credit is due, science has helped humans no end in advancement, without science we wouldn't have cars, TV, medicines, computers, the internet, social media, and you wouldn't even be reading this book…

However, let's not be too one-sided, and biased - is science the shining crowning successor to religion as it first appears?

Science, like religion and any other human endeavour, when in the wrong misguided and misdirected hands can be destructive, harmful, and violent. Let's have a look at a few examples of the shadow-side of science that destroy, harm and control individuals, groups, and nations:

1. Weaponizing – humans have created and use those things discovered and created by science as weapons, e.g., guns, chemicals, machines, bombs, drones, missiles, and nuclear arms.

2. Pollution – air pollution (chemicals, gases, particle); electromagnetic pollution (radio and TV transmissions, Wi-Fi, Microwaves – radiation); litter; Plastics; Water; Noise; Radioactive contamination; Thermal and Soil pollution.

3. Medicines – Alcohol, Fentanyl, Heroin, Hydrocodone, Methadone, Morphine, Oxycodone, Cocaine, Methamphetamines, Alprazolam (Xanax), Diazepam (Valium), Nicotine, and any anti-psychotic drug.

4. Genetic and biological engineering – ethical, ecological, health and economic concerns.

5. Addiction – medicines, drugs, gambling, shopping, sex, food, exercise, and gaming – all facilitated and supported through online and offline activity.

6. Online and cyberspaces – addiction, control, oppression, bullying, harassment, pollution, dark-web, people trafficking, weapons/arms sales, drug sales, pornography, discrimination (including all the 'isms'), radicalising, violence to name a few...

For all sciences wonder and positive advancement, it's by no means 'squeaky clean' and has and still is causing a huge amount of damage, suffering and destruction to human life and planet Earth.

Is spirituality the same as science and religion?

To recap briefly, spirituality from its first human understanding is a way to move beyond the ordinary human experience and the method to experience our true 'connection' (I use this term lightly) to the source of existence. which some people and groups understand as God/Allah/Spirit/Universal Love/Self/Eternal Bliss/All That There Is.

How spirituality is different, say to science and religion, in its purest form is to experience ultimate 'Truth'. To reside in a purely unconditioned experience of completeness that is and of itself Oneness. One could say that finitude or that which is perceived as finite, relative and forever changing (impermanence) is the dream of the source of our existence. This doesn't mean that we don't exist or are only a dream, of course we exist, but we exist in a limited, finite form, through the impermanent (finite and relative) cycles of beginnings and endings, hence the human experience of birth, life, and death respectively. It is not until we experience oneness, absorption, togetherness, Samadhi, pure integration of being that we finally understand the 'Truth' or Dharma of life itself, hence we become enlightened. How this is different from religion and science is that religion and science are a manifestation of relativity that exist in time and space, therefore they are finite and are subject to the rules, laws, and processes of the physical world/reality e.g., physics. They are also subject to human manipulation, again stressing the finitude of them and the relativity of them through the potential to be changed and manipulated by human action, interpretation, and perception. Science and religion are therefore not a true representation of pure existence only a partial representation within

311

the relative laws of time and space. They are not the Whole Truth only a partial representation or part of the Truth. Spirituality is the method to knowing and experiencing the Whole Truth.

Pure Truth or the infinite is not an intellectual concept that can be grabbed, examined, and explored through philosophising, intellectual discussion, objective testing, subjective thinking or researched (Sciences, Social Sciences, Humanities and Mathematics), or can it be artistically or poetically represented (Arts and Languages). Pure Truth has to be and can only be experienced through a spiritualised method of experiential practice, i.e., meditation, which fosters integration of Body/Mind/Spirit. Our limited, incomplete, partial, subjective, and objective experience of the physical world (illusion, delusion, dreamlike state) is made Whole through our spiritualised meditation of Body/Mind/Spirit, and in that moment of Full Integration (Samadhi, Absorption, Nirvana) we experience our True Being, our True Reality, Infinity, Completeness. We experience and know the whole Truth and nothing but the Whole Truth…we go Home…

Let us look at a simple example to illustrate this in action:

If we were to exist only in our living room (physical reality) and were never to leave that reality of the living room and existing only within the four walls of that space, we would be subject (relating only) to that physical reality of our living room and everything that existed in it. That would be all that we would know…we might have a sofa, chairs, table, books, bookshelf, computer, ornaments, pictures, carpets, and windows – those physical objects in that room

312

would also become our reality as we would create a relation to or an attachment to them through our use of our five human senses and our mind. The level of attachment or relationship we have to those objects would be determined by the value we place on these objects in relation to ourselves – we place a personification of being human onto the object – we grasp the object by bringing it closer to us and say, 'this is mine', and by doing so we make it a part of us... The greater the value we place on the object, e.g., *I couldn't live without my sofa because it's so comfy and I love sitting on it to watch TV,* the greater the sense of loss, grief, and suffering we'd experience if our sofa stopped being comfy and didn't offer the comfort it once did due to our personification (making it a part of us) by feeling like we are losing part of ourselves...your isolation within the boundaries and limits of the living room also increases your attachment and identity with the objects around you. We would do this to ease our pain, insecurity and suffering of isolation, loneliness, and separation from others by over identifying with the objects (creating strong value attachments) to ease our sense of disconnect and boundary limited existence in the living room.

A classic example of this was shown in the 2000 movie 'Castaway' starring Tom Hanks, when his character 'Chuck' a FedEx systems analyst, finds himself deserted on a desert island in the Pacific after his cargo plane crashes. Chuck is completely isolated on the island with only a few objects from the plane to help him survive. The island is Chuck's living room (previous example), an isolated, boundary or limited existence. Chuck is confined to the island without anybody else there and can't get off. With time he makes fire, shelter and catches fish to eat to survive (objects of survival) – he adds value and worth to those objects because they are sustaining his life… as time goes on Chuck finds his loneliness and isolation painful and begins to suffer from no other human contact. Chuck finds a volleyball and draws a face on the ball and gives it a name 'Wilson'. To ease the pain and suffering of his isolation Chuck personifies and creates a friend through his projected loneliness and loss of human connection. Chuck projects a personality and character onto 'Wilson' the volleyball to make him human and begins a relationship with 'Wilson' through conversation, discussion, and emotion. Chuck projects his pain, anger, fear, sadness, humour, confusion and every human thought, emotion and feeling onto 'Wilson' to help ease his limited isolated existence on the island. The island becomes Chuck's limited reality, his limited physical world and then because of this limited physical world Chuck finds ways to survive and exist without going completely insane, losing a complete grasp of reality and falling into complete delusional psychosis…his personification of 'Wilson' helps Chuck stay relatively sane through 'Wilson's' personification and Chuck's ability to dialogue and communicate with 'Wilson' and exercise his thoughts, fears and emotions – in all actuality 'Wilson' becomes and is Chuck's therapist…

What this example 'Castaway' and the 'living room' highlights are the universal human condition and existence on and in the physical world. Like Chuck and the person in the living room, we are all living within the physical boundaries and limits of our own existence. For Chuck it was the island and for the person in the living room it was the four walls. Within our physical realities we all have access to and relate to objects or 'things' that we relate to, own, and/or use in our physical worlds. Depending on our social conditioning, preferences, personality, desires, wants, needs, relationships, fears, feelings, emotions and thoughts will determine what value we give to those objects we relate to, e.g., employment, partner, children, ideas, material goods (cars, computers, phone, etc.), feelings, home, country, religion, etc…the human being whilst existing and living in the limits and confines of physical reality will forever give value and attachment to every perceived object or relationship that exists.

Why do we do this?

We do this to ease the existential pain and suffering of isolation and perceived disconnect from our original source of reality – Infinite reality. Just like Chuck on the island and the person in the living room, we are continually personifying every object and relationship around us to ease our isolation and disconnect from our original source of existence…by personifying the objects and relationships around us we are continually going through a cycle of pleasure/pain to help ease our continual suffering and pain of living. Depending on the type of person you are will determine how you do this pleasure/pain cycle, some will throw themselves into work, some the acquisition of money, some fame, some art, some science, some education, some mental illness, some physical illness, some theatre, some recreation, some exercise, some drugs, some alcohol, some shopping, some music, some politics, some finance, some pornography, some inventing, some sex, some religion, some parenting, some family, and some a varied mixture - whatever it is that the human chooses they are all varied degrees of attachment i.e., degrees of addiction and compulsion on some level...the human condition will find a way to utilise it and use it to ease the suffering and perceived isolation of living within the boundaries of physical existence. It doesn't matter if you are living alone on a desert island, or isolated in a living room, or living in a village, or town, or country – no matter where your boundaries are, where you perceive your limits to be – the physical reality is all the same just varying degrees of space and time. One person may never leave the village they were born in, grew up in and then died in that was their limited physical world; another person might live and have homes in different towns and cities in the same country that's their limited physical boundary; another person might be global and jet set across the whole planet, living in different countries and places all over the world and that is their physical limited reality but what is true and limited to all of these people is that no matter where they live or travel to over the course of their life they are all subject and limited to the boundary and limits of planet Earth, the solar system, the universe, i.e., the physical world, and the relationships they create and live throughout their lives in relative time and space.

A Model of Illness/Pathology of the Body & Mind

There are numerous disciplines and frameworks within our cultures that posit, pose and present reasons, concepts, and frameworks for human illness...the medical model focuses on the physical composition of the human body and how this body gets sick and ill through disease, infection, malfunction, and decay. The premise of the medical model is to provide aid and cure to the malfunction, infection, and disease of the human body through medical intervention (e.g., consultation, surgery, etc) and the application of medicine (e.g., drugs and pharmacy). The focus is on the physical body and why it is not functioning at optimum efficiency.

From a mental health/psychological perspective we have practices, interventions and disciplines that focus on the mind, cognitive functioning, emotions and how these relate to the physical organ of the brain. This includes psychology, sociology, neuropsychology, psychiatry, psychotherapies, cognitive sciences, neurosciences, and interpersonal neurobiology. These disciplines, especially within the West, sit either within or alongside the medical model, to support the medical model.

If you are looking for support or guidance in respect to religious and/or spiritual matters, concerns, and angst then you would be advised to see a person, group or organisation that deals with these, e.g., to go to Church, Synagogue, Temple or consult with a Priest, Iman, Rabbi, religious teacher, leader or representative, that could offer guidance, solace, and possible answers to your troubles and angst.

From the above examples we see the three disciplines of the Body, of the Mind, and of the Spirit. Each independently focuses and offers help in relation to issues that humans can experience during their lives. The sciences of the medical model work tirelessly and focus specifically on the human body, looking for answers and ways to help it function healthily and efficiently for the promotion of long-life. The sciences and arts of the Mind offer a similar approach as the medical model, by working tirelessly and specifically looking for answers and ways to help it function healthily and efficiently for the promotion of long-life. The representatives and groups of religion and spirituality also do a similar job but focus solely on religious and/or spiritual matters looking for answers and ways to help support the individual, groups, and nations to find understanding and meaning to life.

So, we have the three major cornerstones to modern and postmodern cultures that help and support individuals and groups in relation to illness, pathology, and wellness.

But is this the whole story…is this the whole truth?

In the previous section on science, religion, and spirituality, I posited how we as humans experience and live in a continual existential crisis of angst (anxiousness and depression) through the human's perceived attachment, and relationship to objects (physical and mental) that exist in our daily lives…alongside this I suggested that it is the human's positive and negative personifying of these objects that keeps humans in the continual cycle of pleasure/pain (highs and lows) due to the finite boundaries of relative time and space. As long as we exist in the relative boundaries of time and space (finite reality) we will forever experience the continual and existential angst of impermanence that we try and remedy and ease through our incomplete and unsatisfactory process of pleasure/pain (highs and lows). What is born must inevitably die, what is created will and must be uncreated (decay, dissolution, diminished). Hence from the physical perspective and by the laws of relative time and space, we are born, we live and then we die in the body and in the mind.

Now what if there is an alternative to this, that the true human experience, the Whole Truth is something very different?

If we look at human existence through the framework of Body/Mind/Spirit, our understanding of human pathology/illness in all its many forms (be it physical, mental or a combination of the two) is all based in and caused by one single premise:

1.   That the human's experience of illness in its myriad forms is due to the perceived disconnection, isolation, and ignorance of not realising that the very core and essence of who we are is Infinite reality - Oneness.

We get ill because we have forgotten through our continual attaching to finite reality that we are infinite reality and that we can experience this on Earth. We exist for the sole purpose to actualise, realise, and fulfil the human conscious embodiment of infinite reality, i.e., to become enlightened and to realise that we are infinite reality, and our sole (soul) purpose is to achieve this whilst we are consciously alive on this planet...

If we put this within the context of science, it is to know and experience Higgs Boson (God particle) through our own experience. From a psychological perspective it is to achieve full integration, become fully-functioning and a united whole. From a religious or spiritual perspective, it is to become Christ, the 'I AM', Krishna, Shiva, to experience Moksha, Liberation, Heaven on Earth...from a philosophical perspective it is to become Self-realised, a Buddha, enlightened and awakened. However, we choose to understand It or present It - the outcome and means is all the same – to 'know thyself' and to realise and become 'That' whilst we are still alive in Body and Mind here on planet Earth.

Now that we know the fundamental cause of why we get ill in Body and Mind, let's look more closely at the processes of illness and how this is manifested and presented.

Why we get ill:

- We get ill due to our perceived disconnect from our original source of existence.

What do we do to try and make this better:

- We personify objects through the 'pulling to' or 'pushing away' from us which produces an emotional value attachment to the object. If we like it, we want it more experiencing a high/pleasure (I like it); if we don't like it, we reject it experiencing a low/pain (I dislike it), and we do this with every object and relationship we experience in our lives. This is understood as the pleasure/pain cycle – samsara cycle.

Why do we do this 'pulling to' or 'pushing away' of objects and relationships?

- We do this because we are constantly in a process of dysregulation (non-equilibrium, Body/Mind tension, incongruence, suffering and pain) and angst (fluctuating anxiety and depression) due to the perceived disconnection, isolation, and ignorance from our original source of infinite reality. Due to this we continually search for relationships and objects that will alleviate and help our Body and Mind regulate. Essentially, we are in a constant process of feeling 'lost in the world' due to our loss of connection or realisation that we are infinite reality, so we attach ourselves to objects and relationships to help us feel connected, safe, and secure, giving us temporary relief from our deep feelings of dysregulation, ignorance, and angst.

Do the objects and relationships offer regulation and ease?

- They do but only temporary due to the relative finite boundaries of time and space. Once the regulation has ended, the person will feel a low and dysregulation once more. This signals the Body and Mind to once again search for a new object or relationship that will ease and regulate them. A classic example of this is the newborn baby, the newborn baby has an innate need to attach itself to the mother (Bowlby's Attachment theory – it's there in the name) for survival but also ultimately to regulate its emotional states. If that mother or primary career can effectively regulate the baby's emotional states then the baby will develop a secure attachment to the mother; if the mother can't regulate the baby's emotional states, then the baby develops an insecure attachment to the mother. Depending on the attachment style - secure or insecure - will determine how the child and eventually the adult will attach to objects in future relationships. Ultimately though, irrespective of the style of attachment – secure or insecure – the human will always have a need to attach to relationships and objects to find some form of regulation in the physical world; the determining factor in attachment theory is the perceived positive or negative degree (secure or insecure) attachment and how this 'plays out' in a person's life.

Does this cause the cycle of pleasure/pain that humans get trapped in?

- Yes, due to the finite regulation of objects and relationships i.e., everything can never last, the human then finds themselves in a constant ongoing cycle searching for objects and relationships to regulate them. This causes a perpetual cycle of pleasure/pain (highs and lows), which the person is constantly playing out as they move from one object and relationship to another, to find regulation and ease from their dysregulation and angst.

Where does illness/pathology come into this system?

- Illness/pathology are decided by two factors: 1. a person's karma, and 2. the person's processes and outcomes of their attachment to objects and relationships for regulation.

How does karma determine illness/pathology?

- The law of karma states that whatever value (positive, negative, or neutral) you give to a thought, feeling or behaviour within relative time and space, will come back to you either in this lifetime or future lifetimes. Energy is cyclical in relative time and space, so whatever you throw out into it, will eventually come back to you in some way, shape or form. If you think negatively about yourself or others, that negative energy will eventually come back to you. If you behave negatively to yourself or others, that energy will eventually come back to you. The same is true from a positive perspective. Be positive and positive energy comes back to you. Whatever you manifest will eventually come to you at some point in your spiritual journey.

So, whatever I'm experiencing is due to some previous manifestation in a past life and this life?

- Yes…If we go back to our example of the new born baby, in cognitive sciences it's believed we are born with a 'blank slate' therefore whatever we experience and develop in the world is solely due to this lifetime, so if we have an insecure attachment to our mother (attachment theory), this is part of the 'blank slate' of our experiences in this lifetime – this is partially true. This theory doesn't consider karma. The law of karma says that we come into this world with accumulated forms of energy positive, negative, and neutral that have an impact and affect our experiences in this lifetime. So, when we are born the accumulated positive, negative, and neutral energy we are born with will have an influence on how we attach to our mothers. There is no predictive determinant of this as we are unaware of our karmic energy when we are born. However, that is not to say karma is fatalistic, it is not, because depending on how we choose to live our lives (Free will), will also have an influence on how our karma is 'played out'. In fact, the more aware we are of karma (know thyself) and its influence will help us think, feel, and behave in ways that can help us complete our karmic debts and neutralise our karmic ties, therefore getting off the cycle of pleasure/pain (highs and lows) of attaching and personifying objects to alleviate and relieve our dysregulation, angst, and ignorance.

What illnesses/pathology can we experience in this lifetime?

- Illness in all its shapes and forms (e.g., disease, infection, mental disorders, body and organ breakdown and failure, etc.) will manifest either in the Body, the Mind, or a combination of the two. The two forms of illness/pathology of the Body/Mind (especially in Western culture) will be either based and understood in science/medicine, and/or psychology, and the practitioners of these disciplines will then name and categorise (diagnose) the problems that the human body and/or mind experiences, and offer appropriate consultations, interventions, medicines, and procedures to 'fix' these Body/Mind problems. An example of these are medical surgery and medicines to help 'fix' problems with the body (e.g., remove cancers, repair a broken bone, etc.), and psychological and psychotherapeutic interventions to help 'fix' the problems of the mind (e.g., anxiety, depression, personality disorders, etc.), and/or a combination of the two to help 'fix' the problems of the body/mind relationship (e.g., physical problems impacting mental health and vice versa).

So, whatever illness I'm experiencing is due to my karma and the outcome and process of my attachment to objects and relationships in my life?

- Yes

So, are you saying it's my fault I'm ill?

- Now that's an interesting position to ask that question from…when we ask that question from the position of blame, fault, and the release of any responsibility – we are positioning ourselves and viewing life from a purely Victim mode. We are playing the Victim and absolving ourselves of any responsibility of our thoughts, feelings, and behaviours. We are not taking any responsibility for ourselves and the part we've played in our past lives and most definitely the part we play in this life – therefore you are arresting and blocking your own physical, emotional, psychological and spiritual growth - you are blocking your own master plan and stopping yourselves from achieving and experiencing the ultimate goal of your existence – to experience Oneness with the original source of your Being – infinite reality.

By taking responsibility of the 'part' I've played and play in past relationships and current relationships – I'm taking responsibility for my physical and mental wellbeing?

- Yes…you are working towards healing yourself in Body and Mind with positive help and interventions of others to facilitate a process of positive living, which will support your physical, emotional, psychological, and spiritual wellbeing, development, and growth.

Next is a working example to illustrate the model of illness/pathology of the Body & Mind:

The case study of Dave:

Dave is a 30-year-old man suffering from relationship breakdowns, depression, and an addiction to pornography. In this life Dave had an initial insecure attachment with his mother, who was an alcoholic, and with his father who was emotionally absent, aggressive and had several affairs with other women. Dave's childhood was difficult, and he didn't experience a great deal of love and emotional support from his parents. He would spend most of his time around his friend's homes looking for support and understanding from his friends, their parents, and families. Dave was a naturally bright student and enjoyed learning at school and escaping into science. Although, he had a difficult childhood with neglectful and abusive parents, he did well at school, managed to get a scholarship to university, and secured himself a good job as a software engineer in a software firm for the last five years.

At university Dave met a fellow student Hugh, which turned into a romantic on-off relationship with Dave identifying as a gay man and with Dave socialising and embracing the local LGBT+ scene. After university Dave and Hugh had an open relationship, which turned toxic with Hugh becoming aggressive after drinking alcohol and physically/verbally abusing Dave...Dave found this difficult and ended his romantic relationship with Hugh, which caused Dave a lot of anxiety and confusion. Dave became depressed and started to engage with a lot of online porn and have one-time 'meet-up' sexual relationships with other gay men through a 'meet-up' app.

This went on for a couple of years until Dave's depression got so bad that he stopped socialising with friends and now spends his evenings watching porn, eating 'take-out', and over-working.

Dave's key issues in this life:

- His insecure attachment style
- His inability to find secure emotional and psychological regulation
- Past abuse
- His addiction to pornography
- His isolation from others
- His over-working
- His poor diet – feeling tired, constipation, dry skin, and hair
- His depression

What has caused Dave's issues?

1. The main cause of all of Dave's issues is his perceived disconnection, isolation, and ignorance from his original source of existence – infinite reality
2. The karma that Dave has accumulated in other lifetimes, which he's brought in with him
3. Dave's insecure attachment and personification of relationships and objects that Dave engages with, i.e., work, pornography, 'meet-ups', junk food and isolation.

How do we help Dave understand his issues and the cause of his issues?

- This is dependent on Dave's awareness, openness, and willingness to engage with therapeutic approaches that can help Dave make sense of his issues.

What are the possibilities open to Dave?

- He could look at support groups for pornography addiction
- He could get psychotherapeutic help from a psychologist, psychotherapist, or counsellor
- He could get spiritual help from a prana/energy healer or other spiritual therapies
- He could join or follow positive online groups that advocate positive lifestyles and activities
- He could try positive alternative support and activity – (e.g., eating healthily, joining a gym, walking in the city-park, taking up an out-door activity, reading positive literature, studying further, practicing yoga)

Is Dave in Victim mode?

- Yes...Dave is very much entrenched in Victim from the result of his karma, his childhood attachment styles and his negative use of objects and relationships in his life to regulate his fear, anguish, pain, and suffering. Dave is stuck in the perpetual cycle of pleasure/pain (highs and lows), which is manifested and supported through the choices he makes in his life. The negative choices Dave makes reinforces how Dave thinks, feels, and behaves toward himself and others in his life...setting up a negative perceived and experienced self-image of, *'Life is rubbish, people think I'm rubbish – I must be rubbish – I am rubbish'*...

How does Dave get out of Victim?

- The only person that can get Dave out of Victim is Dave…this doesn't mean Dave has to do it alone. It means that Dave must want to make his life better and then do what is necessary, by engaging with the right people and positive lifestyle choices that will support and help Dave do this. Getting out of Victim is a life choice and a process of continual development, commitment, and positive change. For Dave to feel better about himself, his life and relationships, Dave must take responsibility for his own change, development, and lifestyle choices. This must be a conscious process through thought, word, and deed. Remember, Rome wasn't built in a day and nor will Dave's positive change but with the right people and support in place, Dave will eventually get and be the change he wants to be…

A Model of Wellness/Health/Wholeness of the Body & Mind

When we look at the human experience and lifestyles in our cultures, we have an opportunity to view their experiences and relationships from two positions or frameworks: 1. Wellness/Health, or 2. Illness/Pathology. In the previous section we looked at the human experience and framed it in the model of illness/pathology and explored the processes and interventions that could remedy/cure the illness/pathology that humans can experience. In this section we are going to 'flip' this model and frame it from a position of wellness and health.

This is a very simple and straightforward model and a model that could be understood as preventative, restorative and reparative. In the previous model of illness/pathology we understood the primary cause and reason people experience and manifest illness/pathology is due to:

1. The perceived disconnection, isolation, and ignorance of not realising that the core and essence of who we are is Infinite reality.

If we understand and accept that this basic premise is the fundamental root of all forms of illness/pathology in the body and mind then all we need to do to live a healthy, content, non-ill life is to direct our life course, relationships, and experiences toward the fulfilment of realising and experiencing our original source of existence – Infinite reality.

If we can direct all our life toward that one goal then we are on our way to living a positive, fulfilling, and joyous life.

But what about karma and the processes and outcomes of our attachments to objects and relationships for regulation?

- If we accept that Illness/pathology are determined by the two factors of: 1. a person's karma, and 2. the person's processes and outcomes of their attachment to objects and relationships for regulation. Then our knowledge and understanding of this directs and motivates us toward actively engaging with people, study, practices, and processes that can help us explore these two factors. We do this to develop awareness, gain self-knowledge and self-mastery, and to help us integrate positive lifestyle choices, relationships and practices that will aid our positive journey toward fulfilling the premise of our existence: to experience and realise that the core and essence of who we are is Infinite reality.

Karma and our attachment to objects is a process that allows us to physically, emotionally, psychologically, and spiritually grow. By taking full responsibility of our life course and directing it toward the premise of infinite reality, we are consciously and actively deciding to step out of Victim and to engage with our Master Plan. Your energy and choices are now working for you, instead of working (self-sabotage) against you, which in turn foster positive life experiences and relationships that nurture you, support you, and enhance you i.e., that make you Well/Healthy and Whole...

Now we understand the model of wellness, let's revisit the case study of Dave to see how things could be different. We will pick up the case study from the point of Dave leaving university and starting to live an independent adult life and show how Dave's issues and choices can now be different.

The case study of Dave revisited:

Dave's main issues at this stage of his life:

- His insecure attachment style
- His inability to find secure emotional and psychological regulation
- Past abuse
- His anxiety

The issues at this stage of Dave's life are based within four factors above, as we can see Dave's life hasn't spiralled down into the depressive state of isolation, over-working, porn addiction and poor health at this point. Dave's life takes a potentially different turn when positive relationships and opportunities are experienced.

The factors that will assist and support Dave:

- Positive thinking
- Supportive friendships
- Awareness of positive ways to live
- Active engagement with positive/nurturing activity
- Self-belief

Given the supportive factors above, let's now look at Dave's life as it develops through the model of wellness/health:

- Dave was feeling anxious at work. The relationship break-up with Hugh had hit him hard and he was beginning to feel anxious around other people and feeling sad. Dave began to have moments when he'd have to take himself off to the toilets where he'd cry for 10-15 minutes, feeling lost and the pain of the break-up with Hugh.

The help from a new friend and a positive support for Dave:

- Clara is a work colleague of Daves, she noticed the change in Dave, and was aware he'd often leave the office and look upset and sad on returning. Clara plucked up the courage to go and speak to Dave by the coffee machine. Dave at first felt uncomfortable…Clara had said she'd noticed that he wasn't the same and was concerned for Dave. Dave dismissed Clara and said he was fine and didn't want to discuss it further…the following week for some unknown reason, Dave kept hearing the voice of his old high-school basketball coach in his head, *'remember team no man is an island, to work efficiently and to be our best we need to support each other and work together'*. Dave couldn't get this out of his head, and it sat with him for about a week…the following week, Dave saw Clara at the coffee machine, and he approached her. He thanked her for her concern and explained he was feeling low from a recent relationship break-up, and it has hitting him hard. Clara expressed her understanding and asked if Dave wanted to go for a drink after work no strings attached just as friends. Dave accepted the invitation and Clara and Dave started a good friendship.

Engaging with positive activity:

- Through their friendship and 'talks' Clara and Dave realised they had shared interest in sport. Clara used to be in the university swim team and swims every morning before work. Dave was a good basketball player and played at university. Clara invited Dave to swim with her, which Dave decided to do. Dave also noticed at the local community centre there were basketball courts. So, he'd go and shoot some hoops a couple of days a week after work.

Turning points and developing positive change:

- The local basketball coach at the community centre noticed Dave practicing and playing the odd game with some of the local kids there and went over to introduce himself. He was looking for an assistant coach to help with the kid's team and had noticed Dave's skill and ability...

Checking in with nurturing friends and support networks to help with decisions:

- Since becoming friends with Clara, Dave had been having therapy through his work insurance. Clara had used it and recommended it after she'd lost a good friend to suicide, and the therapy had supported her to make sense of her feelings and thoughts. Dave was very sceptical at first and wasn't sure therapy was his thing…but trusted Clara and her friendship and decided to give it a go…at first it felt uncomfortable to discuss his worries and concerns but with time and trust he started to feel better and even began to talk about his parents…

- Dave discussed the assistant coach position with Clara and brought it to therapy to explore the pros and cons and if it was the right thing for him…Dave after much reflection began to see the benefit of nurturing relationships and how they were making his life better and happier. He accepted the assistant coach position and began to help coach the local kid's basketball team. Dave surprised himself how much satisfaction and joy he got from supporting others, especially with an activity he enjoyed himself.

Challenges along the way:

- A few months down the line Dave was enjoying his life and had positive friendships and relationships. His bosses at work had been so impressed with Dave's new outlook, quality of work and leadership skills that they offered him a promotion and pay rise.

- One day Dave got a call from his ex-boyfriend Hugh. Hugh was in town and wanted to meet. Hugh explained he was sorry for how he'd treated Dave and wanted to make amends. Dave decided to meet with Hugh. They met at a local LBGT+ bar. Things went well to begin with Hugh apologised for the way he'd treated Dave and said he'd turned over a new leaf. They decided to meet again, as friends, and things were ok for a few weeks. However, Hugh was using a lot of porn and asked if Dave wanted to share in this with him, he'd also noticed Hugh becoming judgmental and unkind to others around him when he was drinking alcohol.

Dave's dilemma:

- Dave was starting to feel pressurised by Hugh and Hugh was coming round more and asking more of Dave. Dave had noticed he was drinking more than usual and his coach and Clara had noticed that Dave seemed tired and a little 'out-of-sorts' and were concerned for Dave...Dave explained to Clara that Hugh was back in town and what had been going on...he'd also mentioned this to his therapist and wasn't sure how he was feeling about Hugh, although he was aware that he was drinking more, feeling tired, and his focus for work and coaching the kid's basketball wasn't at the standard he wanted it to be...

Dave's growing awareness and understanding of himself and relationships:

- Through his positive friendships (Clara and Coach) and activities (i.e., coaching kid's basketball, his managerial role at work) and his decision to engage with therapy, Dave had been developing and understanding his attachment styles and the impact his past abuse had been having on his choices and relationships. His growing self-awareness was helping him make better choices and develop better relationships with people, it was also helping him become aware when choices and people were not enhancing his life and were having a negative impact on him and on others around him. Dave knew that his relationship with Hugh was not supporting him and his lifestyle, in fact it was doing the opposite, yet Dave still felt a 'pull toward' Hugh and felt guilty for not wanting to be there for him and support him…

Understanding boundaries in relationships:

- From Dave's past abuse and relationship with his parents and Hugh, Dave was realising that his boundaries with others had not always been supportive, and in fact had caused Dave to feel low self-worth and 'rubbish' about himself. Since making more positive choices Dave was beginning to understand that to feel secure, safe, and happy he needed to develop boundaries in relationships that would support his positive lifestyle and choices. This meant that Dave was going to have to change the boundaries with Hugh.

What these new boundaries could look liked:

- The options open to Dave regarding the new structuring of boundaries with Hugh, is dependent on Dave's ability to manage the boundaries effectively.

Possible options:

- Decide to end the relationship with Hugh
- Make clear times and places to see Hugh
- Limit the times Dave sees Hugh
- Put conditions on Hugh seeing Dave (e.g., Hugh stops drinking, Hugh doesn't drink if he sees Dave)
- Only see Hugh when in the company of others

These are a few possible options, that show what needs to be put in place to assist Dave in managing the boundaries. With the implementation and managing of the new boundaries that Dave decides, and Hugh agrees to will help support Dave's positive lifestyle choices. If Hugh cannot commit or breaks, abuses, or oversteps the new boundaries then the relationship needs to be reevaluated and new choices and decisions need to be made by Dave and Hugh.

New boundaries and the way forward:

- Dave discussed with Hugh that he could only see him for limited times a week and that if they were to meet then Dave didn't want to drink or Hugh to drink. Hugh struggled with this conversation and took it personally; he became verbally abusive and said that was the end of their relationship.

- Dave felt hurt, abandoned, and rejected by Hugh (Hugh felt this way too due to his own issues).

What Dave learnt from his relationship with Hugh:

- Dave discussed what happened with Clara and took it to therapy. With time Dave understood and unpicked his insecure/unhealthy attachment to Hugh. Dave began to realise the harm and low self-worth he'd been experiencing in relationship with Hugh and understood that due to his own past abuse, and Hugh's past abuse, they'd been 'playing out' their own trauma, fear, and abandonment issues on each other through their toxic relationship. Since the break-up with Hugh, Dave had been progressively feeling better, his energy levels had come back, his focus and his general sense of wellbeing improved, and he'd never felt better.

Is Dave in Victim mode, is he accessing his Master Plan?

- In some respects, yes Dave is still in Victim due to his lack of awareness regarding his spiritual path, spiritual development, and spiritual knowledge. However, from his positive engagement in his life and his choice to be responsible for himself and his relationships, he is well on his way to stepping out of Victim. Regarding his Master Plan, yes Dave is accessing his Master Plan, this is evident from the positive choices Dave is making in his life and from the positive relationships in his life. His experience with Hugh and how Dave managed that relationship clearly shows that Dave is taking a mature, positive, and considered approach toward himself and others. Dave is learning about himself, how his past relationships and experiences have shaped and shape him, and why he's more prone to thinking, feeling, and behaving in certain ways. Dave is also learning that these past relationships and experiences do not have to define and cement his future. We all have 'free will' and choices even if we don't believe we have, but with the right people and relationships around us we can begin to learn and understand that we can change for the better and that we don't have to be unhappy, stressed, and in pain forever. Dave realises this now and is enjoying and working toward being *the best version of himself*, becoming integrated, becoming Whole. Dave is embracing and taking responsibility for his life by accessing his Master Plan and living more positively…

A Model of Illness/Pathology or A Model of Wellness/Health?

This seems an obvious choice – A Model of Wellness/Health every time…Yet for others I appreciate this isn't an easy option, or even possible. It is only until we find ourselves in the deepest depths of despair, physical illness and/or profound physical and psychological suffering do we become aware or realise that now is the time to act, to seek help, to do something to resolve the distress, fear, and pain.

Either way, a model of illness or a model of wellness, the goal is to take-stock of the situation you're in and to do something about it. If you find yourself in the grips of cancer, disease, body breakdown or physical pain then a trip to the GP and healthcare consultant is needed with the help of a psychologist or psychotherapist/counsellor to support you with the mental anguish. If you find yourself in the grips of psychological breakdown after the loss/death of a loved one and feel like your life just can't go on, then maybe it's time to seek help from a bereavement counsellor, psychotherapist, or support group. If you're struggling with addiction issues and causing yourself and those around you continual distress and grief, seek help from your local addiction agency/services, support groups (e.g., AA, NA, etc.), a therapist and/or alternative therapies…whatever distressing situation or circumstance you find yourself in, then please do something about it…it doesn't have to be your life, or the end of your life…there are always options and choices that will help, alleviate and support you through the illness and pain.

If, on the other hand, you are going along and generally life seems ok…but you feel on the odd occasion that something seems to be missing. You can't quite put your finger on it, or even define what it is but somewhere deep inside of you, you have that niggling doubt, that 'itch you just can't scratch'… then perhaps it's time to be brave, and time to take responsibility for 'That' and begin to listen to yourself. Reflect on those questions: Who am I really? What is the point of life? What is my purpose and the purpose to all of this? Begin to look for ways to answer these questions - look to practices, study, people and most importantly yourself to help you make sense of this reality and to help you find a deeper purpose to your life and journey, just like Dave. Take up the mantle of wellness/health and begin to access your Master Plan step out of Victim and move ever closer to lifting the veil of ignorance/illusion and experiencing who You really are…

The Tree of Life/Garden metaphor

Metaphors are wonderful ways to illustrate learning, if you investigate the Vedanta philosophy, Yoga scriptures, the sutras of Buddhism, and the teachings of Christ they are abound with many profound and deeply meaningful analogies and metaphors to instil knowledge and to guide us.

A metaphor that I use and have found very useful over the years is the metaphor of the 'Tree of Life/Garden'. We are organic creatures in the Body, so I find the organic image of life, growth, and maintenance very useful in the image of the garden.

The Tree of Life/Garden:

 The first decision we encounter when approaching our growth and development is one of choice. You have a choice to actively embark and take responsibility for your growth/development or to not…so, when we approach the metaphor of the Tree of Life/Garden the first decision/choice is to take responsibility for your life (the garden) or not. The second responsibility is the growth/development of this (the Tree). The third responsibility is choosing the means to do this (be the gardener). The fourth responsibility is actively engaging and nurturing your growth (the gardening).

- The Tree is Your physical, emotional, psychological, and spiritual development.
- The garden is your life.
- The weeds are all the negative energies/vices i.e., lust, greed, hate, anger, selfishness, envy, jealousy, egotism, laziness, arrogance, materialism, pride, gluttony, wrath, vanity, avarice, self-pity, self-harm, self-punishment, deceit, and dishonesty…
- The gardener is You.
- Gardening is the positive nurturing, up-keep and maintenance of your life and the tree.

Depending on where you are along the journey of physical, emotional, psychological, and spiritual growth will determine how your garden looks, at what stage of life the tree is at and what level and practice of gardening you apply each day. For some that feel so disillusioned and in pain, the thought of the garden or tree seems a lost forgotten dream, overgrown unkept and left to its own wild uncontrolled devises – if this is the case then hopefully in time, you'll find someone or something that will help you remember your garden and support you to look and take responsibility once more. Others might have young saplings that still need a lot of time and attention with a general day-to-day weeding to keep it healthy. Others might have a mighty Oak strong, solid, and powerful that overshadows any weeds that grow but that is not to say that we don't keep a weekly or two weekly maintenance and up-keep of our garden and mighty Oak. Some others might be at the clearing and weeding stage making good fertile ground to plant the tree seed, to help grow the tree and nurturing the tree…

Whatever stage you are at is Ok…it's not about evaluation…whatever stage you are at is your stage and is right…the key to the growth, nurturing and maintenance is continual committed care. Whenever we see a weed, we must pluck it out and put it on the compost heap being continually watchful, careful, and using good discernment each day to notice and be ready to pluck out those weeds when they appear. The compost is our recycling station that breaks down the weed and turns it into necessary fertiliser to help our tree grow healthy and strong. So, nothing is wasted, just transformed into useful energy for the development of our tree and garden…Every weed is our opportunity, our gift to self that gives us the means to learn, to grow, to transform into an even stronger, caring, loving, and committed gardener. By knowing our weeds we have an opportunity to transform them into their opposites and to live a life more virtuous and grounded in non-harmful, more truthful, more ethical and non-selfish ways…However, there are those times in the life when outside forces hit our garden hard, strong winds and storms that seem out of our control that we didn't predict or even imagine would affect us…these forces feel so strong that they even threaten the life and existence of our tree and all the positive work we've achieved…it's in these times we must remember that whatever is happening is part of our plan and due to karma, so if they seem to be beyond our control or beyond our capability, they are of our own making and are the necessary means to assist our growth even more – there's nothing in our existence that we experience or perceive that we can't deal with and grow from however extreme, and once we've weathered the storm and come through the other side, we start again and pick up the necessary pieces to carry-on. If our tree is a young sapling and has snapped in the wind, then we know the roots are ok and we can still nurture growth. If our tree has been uprooted and looks close to death, then it's time to embrace that tree, show it the love and respect it deserves and after we've grieved, we can plant a new tree. Whatever the outcome, whatever the change or perceived devastation, we always regroup, reach out to those that can help and begin again…the key is to never give up, never be defeated, never fall into complete hopelessness or helplessness (Victim)…remember this is your journey, your life, your opportunity to grow physically, emotionally, psychologically and spiritually – there is no other reason for you existing on this planet – if we go back and revisit the Principles of Life/Existence:

1. First Principle: You are Infinite Reality - You are Not the Body – You are Not the Mind – You are Not the - I Am.

It is due to this First Principle that you exist. This is why you are here on Earth. The Second Principle is why you do not realise this:

2. Second Principle: You are trapped in a cycle of ignorance and delusion that blinds you to the First Principle.

Your tree and garden, the Third Principle, are your way out of the Second Principle:

3. Third Principle: There are means and ways to gain knowledge and experience that will bring realisation and experience of the First Principle.

So, whatever you experience, whatever life throws at you, whatever you encounter along your way, remember the Third Principle, and remember why you are here in the first place…

Know thy Self – Revisited

To know thy self, self-knowledge, is the fundamental premise to the principles of life/existence and that underpin the whole process of physical, emotional, psychological, and spiritual growth, i.e., accessing your Master Plan. The tree of life/garden metaphor is a method and symbolic representation of this process, and the art of listening is a practical method of application to assist you in developing, understanding, and experiencing self-knowledge. Self-knowledge is the ultimate key to self-realisation. It is from self-knowledge that we finally realise and experience infinite reality understanding that we are not the body, not the mind, and not any finite representation or symbol of name and form manifested in Consciousness, Maya, Prakriti, Relative Time & Space. We are as principle one states, infinite reality, which cannot be known, it can only be realised in 'Being' and when this is realised, then and only then is self-realisation, God-realisation, nirvana, Samadhi realised.

Knowledge, intellect, naming, and evaluation is the playground of the Mind. Infinite reality is not mental or intellectual gymnastics. It is a full complete whole Body/Mind/Spirit integration realisation called samadhi, nirvana, self-realisation, again it's Not any of these names as these are symbolic manifestations of the Mind, and as we know it's Not the Mind, we know it's Not any of these names...

Humans have a strong over identification with the Body and the Mind; they believe through perceived repetition in relative time and space that the Body and the Mind are permanent. This is a delusion as relative time and space is impermanent (forever changing), therefore as the Body and the Mind are products of relative time and space (impermanence) they are subject to the laws of time and space. So, to identify with the Body and the Mind and to perceive and believe it is permanent (does not change) is a delusional state of ignorance. Then through the added personification of naming, e.g., 'I am Michael', 'I am a teacher', 'I am Jane', I am a lesbian', we create value attachments that hold and create a bond (bondage) to the named Body and/or named Mind that we believe is real and who we are...this is the trap of relative time & space, this is the delusion/illusion of the material world...the trap of suffering/pain of perceived life...the only way to get out of this trap, to relieve and stop the suffering is through realising nirvana/samadhi.

We do this this through the process of negation, therefore 'I AM Not' we understand and know what is 'Not I AM' which finally leads us to the experience of realising what is the 'I AM' therefore the 'I AM' in and of itself...

Meditation is the means and method to help us through the discrimination of thoughts, feelings, emotions, and all that is the Body and the Mind. We examine and begin to know what is Not the 'I AM' e.g., 'I Am Not this hand', I Am Not this Body', 'I Am Not that anger', 'I Am Not that name', 'I Am Not this feeling', 'I Am Not the Mind'…then we begin to understand what we are Not, and by knowing what we are Not we are led to a realisation of what we truly are…

Silent Witness:

Once we examine the Body and the Mind through the process of negation, understanding that we are Not this or that, we are Not of the Body or Mind or anything else that has name or form, we are led and begin to realise and experience our process of 'Witnessing' the perceived action of the Body and the Mind. Just as the audience member sits in the seat and watches and witnesses the movie or stage play silently, the negation of name and form leads us to experience the world as a 'Silent Witness'. It is the 'Silent Witness' that is the gateway (although these terms in and of themselves are creations of the Mind, illusions and delusions that are Not the 'I AM'), however they can be used as a guide, a pointer to experience the world as the 'Silent Witness' that leads us to finally experience the ultimate realisation that we are Not the Body and Not the Mind. We are in fact Not even the 'I AM' and we are 'silently witnessing' the outward play of the Body and the Mind – as if we are a performer in a play or movie and we are watching the play and movie whilst being in the play and movie – we are in fact witnessing the body and the Mind manifest action, thought, feeling, word and deed, witnessing the body and mind that we are 'in' perform speech, thought, behaviour with what we **mistakenly believe is our body and mind** with other objects in our world e.g., 'people', 'animals', 'plants', 'life forms', 'cars', 'TVs', 'Computer'. It is our mistaken belief that we are the doer, enjoyer, experiencer of these processes through our over identification and personification of the Body and Mind. The taster of the sugary desert, the taster of the bitter drink, the drinker of the coffee, the hand that presses the keys on the computer or swipes the screen, the eyes that 'see' the sunset, the legs that walk – these are products, perceived actions of the Body and the Mind, these are Not You...You are the 'Silent Witness' that witnesses these processes, thoughts, feelings and actions. The danger and trap of relative time and space is your perceived over attachment and identification that leads to the mistaken belief (your delusion/illusion) that these are You and that You are doing them and thinking them and feeling them. You are Not. It is the Body and Mind that you are 'in' (although this again is a misnomer in of itself, for in fact You are not in anything, again another delusional trap) that is doing all these – You are the 'Silent Witness' that witnesses all these things as they are happening...a constant beginningless and endless ongoing movie through the constant appearing and reappearing of the delusion of time and space that gives the impression of a constant Body and constant Mind. A constant story (permanence) but in actuality it is impermanence (forever changing) forever disappearing and reappearing always changed, never permanent, never the same, always impermanent, forever different...and as mentioned in previous sections it is this mistaken belief of permanence and attachment to the Body and Mind that traps us into the ultimate fear and belief that we will finally come to an end, the annihilation of Body and Mind with what we believe is Our Death...but in actuality the source of 'I Am' is eternal/absolute, is beyond time and space and therefore not subject to the laws of impermanence (beginning and ends) to death – it never dies because it was never born - so, therefore is Absolute...

Method of Negation:

1. First Principle: You are Infinite reality.
2. Second Principle: 'I AM Not' i.e., illusion/delusion, material world, relative time & space.
3. Third Principle: Meditation on 'I Am Not' – leads to realisation of the first principle.

You are the Silent Witness, it is your life, witness the life you want – witness a good life and it will be so...

Matthew S.V.

Conclusion

I hope you've found the book informative, useful and a friendly guide. The book is a personal journey and signpost to what is available and what can be used and integrated into your current lives.

Body/Mind/Spirit is the only framework human beings need and it's been with us through our entire history as a species. To miss out one of these components is to live an unintegrated, incomplete, and fractured existence. We as human beings need to structure our lives and existence through the lens of Body/Mind/Spirit, if we are to fulfil our integrated sense of wholeness, completeness, and self-realisation. How you do this is unique, personal, and individual to You. No one can tell you how to do this, no one can make you do this, and no one has the power to do this either…the only person that has the power, capability and potentiality to do this is You…and when you start to live Body/Mind/Spirit by accessing your Master Plan, you are living your unique physical, emotional, psychological and spiritual existence that is You. It is You existing in your authentic, unique, perfect way…

Remember - You are Not the Body – You are Not the Mind – You are infinite reality manifested as a finite Body, as a finite Mind – stop identifying with the Body, stop identifying with the Mind – these are your tools, your instruments, to use, to play with, for you to utilise…take care of them, look after them, learn how to use them effectively, and to control them effectively – make them work for You not the other way round. Realise how being authentic is a process, is flow and rhythm. Develop the art of listening and tune into the vibrational flow of life, harmonise with it, become it, and when you do everything in your life will flow naturally, authentically and with ease…

Glossary:

Absorption: a process of samadhi when your energy system is integrating body/mind/spirit.

Addiction: the use, taking or engaging with a substance, activity, behaviour, thought process and/or object, whereby there is perceived to be no control.

Administration: managing and administrating the processes involved in running an office, business, and organisation.

Advaita: non-duality, literally, 'not two.'

Aham: the individual soul, self-consciousness, the inner Self.

Ahimsa: non-injury in thought, word, and deed - non-violence, non-killing, not harming others.

Ajna chakra: the third eye, energy centre located between the eyebrows.

Ananda: Bliss, happiness, joy.

Anandamaya kosha: 'The sheath of bliss (Ananda).' The causal body. The borderline of the Self (Atman). The fifth kosha/sheath.

Annamaya kosha: 'The sheath of food (Anna). The physical–or gross–body, made of food. The first kosha/sheath.

Aparigraha: non-possessiveness, non-greed, non-selfishness, non-acquisitiveness.

Aphorism: a general truth written or spoken.

Art of Listening: the ability to attune to the vibrational energies of other forms of existence (e.g., humans, animals, plants, etc…)

Asana: posture, seat Hatha Yoga posture.

Ashtanga Yoga: The 'eight-limbed' Yoga of Patanjali consisting of: 1. Yama – restraints/ethical, behaviours, 2. Niyama – observances/practices, 3. Asana – postures, 4. Pranayama – breath control, 5. Pratyahara – withdrawal of the senses, 6. Dharana – concentration, 7. Dhyana – meditation & 8. Samadhi – absorption/oneness.

Asteya: non-stealing; honesty; non-mis-appropriateness.

Astral Body: the second major body of yoga, corresponding to the astral plane. The subtle/astral body like the physical body is constituted with a system of channels and organs that are used to circulate energy to keep the body alive and healthy.

Attachment: an emotionally charged relational connection to an object either organic or non-organic (e.g., another human, animal, plant, non-organic object, conceptual, instrumental, etc.)

Attachment Theory: the relational attachment between humans to sustain and regulate psychological, physical, and emotional states.

Atman: the individual spirit or Self that is one with Brahman. The true nature or identity.

Avatar: a fully liberated spirit (Jiva) (e.g., Buddha, Christ) born into the world to help others attain liberation. Referred to as a divine incarnation, an avatar is total God-Consciousness, and therefore God-realised.

Avidya: Ignorance nescience, unknowing, literally: 'to not know.'

Awareness: the ability to be conscious of one's existence.

Baba: A title often given to sadhus, saints, and yogis, meaning 'father.' (e.g., Sai Baba of Shirdi).

Bhagavad Gita: 'The Song of God.' The sacred Hindu philosophical text.

Bhakti: devotion, love of God, All That There Is – Brahman.

Bhava: subjective state of being (existence), an attitude of mind.

Body: pertaining to and/or encompassing a system relating to a sum of (e.g., human body).

Boundaries: creating and knowing where something begins and where something ends – personal boundaries (the ability to create relationships that foster positive wellbeing).

Brahmacharya: continence, self-restraint on all levels, celibacy, discipline.

Brahman: The Absolute Reality - the Truth proclaimed in the Upanishads - All That There Is, Infinite Reality, Supreme Reality - Satchitananda pure existence, Knowledge, and Bliss

Breath of Life: prana, life force, Chi, Ki – infinite energy.

Buddha: The Enlightened One.

Buddhi: intellect, understanding, reason, the thinking mind.

Buddhism: a philosophical tradition realised through the teachings of Buddha pertaining the Dharma – the absolute Truth.

Causal Body: the most subtle of the three bodies (Physical, Astral & Causal). It is believed to be the contain the Soul and houses the energies that get reincarnated from one life to another.

Capitalism: the free market, it's the place where anyone with an idea, strong business acumen and a driven mindset for production, sales and marketing can make a profit and collect financial gain.

Case Study: an illustrative detailed study of a person, place, group, or phenomena, used in social sciences, business, education, and clinical research.

CBT: Cognitive behavioural therapy is a psychological therapy used to help clients/patients change from negative thinking and behaviour to positive thinking and behaving leading to positive lifestyles choices.

Charismatic leader: a person that adopts and uses charm and charisma to persuade others to follower their ideas and beliefs.

Chakra: wheel - centre of psychic energy in the human system found in the astral body.

Chitta: the subtle energy that is the substance of the mind.

Christ-ed: the anointed one, the self-realised one – the Messiah.

Christianity: the religion based and founded through the teachings of Jesus Christ.

Concentration: see Dharana – the ability to focus one's energies on a single point.

Consciousness: with a big C is the ground of all existence.

Consumerism: the consuming of goods and services through the Capitalist 'Free Market'.

Corporeal: pertaining to physical reality (e.g., Earth, the Body)

Cosmic Love/Universal Love: the ultimate expression and body of Supreme Being/God/All That There Is/Para-Brahman.

Cosmology: the origin story and structure of the Universe, Humans and Life grounded in a belief system.

Dalia Lama: the head of the Tibetan Buddhists and the manifestation of Avalokiteshvara or Chenrezig, the Bodhisattva of Compassion and the patron saint of Tibet.

Dharana: is concentration or 'single-pointedness'. It is the ability to focus on one object or point through yoga practice.

Dharma: the Truth of reality, the righteous way of living.

Dhyana/Dhyana Yoga: Meditation; contemplation.

Drama Triangle: a diagrammatic overview of how we as humans perpetuate the drama roles of Victim, Persecutor and Rescuer relationships in human life.

Divine Plan: the continual unfolding of Divine Will.

Dualism: 'of two parts' – distinction between opposites -Body & Mind.

Dukkha: pain, suffering, distress.

Eco-living: adopting a lifestyle that incorporates positive connections and living with the natural world.

Ecology: studying the relationships between different organisms and species in their environments.

Ego: little self, limited perspective on reality fostering selfish and defended ways of existing.

Egoism/Egoistic: pertaining to one that lives life through their ego perspective.

Eight-Fold Path: Buddha's pathway to the cessation of suffering.

EMDR: eye movement desensitization and reprocessing therapy used to release and resolve trauma in clients/patients.

Empathy: the ability to understand one's viewpoint and another's viewpoint.

Energy-Healing: a form of therapy that supports the person's 'life force, prana, Chi, Ki' to assist healing.

Existence: the perceived quality of life that a human experiences.

Experiential: the lived experiences of a person's life that informs their understanding and evaluating of their existence.

Evidence Base: the rigorous testing, observing, and researching of a subject and practice that establishes valid knowledge.

Evolution: the continual unfolding and progressive development of a species and life forms.

External teachings: pertaining to spirituality and religion – the literal meanings to teachings usually based in morals and ethics.

Fear: the universal process that creates defensive and risk management behaviour in humans.

Formulation: a structured therapeutic plan based on three underpinning questions: 1. what has caused the client's problems? 2. what factors are maintaining the client's problems? 3. what might facilitate change? To gather information to create relevant interventions for positive therapeutic outcomes.

Framework: a conceptual or physical structure that supports relevant theoretical principles leading to a desired outcome.

Free Will: the human ability to make choices.

Fully functioning: Carl Rogers' (1959) theory of the human being that has evolved and is potentially able to transcend Fear. The human being is so accepting of experience, self and other, is so open to experience, self and other, so integrally attuned to experience, self and other that Fear is a non-entity.

Gayatri Mantra: A Rig Vedic mantra in the gayatri meter invoking the solar powers of evolution and enlightenment, recited at sunrise and sunset.

Gospel: the teachings of Christ 'good news'.

Guru: Teacher, preceptor, spiritual teacher.

Hatha Yoga: a system consisting of physical exercises, postures, and breathing exercises for gaining control over the physical body and prana.

High Self: the personification of one's higher power – see Atman.

Hinduism: an Eastern religion that developed from the Vedic traditions.

Ideology: a set of beliefs that underpin a person's worldview.

Indoctrination: to teach a set of beliefs that are accepted without question or criticism.

Indra's Net: a metaphor that is used to symbolise the fundamental interconnectedness of all reality and the things in reality. In Hinduism it purports to a Vedic cosmology as a web of interdependencies and connections among all its parts, therefore every part is both a manifestation of the whole and inseparable from the whole. This is also later seen in Hua-yen Buddhism and taken from the *Avatamsaka Sutra* ('Flower Garland') of Mahayana Buddhism.

Integration: to simply combine or bring together two or more things.

Integrative Practice: to integrate different forms of therapeutic practice to foster a positive therapeutic outcome.

Internal teachings: the 'hidden' under the surface meanings of religious teachings.

Involution: in spirituality an inward expression of turning back toward a higher focused outcome.

Ishwara: 'God'/'Lord' in the sense of the Supreme Power, Ruler, or Controller of the cosmos. 'Ishwara' implies the powers of omnipotence, omnipresence, and omniscience.

Janaka: the royal sage (raja rishi) who was the king of Mithila and a liberated yogi.

Japa: repetition of a mantra.

Japa Mala: A string of beads, usually one hundred and eight, on which repetitions (japa) of a mantra are counted to help the yogi remember to do japa.

Jesus the Christ: in Christian religion the son of God and head of Christianity.

Jiva: the immortal principles of consciousness that constitute individuality through the limitations of relative time and space i.e., mind and body - psychological and physical. See also Soul.

Jivanmukta: One who is liberated here and now in this present life.

Jivanmukti: Liberation in this life.

Jnana: knowledge, wisdom of the Reality or Brahman, the Absolute.

Jnana Yoga: The path of knowledge, meditation through wisdom, constantly and seriously thinking on the true nature of the Self as taught by the Upanishads.

Jnani: A follower of the path of knowledge (jnana) - one who has realised - who knows - the Truth (Brahman).

Juliana of Norwich: English anchoress and mystic of the 14th century. Writer of the 'Revelations of Divine Love' an important religious and mystical classic.

Kabbalah: Jewish esoteric teachings and method that fosters a pathway to Infinite God.

Kama: Desire – passion - lust.

Karma: to act, do, or make, therefore action, including thought and feeling. Karma is also the 'effects of' both action and reaction – the law of moral causality.

Karma Yoga: The Yoga of selfless unattached action - performance of one's duty - service of humanity.

Krishna: A Divine Incarnation born in India about three thousand years ago. Whose teachings are spoken and discussed with his disciple Arjuna and comprise the Bhagavad Gita.

Kriya: Purificatory action and practice. The Kriyas purify the body and nervous system as well as the astral body to enable the yogi to reach and hold on to higher levels of consciousness and being.

Kundalini: The primordial cosmic consciousness/energy located in the individual. It is believed to be at the base of the spine in the 'sex chakra', analogised as a coiled serpent.

Kundalini Yoga: the spiritualised practice through meditation of transmuting one's sex energy into spiritual energy for the benefit of one's spiritual development.

Mahatma: literally - 'a great soul [atman].' Usually a designation for a sannyasi, sage or saint.

Manomaya kosha: The sheath of the mind. The third Kosha.

Mantra: Sacred syllable or word or set of words through the repetition and reflection of which one attains Self-realisation.

Mara: cosmic evil, illusion, and delusion.

Master Plan: is the genetic blueprint that exists within all of us. Each person has their own unique Master Plan that is designed for the person to achieve their spiritual growth in this lifetime.

Maya: ignorance - delusion.

Mental Illness: the dysregulation, incongruence, and distressing processes of the mind.

Metaphor: the comparison of two different objects with an underlying illustrative point of one object describing another.

Mind: the conceptual platform that humans use to make sense of reality.

Moksha: liberation, Samadhi, enlightenment.

Mysteries: the hidden internal teachings of religion.

Mysticism: the practice of divine spiritual union with Absolute infinite reality.

Nada: sound, the primal sound or first vibration from which all creation emanates, a mystic inner vibrational sound.

Noble truths: the four noble truths as expounded by Buddha: 1. Dukkha (suffering), 2. Samudaya (origin of suffering – samsara), 3. Nirodha (Cessation of suffering), 4. Marga - eight-fold-path (the path to cessation of suffering).

Non-Dualism: Advaita, wholeness, Absolute.

Neuroscience: scientific study of the human brain and nervous system.

Neuropathways: a series of neural connections/pathways (neurons) that send signals from one point of the brain to another.

Neuroplasticity: the organism's ability to reshape neural pathways in response to their relational and environmental existence.

Nirodha: number three of Buddha's four noble truths – the cessation of suffering.

Nirvana: liberation, final emancipation from the bonds of relative time and space. See Samadhi, Moksha.

Nirvikalpa samadhi: this is complete absorption into Oneness, where distinction between body, mind and spirit is not experienced, only a complete Divine state of enlightenment. The highest state of samadhi in the Hindu system.

Niyama: the five Do's of Yoga: 1. Saucha - cleanliness; 2. Santosha - contentment, gratitude; 3. Tapas - austerity, self-discipline; 4. Swadhyaya - Self-reflection, spiritual study; 5. Ishwarapranidhana – devotion, offering of one's life to God.

Oneness: fundamental connectedness of all forms of existence.

Para-Brahman: Supreme Brahman, Supreme Being/Reality.

Parable: the teachings of Jesus the Christ in story form.

Para(ma): highest, universal, supreme.

Paramatman: The Supreme Self, God.

Past Lives: according to the laws of reincarnation the living of a previous life in a different body.

Patanjali: A yogi of ancient India, the author of the Yoga Sutras.

Pathology: the study of diseases in body and mind attributed as illness.

Personifying: to attribute human characteristics and form to an object.

Pineal gland: a tiny gland at the back of your brain beneath the corpus callosum that helps regulate melatonin and sleep.

Prakriti: material reality, the absolute power (shakti) of Infinite reality from which the entire finite reality is formed – made up of the three qualities/gunas: sattwa, rajas, tamas.

Prana: life force, vital energy, life-breath.

Prana-Healing: therapeutic practice that utilises life-force/prana to heal.

Pranamaya kosha: 'The sheath of vital energy (prana)'. The second sheath/kosha.

Pratyahara: abstraction or withdrawal of the senses from their objects - the fifth limb of Patanjali's Ashtanga Yoga.

Process-orientated: focusing on the 'how you do things' including the dynamics, relationships and pathways involved.

Programmes: negative energy blocks that inhibit a person's physical, emotional, psychological, and spiritual development.

Psyche: the totality of the human mind – the conscious and unconscious.

Psychological: pertaining to the psychological world and process of the human mind.

Psychologist: a practitioner that studies and offers psychological help to clients/patients.

Psychotherapist: a practitioner that helps people deal with their psychological, emotional, and mental distress.

Raja Yoga: yoga of self-control.

Reflection: the ability to turn in on oneself to enquire on one's experiences, relationships, and processes of existence.

Reflective Task: an exercise that focuses on a particular experience, relationship and process of human existence that has happened for one to remember and evaluate.

Research: a systematic investigation into phenomena (e.g., subject, observation, material, object, experience, etc.) for the understanding and pursuit of new knowledge.

Rig Veda: an ancient collection of sacred Hindu texts composed as hymns.

Sacred Geometry: the study and engagement with geometric mathematical shapes that have certain rules and laws that are significant to them. These shapes when understood and actively engaged with help us connect to the infinite universal structure of life.

Sadguru: True guru, or the guru who reveals the Real (Sat–God).

Sadhana: spiritual practice.

Sadhana-Chatushtaya: the four pillars of spiritual practice: 1. Viveka - the ability to discriminate between self and non-self. 2. Vairagya: non-attachment stepping of the pleasure/pain cycle; 3) Shat-sampat: the embodiment of the six virtues – *Shama*, or the ability to be calm and keep a peace of mind, *Dama*, or the ability to control the senses and, therefore, reactions to external stimuli, *Uparati*, or renouncing anything that doesn't fit your dharma (duty), *Titiksha*, or persevering through suffering, *Shraddha*, or trusting and having faith in the path of Jnana yoga, *Samadhana*, or total concentration and focus of the mind; 4) Mumukshutva: an intense desire for liberation/freedom from suffering.

Sahasrara: the twelve chakras, the highest point of consciousness at which the spirit (atman) and the bodies (koshas) are integrated and from which they are disengaged.

Samadhi: super consciousness where Absoluteness is realised with all-knowledge and joy - oneness, complete absorption, realisation of Self, Unification of Body/Mind/Spirit, Non-duality.

Samsara: the wheel of birth, death and rebirth, the process of corporeal existence.

Samudaya: second noble truth of Buddha, where suffering arises from.

Sanskaras: psychological imprints, memories, impressions on the mind.

Sanskrit: The language of the ancient sages of India and therefore of the Indian scriptures and yoga.

Sat Chakras: The six chakras: Muladhara, Swadhishthana, Manipura, Anahata, Vishuddha and Ajna.

Satchidananda: Existence-knowledge-bliss Absolute, Para-Brahman.

Satsanga: literally – 'in the company with Truth.' Groups of people that are self-realised focused. In the company of saints and devotees.

Science: the study of the natural and social worlds of finite reality.

Self: with a big S is the Absolute, Para-Brahman – the Atman.

Self-awareness: the ability to know thy self – having awareness of Being that pertains to You.

Self-worth: a sense of value of the self, usually linked to conditional relationships that foster worth or value of self through meeting the needs of others.

Shakti: power, energy, the Absolute expression of Divine power.

Shadow side: in Jungian psychology that aspect of self that is usually deemed unacceptable to oneself and others.

Silent Witness: the watcher, the observer, the witness that experiences the processes of the Body/Mind - the Atman.

Sivananda (Swami): A great twentieth-century Master, founder of the world-wide Divine Life Society, whose books on spiritual life and religion are widely circulated in the West as well as in India.

Sivananda Yoga: the pathway of yoga founded by Swami Sivananda.

Soul: the immortal aspect of sentient life – consciousness manifested as the individual. See Jiva.

Spirit: God, Brahman, Absolute, Infinite reality, All That There Is.

Spirituality: the study of and engagement with that which is beyond finite reality.

Spiritual Response Therapy: a spiritual therapy founded by Robert Detzler that incorporates the removal of negative energy blocks and working on past lives.

Subtle/Astral Body: in yoga the second body that houses the chakras and energy channels – the bridge between the physical and spiritual bodies.

Sufism: a form of Islamic mysticism and ascetism that brings practitioners closer to God-realisation.

Synchronicity: unity in diversity – everything is connected and therefore dependent on each-other. The process whereby things happen in meaningful ways.

Swami: religious Hindu teacher.

Swami Vivekananda: a famous 20th century Hindu teacher, and disciple of Ramakrishna, which was instrumental in bringing Vedic and Yoga philosophy to the West.

Tao: in Taoist philosophy the natural way of the underpinning cosmic energy/power of the Universe.

Tapas: disciplined spiritual practice. Literally - to generate heat or energy, e.g., the burning up of karma.

Theory of Mind (TOM): in developmental psychology, the ability of the individual to attribute mental states to ourselves and others e.g., emotions, beliefs, desires, knowledge, etc.

Therapist: a person skilled in the arts and ways of therapy.

Trauma: an emotional and psychological response to an event that overwhelms a person's sense of self and reality, e.g., traffic accident, abuse, natural disaster.

Trauma-Focused Practice: therapy that focuses on helping a person resolve the trauma they have experienced.

Upanishads: the philosophical teachings of the Vedas, they contain the essence of the Vedas, therefore they are the source of the Vedanta philosophy. They contain two major themes: 1. the individual Self (Atman) and the Supreme Self (Paramatman) are one in essence, and 2. the goal of life is the realisation/manifestation of this unity, therefore Self-realisation realization of God/Brahman.

Vasanas: A bundle or aggregate of samskaras. See Samskaras.

Vedanta: literally - the end of the Vedas - the Upanishads.

Vedas: the oldest scriptures of India, possibly considered the oldest scriptures of humanity – they were revealed in meditation to the Vedic Rishis.

Vegetarianism: non-eating of meat and living this lifestyle.

Veganism: the non-eating of any animal products or by-products of animals.

Vibrational Energy: the energy level of life forms and the structures of life that organic and non-organic matter vibrate at.

Victim: a mental state that is perceived by a person underpinned by a sense of hopelessness and helplessness.

Victim mode/ Victim mentality: the experiencing and living of the state of victim.

Vijnanamaya kosha: The sheath of intellect (buddhi). The level of intelligent thought and conceptualization. The fourth sheath/kosha.

Viveka: discrimination between the Real and the unreal, between the Self and the non-Self, between the permanent and the impermanent - right intuitive discrimination.

Vivekananda (Swami): The chief disciple of Sri Ramakrishna, who brought the message of Vedanta to the West.

Vritti: thought-wave, a ripple in the chitta (mind substance).

Yama: the five Don'ts of Yoga: 1. Ahimsa - non-violence, non-injury, harmlessness; 2. Satya - truthfulness, honesty; 3. Asteya - non-stealing, honesty, non-misappropriateness; 4. Brahmacharya - continence, celibacy; 5. Aparigraha - non-possessiveness, non-greed, non-selfishness, non-acquisitiveness.

Yang: the male aspect of the Tao - Yin and Yang of Taoist philosophy.

Yantra: geometric designs (sacred geometry) - energy patterns made by mantras when they are recited or when concentrated on to produce the effects of the mantras.

Yin: the female aspect of Tao.

Yoga: literally – 'to yoke', union with divine reality – pathway to Self-realisation.

Yoga Sutras: The oldest known writing about yoga, written by the sage Patanjali, a yogi of ancient India, and considered the most authoritative text on yoga.

Yogi: one who practices Yoga - one who strives earnestly for union with Divine reality.

References:

Agdal R, von B Hjelmborg J, Johannessen H. (2011) Energy healing for cancer: a critical review. Forsch Komplementmed. 2011;18(3):146-54. doi: 10.1159/000329316. Epub 2011 Jun 3. PMID: 21701183

Ahmadi, A. (2023) Irfan and Tasawwuf (Sufism) Irfan and Tasawwuf (Sufism) | Irfan and Tasawwuf (Sufism) | Al-Islam.org https://www.al-islam.org/al-tawhid/vol1-n4/irfan-and-tasawwuf-sufism-ahmad-ahmadi/irfan-and-tasawwuf-sufism

Arendt J, & Aulinas A. Physiology of the Pineal Gland and Melatonin. [Updated 2022 Oct 30]. In: Feingold KR, Anawalt B, Blackman MR, et al., editors. Endotext [Internet]. South Dartmouth (MA): MDText.com, Inc.; 2000-. Available from: https://www.ncbi.nlm.nih.gov/books/NBK550972/

Brazier, Y. (2020) What to know about the Vegetarian diet. https://www.medicalnewstoday.com/articles/8749

Brown, H. (2021) What Is Nature and Ecotherapy & How Does It Work? https://positivepsychology.com/nature-therapy/

Bryson. B. (2020) The Body: a guide for occupants. London: Penguin https://www.youtube.com/watch?v=jupcJfqz_O0

Cherry, K. (2022) Types of Non-verbal Communication. https://www.verywellmind.com/types-of-nonverbal-communication-2795397

Cleveland Clinic (2022) https://my.clevelandclinic.org/health/body/23334-pineal-gland

Cline, A (2020). 'What's the Difference Between Religion and Spirituality?" Learn Religions, Aug. 26, 2020, learnreligions.com/religion-vs-spirituality-whats-the-difference-250713.

Cook, F. (1977) Hua-Yen Buddhism The Jewel Net of Indra. The Pennsylvania State Press

Cozolino, L. (2017) The Neuroscience of Psychotherapy, 3rd Ed. New York: W, W, Norton & Company

Hargreaves, S., Raposo, A., Saraiva, A. & Zandonadi, R. (2021) Vegetarian Diet: An Overview through the Perspective of Quality of Life Domains. doi: 10.3390/ijerph18084067

Hull, R. (2016) The Art of Nonverbal Communication in Practice. The Hearing Journal 69(5):p 22,24, May | DOI: 10.1097/01.HJ.0000483270.59643.ccHuntingdon (2023) Fear: Definition, Symptoms, Examples, & Tips. Fear: Definition, Symptoms, Examples, & Tips - The Berkeley Well-Being Institute (berkeleywellbeing.com) https://www.berkeleywellbeing.com/fear.html

Jordan, M. & Hinds, J. (2016) Ecotherapy: Theory, Research & Practice. London: Bloomsbury

K. I. Pargament, J. J. Exline, & J. W. Jones (Eds.) (2013), *APA handbook of psychology, religion, and spirituality (Vol. 1): Context, theory, and research* (pp. 239–255). American Psychological Association. https://doi.org/10.1037/14045-013

Loewenthal, K. M. (2013). Religion, spirituality, and culture: Clarifying the direction of effects. In K. I. Pargament, J. J. Exline, & J. W. Jones (Eds.), *APA handbook of psychology, religion, and spirituality (Vol. 1): Context, theory, and research* (pp. 239–255). American Psychological Association.
 https://doi.org/10.1037/14045-013

Mate, G. (2023) Human development through the lens of science and compassion https://drgabormate.com/

Miller, K. (2020) Science of Spirituality (+16 Ways to Become More Spiritual) https://positivepsychology.com/science-of-spirituality/

National Geographic (2023) Biosphere
https://education.nationalgeographic.org/resource/biosphere/

Nittur,A. Ganapathi,R.(2020).*Pranic Healing as a Complimentary Therapy in Stage-4 Metastatic Cancer-A Case Study, J Clin of Diagnosis Res. 14*(1), XD03-
XD04. https://www.doi.org/10.7860/JCDR/2020/42423/13432

PBS (2023) World Religious Map
https://www.pbslearningmedia.org/resource/sj14-soc-religmap/world-religions-map/

Psychology Today (2023) Integrating Therapy https://www.psychologytoday.com/us/therapy-types/integrative-therapy

PsychCentral (2023) 'What are the signs of Victim Mentality'. https://psychcentral.com/health/victim-mentality#causes

Rudd, R. (2015) The Gene Keys. London: Watkins Publishing

Ruhl, C. (2020). Theory of mind. Simply Psychology. www.simplypsychology.org/theory-of-mind.html

Rye, M. S., Wade, N. G., Fleri, A. M., & Kidwell, J. E. M. (2013). The role of religion and spirituality in positive psychology interventions. In K. I. Pargament, A. Mahoney, & E. P. Shafranske (Eds.), *APA handbooks in psychology. APA handbook of psychology, religion, and spirituality (vol. 2): An applied psychology of religion and spirituality* (pp. 481–508). American Psychological Association

Sabharwal Pooja, Naik Bibhu Prasad, and Sharma Akanksha. (2019) Pranic Healing: A Stress Buster for Cancer Patients. *Int. J. of Adv. Res.* 7 (Jan). 380-384] (ISSN 2320-5407). www.journalijar.com

Schilbrack, K. (2022) "The Concept of Religion", *The Stanford Encyclopaedia of Philosophy* (Summer 2022 Edition), Edward N. Zalta (ed.),

https://plato.stanford.edu/archives/sum2022/entries/concept-religion/

Schore, A. (2012) The Science of the Art of Psychotherapy. New York: W, W, Norton & Company

Seyfarth, R. (2010) Theory of Mind. Richard Dawkins Foundation for Reason and Science.
https://www.youtube.com/watch?v=XDtjLSa50uk&t=16s

Siegel, D. (2012) Pocket guide to Interpersonal Neurobiology: Integrative Handbook of the Mind. (Norton Series on Interpersonal Neurobiology). New York: W, W, Norton & Company

Siegel, D. (2016) Mind: A Journey to the Heart of Being Human (Norton Series on Interpersonal Neurobiology). New York: W, W, Norton & Company

Sims, M. (2022) Humanistic Approaches. In A, Reeves (ed.) *An Introduction to Counselling and Psychotherapy: from theory to practice* (3rd ed.) London: Sage Publications

Spiritual Response Association (2022) SRT.
https://spiritualresponse.org/srt-class-information/

Stricker, G. (2001) An Introduction to Psychotherapy Integration
https://www.psychiatrictimes.com/view/introduction-psychotherapy-integration

St John V (2023) Hierarchy of the Catholic Church
http://stjohnv.org/parish/files/2017/01/Priest-Hierarchy.pdf

Tariki Trust (2023) Ecotherapy https://www.tarikitrust.org/what-is-ecotherapy

Van Der Kolk, B. (2015) The Body Keeps the Score. London: Penguin

Van Der Kolk, B., McFarlane, A. & Weisaeth, L. (2007) Traumatic Stress. London: Guildford Press

WallStreetmojo (2023) Consumerism
https://www.wallstreetmojo.com/consumerism/

Weller, M. Vegetarian diets and cancer risk. *BMC Med* **20**, 81 (2022). https://doi.org/10.1186/s12916-022-02282-8

Wilkinson, L.A. (2011). Systems Theory. In: Goldstein, S., Naglieri, J.A. (eds) Encyclopaedia of Child Behaviour and Development. Springer, Boston, MA. https://doi.org/10.1007/978-0-387-79061-9_941

Appendix 1. Diagram of Existence

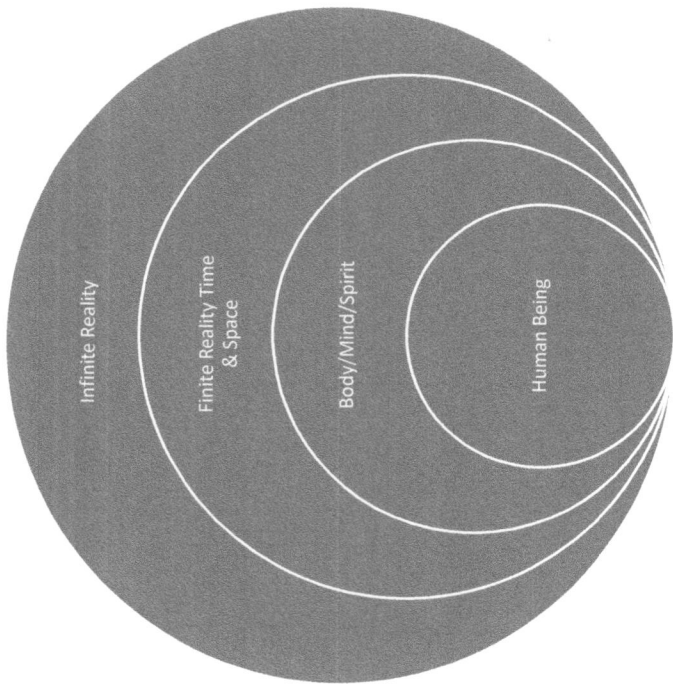

Infinite Reality

Finite Reality Time & Space

Body/Mind/Spirit

Human Being

Appendix 2. Map of Infinite & Finite Reality

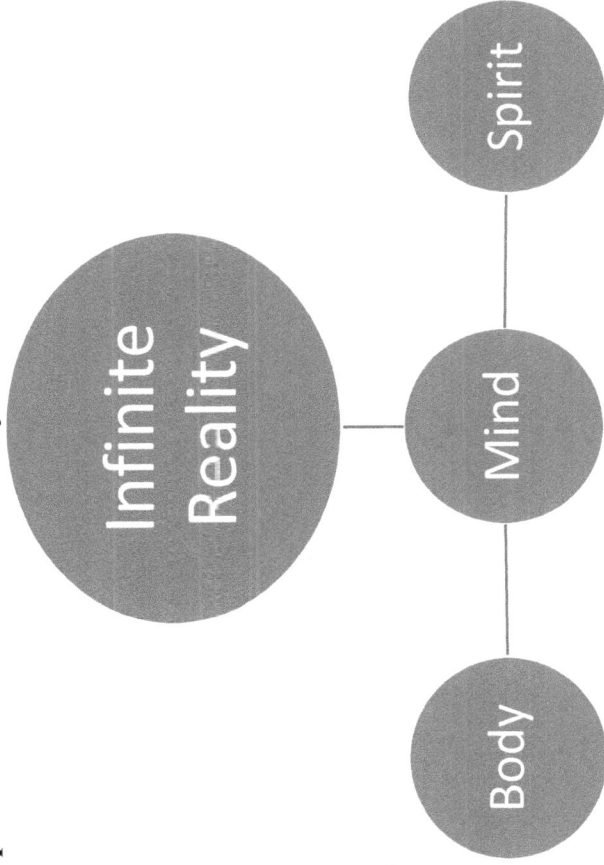

Appendix 3. Diagram of Infinite & Finite Reality

	Infinite Reality Satchitananda Pure Existence/Consciousness/Bliss		
	Finite Reality – Relative Time & Space		
	Body	Mind	Spirit
	Physical world	Mental/Psychological world	Spiritual world
	Natural Sciences, Computer Sciences, Engineering, etc.	Social Sciences, Humanities & Religion	Spirituality

378

Appendix 4. Diagram of Infinite Reality

Infinite Reality
Pure Existence/Consciousness/Bliss

Science	Religion	Philosophy/Spirituality
• Higgs Boson (God Particle) • First Principle • 'Big Bang' • Pure energy	• God • Brahman • The Trinity • Christ • Allah • Grace • Divine Providence • Shiva • Krishna • The Light • El (god) YHVH	• Satchitananda • Para-Brahman • All That There Is • Divine Spark • Paramatma • Bliss • Supreme God • Ain Soph or Ein Sof • Nothingness • Self (big S) • Śūnyatā

Appendix 5. Diagram Finite Reality – The Body

Sciences & Humanities	Religion	Finite Reality Relative Time & Space The Body – Physical World	Philosophy/Spirituality
• Biology • Physics • Neuroscience • Natural Sciences • Computer Science • Engineering • Communication Systems • Global Markets • Law • Art	• Man • Woman • Material World • Vice • The Fall • Lust/Desire/Flesh • Sin • Temple • Vehicle • Temptation • The Devil/Satan		• Materialism • Consumerism • Physical body • Annamaya • Kosha • Food • Gross Body • Maya • Matter • Prakriti • Dualism

380

Appendix 6. Diagram Finite Reality – The Mind

Finite Reality
Relative Time & Space
The Mind – Mental World

Science/Social Science/ Humanities	Religion	Philosophy/Spirituality
• Mind	• Angels & Demons	• Manomaya Kosha
• Mind-Set	• Voice of Gods	• Mind-Net
• Ego	• Deities	• Intellect
• Thinking	• Mysticism	• Citta
• Psychic Structure	• Transcendental	• Awareness/consciousness
• Self-Concept	• Esoteric	• Astral/Subtle Body
• Psychology	• Ritual	• Egoism
• Brain	• Manas	• Dualism
• Psyche	• Laws	• self (little s)
• Reason		• Perception
• TOM -theory of Mind		• Relational Being
• Inter-relational		• Ethics

Appendix 7. Diagram of Finite Reality – Spirit

Finite Reality
Relative Time & Space
Spirit – Spiritual World

Science/Social Science/Humanities	Religion	Philosophy/Spirituality
• Wholeness • Integration • Fully Functioning • Alignment • Self-actualisation • Individuation • Self-realisation • Divinity • Spirituality • Pop Psychology (Best version of Self, Awesomeness, True Self, Authentic Self)	• God • Scriptures • Sacred Books • Resurrection • I Am That I Am • Celestial Beings • Heavenly realms • Divinity • Soul	• Anadamaya Kosha • Self-realisation • Nirvana • Liberation • Enlightenment • Tao • Satchitananda • Non-dualism • Atman • Moksha • Yoga

382

Appendix 8. Structured Study Guides and Examples

1. I AM Not	2. Meditation	3. Yoga	4. Eco-approach	5. Sacred symbol/ Mantra 6.	7. Combination

The above six study guides are examples and not prescriptive. They are illustrations to give ideas and structure to your development and study to integrate the Body/Mind/Spirit framework. You might find that one system works for you and you stick to it, others might find a combination, or change from one system to another as your inner guide and development progresses. As I have stressed throughout the book there is no definitive way to practice and use the Body/Mind/Spirit framework. It is a personal process that one develops and attunes, to enhance one's wellbeing and positive living.

The overall test of this is your own self-evaluation. Engage and take moments to reflect throughout your day, week, month, and year by asking pertinent self-reflective questions:

- Am I feeling more positivity in my life?
- Are my relationships with others improved?
- Am I dealing with stress more calmly?
- Am I communicating in positive ways with myself and others?
- Do I feel an overall sense of 'Ok-ness'?
- Are others responding more positively to me?
- Do I feel more robust and resilient generally?

The guides below are structured in a time frame of morning, lunchtime, and evening. The emphasis is to practice these approaches daily and continue to practice daily. Obviously, your own personal timetable, work commitments, family and personal life will influence how you integrate the approaches, but the general emphasis is on daily continual practice so that you gain the maximum benefit....

5. Sacred Symbols/Mantra

This is the practice of visualising sacred symbols in your mind or repeating a mantra either verbally or silently.

Examples:

- Repeat the mantra: Om Mani Padme Hum in your mind throughout the day.
- Repeat the mantra: Namo Amida Butsu in your mind throughout the day.
- Visualise the sacred symbol 'Om' in your mind throughout the day.
- Visualise the sacred Hexagram/Star of David symbol in your mind throughout the day.
- Recite the Gayatri mantra in the morning, lunchtime and in the evening before bed.

AM	Lunchtime	PM
Visualise sacred symbol in your mind or repeat mantra either verbally or silently in your mind	Visualise sacred symbol in your mind or repeat mantra either verbally or silently in your mind	Visualise sacred symbol in your mind or repeat mantra either verbally or silently in your mind

A note on commitment, perseverance, and application:

To gain any benefit from any approach takes commitment, perseverance, and application – in other words **'don't give up'**. If you want to gain from your practice you need to be consistent (keep doing it), focused (don't lose sight of it) and committed (steadfast in your approach). The hardest thing that most people find to do is not the actual practice but the continued 'doing of it' daily, weekly, monthly, and yearly. Remember this is a lifestyle choice and change, not a faddy trend that gets picked up and dropped like a child when they see the next new toy that comes on the shelf. Be the Adult, time to grow-up, yes by all means have fun and enjoy life but not at the expense of your physical, emotional, psychological, and spiritual growth.

1. I Am Not

This is the simplest – yet potentially the hardest to do…however with commitment and perseverance the most effective…

AM	PM
Keep awareness of the 'I AM Not' in your Mind in every moment of your existence	Keep awareness of the 'I AM Not' in your Mind in every moment of your existence

2. Meditation

The times of the meditation can be up to you, make them fit in your day - duration of meditation is dependent on your level and confidence…beginners start with 10 minutes for week one, then 20 minutes week two, 30 minutes week three and so on adding 10 minutes a week. Intermediate/Advanced meditators start at your preferred duration and progress in your own way…

AM	Lunchtime	PM
Meditation	Meditation	Meditation

3. Yoga

Whatever style of yoga you are engaging with Hatha, Karma, Bhakti, Raja, or Jnani or a combination – apply it throughout your daily life.

Examples:

- Morning: Hatha yoga, Lunchtime: Raja yoga, Evening: Bhakti worship.
- Morning Hatha, Lunchtime: Hatha, Evening: Hatha.
- Karma yoga practiced throughout the day.
- Jnani yoga practiced throughout the day.

AM	Lunchtime	PM
Yoga practice	Yoga practice	Yoga practice

4. Eco-approach

This is incorporating and connecting to the wider eco-worlds that we live in, to help bring a greater sense of connectedness and centredness through one's engagement with nature and the natural world.

Examples:

- Morning: go for walk in a park or woodland, Lunchtime: watch the birds out of your window, Evening: sit in your garden and experience the world around you.
- Morning: take your dog for a walk, Lunchtime: water your plants and have a chat with them, Evening: plant vegetables.
- Morning: set up a nature camera in the garden and monitor it, Lunchtime: go for a walk in a park, Evening: find a river near you and 'hang out' there.
- Morning: create a home garden, Lunchtime: sit in a park, Evening: go for a walk in nature.

AM	Lunchtime	PM
Connect & engage with nature and the natural world	Connect & engage with nature and the natural world	Connect & engage with nature and the natural world

6. Combination

This is where you can choose and apply a variety of combinations of the previous examples. The application of this is varied and diverse depending on you and what resonates and feels right for you.

Examples:

- Morning: Hatha yoga, Lunchtime: go for walk in the park, Evening: meditation
- Morning: meditation, Lunchtime: recite Namo Amida Butsu, Evening: sit in your garden
- Morning: take the dog for a walk, Lunchtime: meditation, Evening: recite Gayatri mantra before bed
- Morning: recite Om Mani Padme Hum on a morning walk, Lunchtime: sit in a park watch the wildlife, Evening: meditation before bed

AM	Lunchtime	PM
Combining varied and different approaches that resonate and feel right	Combining varied and different approaches that resonate and feel right	Combining varied and different approaches that resonate and feel right

Dr Michael Sims is a prominent psychotherapist, lecturer, ecotherapist, yoga teacher and author. He lives just outside Salisbury with his wife and four children.